Making Poetry Happen

ALSO AVAILABLE FROM BLOOMSBURY

Making Poetry Matter, edited by Sue Dymoke, Andrew Lambirth and Anthony Wilson

MasterClass in English Education, edited by Sue Brindley and Bethan Marshall

Teaching English Texts 11–18, Sue Dymoke

The Poetry Toolkit, Rhian Williams

Making Poetry Happen

Transforming the Poetry Classroom

EDITED BY
SUE DYMOKE, MYRA BARRS, ANDREW LAMBIRTH AND ANTHONY WILSON

Bloomsbury Academic
An imprint of Bloomsbury Publishing Plc

B L O O M S B U R Y
LONDON · NEW DELHI · NEW YORK · SYDNEY

Bloomsbury Academic

An imprint of Bloomsbury Publishing Plc

50 Bedford Square   1385 Broadway
London   New York
WC1B 3DP   NY 10018
UK   USA

www.bloomsbury.com

BLOOMSBURY and the Diana logo are trademarks of Bloomsbury Publishing Plc

First published 2014

British Library Cataloguing-in-Publication Data
A catalogue record for this book is available from the British Library.

ISBN: HB: 978-1-4725-0805-8
PB: 978-1-4725-1238-3
ePDF: 978-1-4725-0948-2
ePub: 978-1-4725-1026-6

Library of Congress Cataloging-in-Publication Data
Making poetry happen : transforming the poetry classroom / edited by Sue Dymoke,
Myra Barrs, Andrew Lambirth and Anthony Wilson.
pages cm
Includes bibliographical references and index.
ISBN 978-1-4725-0805-8 (hardback) – ISBN 978-1-4725-1238-3 (paperback)
1. Poetry–Study and teaching. I. Dymoke, Sue, 1962- editor. II. Barrs, Myra, editor.
III. Lambirth, Andrew, 1959- editor. IV. Wilson, Anthony, 1964- editor.
PN1101.M26 2014
808.1'071–dc23
2014028031

Typeset by Integra Software Services Pvt. Ltd
Printed and bound in Great Britain

i.m. Seamus Heaney

CONTENTS

LIST OF FIGURES
AND TABLES

PUBLISHER'S ACKNOWLEDGEMENTS

The editors and contributors of this book are very grateful to all the students and teachers who have kindly given their permission for their poetry to be included here.

'In a Rush' by Agnès Lambert was highly commended in the Foyle Young Poets of the Year Awards 2008; 'James Bond' by William Kerley was selected for the *Times Educational Supplement* Young Poet feature on 22 May 1998 and was also published in *The TES Book of Young Poets* (Grogan, 1999); 'Weed Wants to Travel' by Ruth Yates was an overall winner of the Foyle Young Poets of the Year Awards, 2001. Their poems are reprinted here with their kind permission.

ABOUT THE CONTRIBUTORS

Brenda Ainsley teaches at the Sir William Robertson Academy in Lincolnshire, UK. She has previously worked as an English consultant and for the Basic Skills Agency and the Specialist Schools and Academies Trust.

Myra Barrs is a freelance writer, consultant and researcher. Formerly director of the Centre for Literacy in Primary Education and visiting professor at the University of East London, UK, her publications include *Educational Blogs and Their Effects on Pupils' Writing* (2014) and *The Reader in the Writer* (2002). Her projects include the QCA Reading Differences Project and the CfBT Project on Assessing Learning in Creative Contexts.

Emma Beynon is a freelance creative practitioner working in a range of educational settings at www.opengroundwriting.co.uk. She is leading muddy writing trails for The Wild Wye Web at the Hay Festival 2014.

Julie Blake is the Education Director of the Poetry Archive and co-founder, with Andrew Motion, of the Poetry By Heart poetry recitation competition for schools and colleges in England.

Jane Bluett is a writer, teacher and poet with a PhD in the Practice of Poetry. Currently she is teaching English and Creative Writing at Bilborough College, Nottingham, UK. She is also the Principal Examiner for A Level Creative Writing.

Jennie Clark has taught for over thirty years in the London Borough of Redbridge, UK. She is at present the English coordinator in a large infants school and a leading practitioner of English, supporting local authority schools.

Amy Clifford has taught in primary schools and at the Centre for Literacy in Primary Education and is now Deputy Headteacher of Torriano Infant School, London Borough of Camden, UK.

Mandy Coe is a poet and educationalist who writes for adults and children. A Hawthornden Fellow and Visiting Fellow of the Manchester Writing School, UK, she works with schools, community groups and universities.

Andy Craven-Griffiths is a poet and performer who works freelance in schools across England and with his band, Middleman. He was a lead poet on Shake the Dust (2012), the largest UK Youth Slam Poetry project to date.

Sue Dymoke is Reader in Education and a National Teaching Fellow at the School of Education, University of Leicester, UK, where she co-leads the Secondary PGCE programme. She was a co-convenor of the ESRC *Poetry Matters* seminar series. Her publications include *Teaching English Texts 11–18* (2009) and *Moon at the Park and Ride* (2012). Her blog is suedymokepoetry.com

Sue Ellis was formerly Co-Director of Centre for Literacy in Primary Education. She helped initiate the Children's Poetry Award, edited the Southwark Children's Poetry Anthologies and set up the National Poetry Centre for Primary Schools and Poetryline website.

Janette Hughes is Assistant Professor at University of Ontario Institute of Technology, Faculty of Education, Canada. She leads the Social Sciences and Humanities Research Council Project, which investigates the relationship between new media and adolescents' writing of poetry.

Andrew Lambirth is Professor of Education in the Faculty of Education and Health at the University of Greenwich, UK. His publications include *Teaching Early Reading and Phonics: Creative Approaches to Early Literacy* (2011) and *Literacy on the Left; Reform and Revolution* (2011). He was a co-convenor of the ESRC *Poetry Matters* seminar series and is currently President Elect of the United Kingdom Literacy Association.

Vicky Macleroy is Senior Lecturer in English in Education at Goldsmiths, University of London, UK. She is joint co-ordinator of the PGCE English programme and tutors an MA in Children's Literature.

Nicholas McGuinn has been involved in English teaching at the school and university levels for almost forty years. His most recent book, *The English Teacher's Drama Handbook*, was published in 2014.

Christopher Parton teaches English at Blessed Robert Sutton Catholic School in Burton-on-Trent, Staffordshire, UK. He has previously taught English as a Foreign Language and worked as an editor in London and Lithuania.

Susanna Steele is Senior Lecturer in Primary English at the University of Greenwich, UK. She also works with teachers as part of the education programme at the Unicorn Theatre for Children.

Joelle Taylor is a freelance poet and Artistic Director and National Coach of SLAMbassadors UK. She is the author of *Ska Tissue* (2011) and *The Woman Who Was Not There* (2014).

Jenny Vernon is former Leading Advisory Teacher at the Centre for Literacy in Primary Education and co-author of *Book Power Year 2: Literacy Through Literature Year 2* (2000) and *Book Power: Literacy Through Literature Year 3* (2012).

Anthony Wilson is Senior Lecturer at the Graduate School of Education, University of Exeter, UK. He was a co-convenor of the ESRC *Poetry Matters* seminar series. His most recent books are *Riddance* (2012) and *Love for Now* (2012), a memoir of cancer. He blogs at www.anthonywilsonpoetry. com

Daniel Xerri teaches English at the University of Malta Junior College, Malta. He is currently completing doctoral research at the University of York, UK.

Cliff Yates wrote *Jumpstart Poetry in the Secondary School* during his time as Poetry Society poet-in-residence. His poetry collections include *Henry's Clock* (1999), winner of the Aldeburgh First Collection Prize.

CHAPTER ONE

Introduction

Sue Dymoke, Myra Barrs, Andrew Lambirth and Anthony Wilson

In *Preoccupations*, the much-loved poet and teacher Seamus Heaney writes: 'The power and scope of poetry depend upon individual poets, what they are prepared to expect from it and how they are prepared to let it happen or to make it happen in their lives' (Heaney, 1980: 221). *Making Poetry Happen* exemplifies how poetry can empower and transform – how young people and their teachers can find their voices as poets in the making and discover the sustaining power of poetry. Drawing on research from the *Poetry Matters* seminar series which was funded by the Economic and Social Research Council (ESRC), this text argues for a distinctive pedagogy for poetry and presents practical classroom-based approaches that enable students and teachers of different levels of experience across the 5–19 age range to engage confidently with poetry.

Making Poetry Happen works alongside its companion volume, *Making Poetry Matter: international research on poetry pedagogy* (Dymoke et al., 2013), but also independently. The *Poetry Matters* seminars were the first of their kind. They drew on the research and experience of both established and new researchers in the field, together with contributions from teachers, practising poets and writers in schools and other educational settings. The objective of the seminar series and these new poetry books is to rekindle a love for poetry and to regenerate the passion for introducing poems to young people. *Making Poetry Happen* makes aspects of the seminars real in the classroom by showcasing both the immediate and lasting impact of the seminar series. Our book looks beyond the series to consider how practices in poetry teaching can now be developed in order to transform the classroom experience of poetry, particularly for pupils, teachers and those beginning teachers who are new to the profession and working within the restrictions of performative 'high-stakes' English curricula around the world. It aims to build young people's and teachers' confidence in the genre and strengthen their relationship with poetry on page or screen, in mind or ear. It provides support for the development of creative and innovative poetry practices across age phases. *Making Poetry Happen* revisits learners' and teachers' perceptions of what poetry teaching is like in many different forms and within a variety of contexts. It includes a multiplicity of teachers' and pupils' voices that show how poetry can and should happen anywhere.

Making Poetry Happen is organized in four parts (Reading, Writing, Speaking and Listening to Poetry and Transformative Poetry Cultures). These mirror the structure of *Making Poetry Matter* and draw on classroom and workshop practices at primary and secondary levels (for young people aged 5–19). Each part includes practical, tried and tested materials, workshop activities and case studies in which teachers comment on how they have adapted workshop materials for use in their own schools and developed their own approaches. Part commentaries provide overviews of emerging issues, synergies and practical implications in each area. The book also contains a useful glossary of poetic and pedagogic terms that may be unfamiliar to readers.

The first part focuses on reading poetry. It draws on the work of teachers and researchers working in primary schools, sixth form colleges and initial teacher education both in the United Kingdom and Malta. All the authors are passionate about encouraging students to enjoy reading poetry. Nicholas McGuinn discusses how students need to recognize the delight that can be found from poems by overcoming notions that poetry must always be read academically. Readers of poems need to relax and ask the questions of the poems they feel personally compelled to ask. In her chapter, Susanna Steele wants poetry to be read away from the more instrumental approaches to schooling and offers ways to do this. She writes an inspiring argument for poems to be given the space they require to be lifted from the page. Daniel Xerri's chapter discusses the ways he has inspired his students to read poems in a post-sixteen college in Malta. In his chapter, he describes how, as a teacher, he wanted to break down some of the barriers between teachers and students and for his students to take more personal ownership over the poems they read and discussed together. Andrew Lambirth's case study presents a description and analysis of a primary school teacher's changing perception of poems that occurs because of interactions with his children in the class when they read poems together. Each chapter offers exciting insights into ways to enrich the reading of poems with young people.

The second part explores writing poetry from many different perspectives. It features the work of two highly acclaimed poets, Cliff Yates and Mandy

Coe, who both have extensive workshop/residency experience in schools and contributed to the *Poetry Matters* seminars. They both offer innovative and accessible approaches to teaching writing that are grounded in the realities of how poets write. Sue Ellis then focuses on the 'memorable music' of poetry. Her article demonstrates how poetry in the primary school can develop some of the essential dispositions for literacy (and literature) learning – a lively interest in language, an enjoyment of language play and a growing responsiveness to the patterns and rhythms of language. In her inspiring case study, infant school teacher Jennie Clark, writing with Myra Barrs, explores poetry's central place in the life of a primary school and describes how a literacy curriculum based on books 'that are worth spending time on', written in 'clear, strong and poetic' language, can lead to searching discussions and provoke the writing of powerful poetry. Jane Bluett, a poet and teacher who has been instrumental in the development of the first Creative Writing course to be examined at post-sixteen level in the United Kingdom, explores how she has taken ideas from the seminar series to challenge her students' views about poetry and to make poetry writing happen in her college.

Speaking poetry and listening to its sounds and rhythms are fundamental activities in engagement with poetry that are sometimes sadly overlooked in classrooms where reading can reign supreme. Two of the authors in Part Three, Julie Blake and Joelle Taylor, write about key initiatives in poetry education in the United Kingdom, namely The Poetry Archive, Poetry By Heart and SLAMbassadors. Each of these organizations is giving poetry a much needed nudge/jolt off the page. The active approach with language is also fully endorsed by poet and performer Andy Craven-Griffiths, whose groundbreaking workshops have enabled students of all ages to listen to their voices and have tremendous fun while learning how they can manipulate rhyme. Blake, Taylor and Craven-Griffiths all led *Poetry Matters* workshops. They inspired audiences, including secondary school teachers Christopher Parton and Brenda Ainsley, to develop poetry schemes and slam events in their very different school contexts. In both of their case studies Parton and Ainsley offer practical suggestions and reflections on how they have refined activities to suit their own contexts and to enhance students' thinking about poetic language.

Many of the activities outlined in this book are having a transformative effect on the students and teachers who are involved in them. The final part reinforces this idea by providing indisputable evidence that creative risk-taking can bring about cultural change in a community. The communities represented here are diverse, urban and rural, UK-based and Canadian. They include primary aged children and their teachers, so-called 'invisible children' and young people for whom English is an additional language to their mother tongue. Emma Beynon, Janette Hughes and Vicky Macleroy show the benefits – social, linguistic, cultural – in the widest sense of learners working alongside poets in an atmosphere of mutual collaboration. Jenny

Vernon demonstrates the impact of the same for teachers. All of the authors were participants in the *Poetry Matters* seminars.

When introducing a fantastic group of young spoken word artists to the annual conference of the National Association for the Teaching of English, Susan Weinstein commented: 'Poetry gives us a space to speak and feel and embrace the full possibilities of language.' She observed the sense of duty that we have to 'pass *that* definition of poetry on to young people through teaching and through our own daily practices' and, in doing so, to invite them in to a conversation 'about what poetry is and why, for each of us and for all of us, it matters' (Weinstein, 2013).

All of the workshops and case studies presented here are informed by and contribute to our ongoing conversation about how poetry does matter and how it can happen. We hope our readers will want to seize the challenge to translate the pedagogic discussions embodied in this book into local conversations and poetry programmes in their own schools and colleges in ways that will have a transformative and enduring impact on young people's lives.

PART ONE

Reading Poetry

CHAPTER TWO

The Challenges and Opportunities for Engaging with Poetry

Nicholas McGuinn

I have always hated poetry. I loathe and despise it, in fact.
I do not like it because I do not see the point of it. I read novels,
I write stories, but I have never written a poem (except when
forced to at school).

These words were written in response to a creative writing task a couple of years ago by a first-year undergraduate who had just begun a course in English and Education. In a more temperate comment on the same exercise, her colleague confided: 'I have never before since primary school dared to write a poem!' A third prefaced her reflections with the words: 'I would not consider myself to be a creative person.'

An emotional antipathy, an inability to 'see the point', a sense that poetry writing – creativity itself, even – are not for the likes of us: comments such as these would have been sadly familiar to Her Majesty's Inspectorate (HMI) when, almost thirty years ago, they noted that 'in national terms, poetry is frequently neglected and poorly provided for; its treatment is inadequate and superficial' (DES, 1987: 4). A decade earlier, *A Language for Life* made the same point: 'in many schools [poetry] suffers from lack of commitment, misunderstanding, and the wrong kind of orientation' (DES, 1975: 137). Twenty years before that, the Ministry of Education complained that there is 'a general uncertainty of touch about the presentation of poetry to children and that a great deal of what is attempted is at best, aimless and fruitless' (MoE, 1954: 141). Going back another three decades, The Newbolt Report still felt the need to quote Matthew Arnold's comments from the previous century, in which he urged the 'extraordinary' importance of poetry teaching in schools and complained that the pupil teachers of 1852 'often cannot paraphrase a plain passage of prose or poetry without totally misapprehending it' (In BoE, 1921: 49, 47).

The English in Education undergraduates cited earlier are clearly writing within an established tradition; and Arnold would no doubt be dismayed to discover that, over 150 years after he wrote his 1852 report, poets still do not seem to have found a more positive story to tell. Commenting in 2010, Andrew Motion, for example, observes:

> Poetry is commonly described as a valuable part of our national life. But by common consent the existing general audience for it is much smaller than it could be, and the enthusiasm for it in schools is less than it should be. Indeed, poetry in schools is often seen as 'a problem' by many teachers, and as a bore by many pupils; outside schools it is often regarded as being on a par with clog-dancing.
>
> (Booktrust, 2010: 4)

Motion's pessimism appears to be supported by research. In a study undertaken with over 17,000 young readers and published a year after Motion's 2010 report, researchers for the National Literacy Trust asked respondents what kinds of materials they read at least once a month. *Text messages, magazines, websites and emails* all scored over 50% (with *texting* at the top on 58%) while *poems* were second from bottom with 16.5% (only *plays or screenplays* scored less with 8.8%) (Clark and Douglas, 2011: 55).

Paradoxically, this seemingly entrenched sense of indifference if not outright hostility persists at a time when the radical changes which technology has brought to the 'previously grooved routines of convention' (Kress and Bezemer, 2009: 171) associated with the construction, mediation and reception of text have provided unprecedented opportunities for access to and engagement with poetry in a wide range of forms. Kress and Bezemer note:

> The *page* is used differently to the way it had been: it now has a different semiotic function. It has become a *site of display* [original italics] with quite specific social and semiotic potentials.
>
> (2009: 167)

Particularly potent is the affordance of 'transduction' (2009: 175), which enables the translation of online written text into visual and aural forms.

Arguing that '*Production* and *participation*' [original italics] are 'the ruling metaphors in communication' (2009: 171), Kress and Bezemer see new possibilities for the democratization of knowledge in favour of young people who increasingly see themselves as 'authors' of 'the kind of texts that meet their social, personal and affective needs' (2009: 180):

> Not only do such sites allow learners to choose themselves the text that they think is apt for their learning, but also allow learners to access all other texts – not only those for other year groups, but also those for teachers or for 'experts'.
>
> (2009: 179)

Kress and Bezemer cite the *Poetry Archive* Internet site as a particular example of good practice; and the poetry community has been quick to seize the opportunities afforded by online literacies. Sites like *Global Poetry System, PoetCasting, Poetry Library, Poets.org, The Poetry Society* and *Poetry Soup* – to name just a few – offer access (often auditory and visual) to a wealth of poems, including highly contemporary work. Whether for good or ill (Thompson, 2013), *poetry slams* attract lively audiences nationally and internationally. Developments in social networking have made the possibility for shared access around the world even more comprehensive and spontaneous; and in terms of engaging with poetry, 'transduction' offers powerful alternatives to the 'grooved routines' of the conventional written response.

So where does the problem lie? A standard answer is to blame national assessment procedures; but even examination boards make some considerable effort to provide detailed and imaginative digital access, not only about the poets their students have to write about, but also about information on how to accomplish that writing successfully. Nor is there, as Thompson (2013) puts it, 'a cabal of posh people' whose task is to make poetry 'unintelligible' – at least, not if the reports published by the examination boards are to be believed. Gratefully noting a general decrease in what it describes as the 'trainspotting approach' to poetry, the 2009 GCSE English Literature report published by the Welsh Joint Education Committee (WJEC) – to cite just one example – describes the 'real pleasure' elicited from reading 'inventive interpretations' of Berlie Doherty's poem 'Quieter than Snow'. The examiners quote, as examples of particularly effective student commentary, statements such as the following:

> *Everything is done in silence as if someone has pressed the mute button.*
> *It creates a very distant, quiet, non-present place as if you were looking in through a window.*

The picture is not entirely positive, however. 'Students' work on poetry', the report continues, 'frequently worries the moderators' because it tends to focus on 'peripheral aspects like line counting, noting of rhyme schemes and punctuation' to the detriment of 'the particular way in which a writer shapes language' (WJEC/CBAC, 2009: 38, 42, 43, 2).

Thinking specifically about the context of England Cremin et al. (2009) would detect here the legacy of two decades of national directives on literacy education that have foregrounded utilitarian reading practices at the expense of interactive and shared engagements with whole texts designed to promote that sense of 'pleasure and purpose', which Beard locates as the *sine qua non* of literacy (1990: 24). The 'last decade of prescribed practice and the pressures of accountability', they argue, 'are likely to continue to exert their influence upon teachers' knowledge and use of literature for some considerable time to come' (2009: 3). This is not the whole story. Almost forty years ago, the authors of *A language for life* argued that in order 'to lead a child to wider reading of fiction through an awakened interest', the teacher 'needs to know what is relevant and available' (DES, 1975: 128). Cremin et al. suggest that the problem is compounded by the fact that knowing what is 'relevant' and 'available' remains an issue for teachers. Commenting on the first phase of their *Teachers as Readers* project, they note that:

> questionnaires from 1200 teachers nationally showed that 62% of the teachers could name only two, one or no children's picture fiction creators, and 58% only two, one or no children's poets. Nearly a quarter of the sample named no writers at all in these two categories. Novelists were better known, but the range was narrow and dominated by Dahl, children's laureates and 'celebrity' authors. (2009: 3–4)

Perhaps part of the reason that students seem apprehensive or indifferent is that – like their counterparts forty years ago (DES, 1975: 136) – they are still not getting enough exposure to poetry in school; and that the poetry they do encounter tends to belong to the same narrow categories – usually a short lyric on the themes of love, death, relationships and the landscape and usually something written by poets from the British Isles. Where are the opportunities to read (and even write) political verse, or satire, or strange, genre-confounding long poems like Tennyson's 'The Princess'? How many students today are aware that contemporary and near-contemporary poets – like Margaret Atwood in *The Journals of Susanna Moodie* or Alan Ginsberg in *The Fall of America* or Derek Walcott in *Omeros* – are engaging with the epic form? One can only repeat what the authors of *A Language for Life* said four decades ago: one of the 'essentials' of any school resource bank should be 'a wide range of poetry gathered through teachers' first-hand reading of the work of individual poets' (DES, 1975: 137).

It is equally important – for many pedagogical and ideological reasons – that teachers should write, and share what they write with their students (Andrews, 2008; Ings, 2009; OFSTED, 2009). OFSTED's observation that teachers who were 'confident as writers themselves, and who could

Teachers as writers

demonstrate how writing is composed, taught it effectively' (2009, p. 5) applies as much to poetry as to any other genre. Andrews notes that teachers who share their writing with students are better placed to draw their attention 'to the act of framing and shaping that is at the heart of composition' (2008, p. 12). Sharing one's own poetry with students can also help to demystify what might otherwise seem to be an arcane process and – perhaps most important of all – reintroduce into the classroom the words which Philip Pullman (2003) felt were missing from early Literacy Strategy documents: fun and enjoyment.

In an attempt to adhere to the principle of practising what one preaches, here is a short piece of nonsense doggerel which I wrote a few days ago:

Auntie Jan

She loves her booze does Auntie Jan
Booze from a bottle, booze from a can
Booze in the back of a transit van
Booze in the arms of her fancy man
'Well, you've got to get it while you can
That's what I say' – says Jan.

Not deathless English verse; but not too difficult or time-consuming to write, either. *Auntie Jan* took five minutes to compose and I enjoyed doing it. It reminded me that clear prompts and structures can facilitate the composition process, especially for inexperienced writers. In this case, the challenge of seeing how many words I could find to rhyme with *Jan* turned the exercise into a game and released the flow of surreal images. Writing humorous doggerel about people and animals is a long-established practice reaching back through Spike Milligan and Mervyn Peake, for example, to Edward Lear and Lewis Carroll. It is one which students could easily engage with for themselves and, by so doing, make pleasurable connections with those particular poets and with others who write humorous observational poetry for young people, such as Alan Ahlberg, Julia Donaldson and Michael Rosen.

Auntie Jan serves a more fundamental pedagogical purpose. It is designed to challenge a way of thinking about poetry which has persisted from Arnold's day to this: the belief that, as Dias and Hayhoe put it, a poem 'is a rather complex way of saying something simple, and the reader's task is one of cracking the code' – to which end they will take 'stabs at meaning in the expectation that somehow the theme will be tapped' (1988: 53). To return to the undergraduate whose quoted hostility to poetry opened this chapter, it transpires that her views are a little more complex than that first statement suggests. Her reflections continue:

> I have always liked *Stopping by Woods on a Snowy Evening* [the poem by Robert Frost], but never understood why. Perhaps I like the ambiguity of the ending with the repetition, and though it seems to describe a simple

incident, there is an almost 'darker' quality to it. I possibly like Frost because I discovered him during a difficult phase of my life.

This student submitted, for consideration with her reflections, the annotated notes she wrote on her copy of *Stopping by Woods on a Snowy Evening* when studying it at school. The two documents make an interesting comparison. The statement quoted above is tentative *(perhaps I like)*, honest *(I never understood why)*, emotionally engaged *(I discovered him during a difficult phase of my life)*, perceptive *(though it seems to describe a simple incident, there is an almost 'darker' quality to it)*, willing to admit and even embrace uncertainty *(I like the ambiguity)*. The school annotations consist of a series of underlinings accompanied by comments which range from reinterpretations of what the speaker of the poem says *(horse uneasy)*, to the elliptical *(ambiguous ending)*, to the obscure *(nihilism – literal to psychological)*. The imaginative possibilities evoked by the famous repeated final lines of the poem are narrowed down by the annotation: *acceptance of his responsibility to carry on living*. Reflecting on what she wrote then from her perspective as an undergraduate, the author draws particular attention to the word *anodyne*, which she wrote under the final line of the poem:

> The notes I wrote in my school copy of the poems were not my own thoughts and feelings but rather they're what my English teacher told us to write. They were his notes that would make us look clever and give us an *A*. I didn't even understand half of the things I'd written down. Under the final line I've written 'anodyne'. I certainly would not have put that, in fact I don't know what an 'anodyne' is! I had to look it up!

Most revealing of all is the paragraph of prose which the student had written at school underneath the annotations of the poem:

> In the winter of 1905 – near Christmas. Frost set off to the nearest town to sell eggs to raise money to buy Crimbo pressies [sic] for his kids. However, he doesn't manage to raise much money. On the way home, he stopped by woods and contemplated taking his own life, in the woods and he decides not to and returns home. Seventeen years later he wrote this poem about the incident.

Such a terse cataloguing of Frost's famous poem brings to mind Woody Allen's 1975 film *Love and Death* and his three-word summary of *War and Peace as being a novel about Russia*. Drama practitioners report a similar kind of response when English students encounter play-texts. Kempe cites J.L. Styan's reference to the famous lines from Act 2 Scene 2 of *Macbeth*, where Lady Macbeth tries to explain her decision not to kill King Duncan:

Had he not resembled
My father as he slept, I had done't

Speculation about 'Lady Macbeth's hidden relationship with her father', Styan argues, is unhelpful because it 'brings us very little closer to the play in question' (In Kempe, 1997: 108). What matters is not how Lady Macbeth might or might not have related to her father but how her words and actions impact on the characters and actions *within the play itself*.

These kinds of errors occur when students try to read play-texts as if they were 'realistic' novels. The same issue can be detected in that piece of narrative prose commentary which accompanies the student's annotations of *Stopping by Woods on a Snowy Evening*. It could be the plot synopsis for a novel or a short story. There is no acknowledgement at all that what Frost has written is a *poem*. This is the mind-set that *Auntie Jan* is attempting to challenge. Nobody could possibly accuse that piece of doggerel of being a 'rather complex way of saying something simple': it just cannot be read in that way. It obliges its audience to stop trying to make the 'stabs at meaning' associated with what Louise Rosenblatt calls *efferent* reading (1978: 24) and to focus instead upon two of the essential qualities of poetry: sound and rhythm. Ideologically, too, *Auntie Jan* challenges 'naturalistic' interpretations of what the Russian Formalists Vladimir Propp and Viktor Shklovsky describe as the tensions between *fabula* and *suzjet* (plot and source material): unlike the prose commentary on *Stopping by Woods on a Snowy Evening*, the lines of *Auntie Jan* could be arranged in any order and there is no neat 'beginning, middle and end', no one, fixed way of thinking about it.

Reporting on the fifteen-month long action research programme *Writing is Primary*, Ings (2009) noted that, initially, teachers felt unconfident about putting themselves on the line by sharing their writing with their students (and perhaps if *Auntie Jan* is anything to go by, one can understand why). A safer alternative approach would be to ask students to listen to a poem in a language they do not understand: can they tell that it is a poem? That exercise would certainly serve to discourage students from making their 'stabs at meaning' and encourage them to exchange Rosenblatt's *efferent* for an *aesthetic* reading: one in which, instead of concentrating on what they might 'carry away' from their encounter with the poem, their 'attention is centered [sic] directly' on what they are 'living through' during their 'relationship with that particular text' (Rosenblatt, 1978: 25). So much more is gained, however, if a teacher can find the courage to share his or her own work with students. Gibson suggests that substituting the word *script* for *text* when studying Shakespeare can have a powerful effect on students' attitudes towards that most formidable of canonical writers: where the word *text* connotes 'authority, reverence, certainty', Gibson argues, 'a script declares that it is to be played with, explored actively and imaginatively brought to life' (1998: 7). The same principle applies to poetry. A poem *script* written by a teacher is unlikely to enter the classroom shielded by a protective screen of scholarly commentaries. This means that students (and teacher) are placed under less pressure to play at being academics when they discuss the writing; and where such pressure is removed, there is more likely to be established that 'inclusive environment of trust and respect', which in turn encourages opportunities for authentic 'dialogic bids' between students and teacher (Irish, 2011: 10). If I were using *Auntie Jan* as a prompt for generating a conversation with students about writing verse, the discourse of 'trainspotting' would, I hope, be replaced by statements like: *I wrote it because it made me laugh and gave me pleasure; no, I have no idea what it means – I just like the surreal images which came into my head as I tried to find words which rhyme with 'Jan'; I also enjoy the driving rhythm, the repetition of the word 'booze', the alliteration, and the enjambment on line five because it slows the pace and allows Auntie Jan to have the last word; yes, I like your suggestion of swapping the first and second lines around – I hadn't thought of that; now, I can't wait to hear what you've written.*

This is *not*, of course, to suggest that all poetry lessons should be given over to writing and sharing doggerel, but it *is* to suggest that discussion of the sounds, rhythms and images of poems is more likely to flourish when the didactic classroom is transformed into a writers' workshop. If the idea of sharing one's own attempts at writing with students feels like a stretch too far, an alternative would be to work with poems where we do still have draft, script-like manuscripts to compare with the published versions – the more scribbles and crossings-out, the better. Randall Jarrell's *The Woman at the Washington Zoo* is a good example. It is even better when we have evidence that poets argue about their work together. Famous examples include Ezra Pound's creative intervention in T.S. Eliot's *The Waste Land*, brought vividly to life in Valerie Eliot's edition of the poem's transcripts (Eliot, 1971). If examples from an examination favourite are required, then the relationship between two poets of the First World War, Siegfried Sassoon and Wilfred Owen, is worth exploring, particularly if it is considered in conjunction with Stephen MacDonald's dramatization *Not About Heroes*. Staying with the First World War, there is the creative dialogue between Edward Thomas and a poet who has already featured in this chapter – Robert Frost. Thomas's story has also been dramatized – in Nick Dear's *The Dark Earth and the Light Sky*.

An alternative approach, again, is to take a poem – particularly one written as a monologue – and 'transduct' it so that it reads as if the lines are providing answers to questions posed by the reader. An example might be Seamus Heaney's poem 'Digging'. The famous opening two lines might be preceded with the question: *Poet, what are you holding in your hand?* The following triplet with: *Poet, what can you see?* The questions, of course, could be made more challenging, more off beat. Perhaps most dramatically intriguing of all, they might not even be answered in the poem. This activity can be developed so that, instead of posing questions, the students echo or challenge the poem's lines with statements of their own – ideally, written in verse.

The purpose behind all this is just to encourage students and teachers to loosen up when they engage with poetry, to realize that poems do not emerge fully formed: they are revised, discussed, argued about, agonized over. They provoke laughter and tears. They can be interpreted in different ways and they defy monologic readings. Their power lies in their ability to move us through the interweaving of sound, rhythm and imagery. It is to suggest, too, that if we can first establish that 'quality of relaxed absorption', which Knight deems necessary for even 'the most concentrated act of attention to literature' (1964: 81), we are more likely to stimulate 'dialogic bids' which address what Wilson suggests are the really interesting questions: '"Why do we write poetry?" "What are the challenges of writing poems?" "What do we learn when we write poems?"' (2009: 389), to which I would add: 'What are the pleasures and excitements to be had from creating and sharing poems?'

I am writing this shortly after the death of Seamus Heaney. Thirty years ago, I was fortunate enough to be able to take my sixth form literature group to meet him at a poetry reading. My students were studying his early work for their exams and after the reading, when he made a particular point of coming to talk to them, they bombarded him with questions about what his poems 'meant'. Heaney listened thoughtfully and courteously and then paused for a moment before replying. 'Jaysus', said this man to whom language and poetry meant so much, 'don't take it so serious!'

CHAPTER THREE

Lifting Poetry off the Page

Susanna Steele

In the mid-twentieth century, in a small seaside town in the north of Ireland, I spent my last year of primary school in Mr Fawcett's class. This was a year dedicated to training us to pass the qualifying exam that would separate the potential grammar school entrants from the sows' ears, as he liked to call them. His approach to English teaching was a rigorous and relentless drill, skill and rehearsal programme of comprehension and grammar exercises, handwriting practice and spelling tests, the result of which was twelve silk purses out of a class of forty, yes forty!, children. I'm not recalling this as a nostalgic reflection of the past or to romanticize the primary education I experienced in the early 1960s. Mr Fawcett's teaching style was harsh, judgemental and arguably ineffectual and the class was held in check by the constant and visible threat of the cane that hung by the blackboard. If I were writing about his impact on my understanding and competence in Maths and the reverberation of feeling that I still experience, I would have a different story to tell.

For the last hour of every Friday he read to us and it was on those afternoons that I had my first encounters with poems such as 'Tarantella', 'Cargoes', 'The Ballad of John Silver', 'Sir Patrick Spens', 'Up the Airy Mountain', 'The Highwayman', 'The Song of Wandering Aengus', 'Kubla Khan', 'There was a Naughty Boy' and 'The Destruction of Sennacherib'. I can still recall getting caught up in being somewhere else when Mr Fawcett read and my memory of John Masefield's 'Ballad of John Silver' is of an experience as vivid as watching scenes from *Pirates of the Caribbean*.

But one thing is clear looking back: Mr Fawcett enjoyed them! He read them with relish and his enjoyment became my enjoyment, his pleasure in reading to us, my pleasure in listening and wanting more.

He chose to read us narrative poems by well-known nineteenth- and early twentieth-century poets, Yeats, Byron and Coleridge amongst them, which were written for adults but regularly selected for school anthologies, including the one he produced from his desk drawer every Friday. They were good stirring stories and I was 'willing to surmount the difficulties of language or understanding to savour the pleasure of a satisfying narrative' (Styles, 1998: 197). I have no doubt that it was the power of the story as much as the compelling regular meter that held me fast. But without hearing the poems read aloud I doubt that I would have been able to release the same experience for myself.

The teachers we encounter and the ways in which they teach can become memorable for many reasons but, in general, they can do one of two things: they can illuminate or they can cast a shadow. Whilst I suspect that Friday afternoon poetry was insufficient to remove the shadow Mr Fawcett cast into the future of majority of the class, for me he shone a light on the possibility of poetry through those times when he read aloud to us for no other reason than pleasure, his as well as mine. Positive encounters with poetry have steered me clear of the fear, and sometimes distain, that seems to grip some people, adults and children alike, when poetry is mentioned. I frequently meet students and teachers for whom poetry at school was never anything other than 'a forced march through enemy territory', an experience that they are, understandably, reluctant to revisit voluntarily.

I would like poetry to become a choice that enriches the time spent within the classroom for teachers and children and extends into lives led beyond it. Intrinsic satisfaction, according to Eisner, is the only reasonable indicator that an activity will be pursued by an individual voluntarily, that is, when they have the freedom to decide for themselves. *It is no great victory*, he points out, *to learn to do something that one will not choose to do given the choice* (Eisner, 2002: 203). Or as John Hegley says

> *A poem is not a Prison*
> *And it shouldn't feel like one either.*

Letting poetry be poetry means working with it, in all its forms, in ways that foster increasingly confident, memorable and informed encounters and what matters is that teachers create satisfying experiences that have the potential to live *fruitfully and creatively in subsequent activities* (Dewey, 1935: 27). It also means not substituting other aims that are about poetry for the experience of poetry. Teachers, Rosenblatt points out (1965: 33), often approach a poem as if it is only *a bundle of literary values to be pointed out to the student*. No poem is merely a combination of material parts that can be *modified to suit human purposes* (Langer, 1953/1979: 40) or, in the case of schools, curriculum purposes.

Poetry, like music, is an expressive form and a poem comes into being when it creates in the reader/listener a mixture of sensations, feelings, images and ideas. But there is an ineluctable and inextricable relationship between a poem's form and the meanings it holds and between the form and our experience of the poem. Discovering this inseparability is central to learning within the arts. Once a poem has come alive, we are up against the mystery of how words that lie silently on the page can make us feel, think and imagine the way we do. Teachers need to be able to empower children *to notice what is there to be noticed*, not to explain the poem but to illuminate how the poet has shaped the everyday stuff of language into *an expressive form that can influence how we feel in its presence* (Eisner, 2002: 17).

The quality of attention the poem requires of the reader is different to other forms of writing. If a poem is to become more than merely the object of critical and discursive attention, it has to be *lifted off the page* (Abbs, 1989: 73) through voicing the text, either out loud or on the inner ear. Teachers' confidence in reading poetry aloud has a central role to play in developing children's pleasure in reading poetry and in developing the feeling for form on which writing depends. Finding times and spaces *betwixt and between* (Turner, 1974) the demands of the formalized curriculum where poetry can have a presence for teachers and children through reading aloud in an atmosphere of mutual enjoyment and challenge is the place where we can make poetry matter most.

So here's to poetry with no tying poems to chairs, no torture and no hosepipes!

Shadows and weights

One of the most challenging tasks for primary teachers in England is wresting poetry out from under the long shadow cast by the National Literacy Strategy (NLS) (1998) and the Primary National Strategy (2005) and rescuing it from the weight of an attenuated pedagogy that has subsumed English literature into genre-based form of literacy. Whilst a new curriculum is now in place, the 'strategy', its subsequent manifestations, supporting documents and commercially produced resources have shaped the way a generation of primary teachers approach teaching English literature.

In 1998, the National Literacy Strategy included poetry as 'a central aspect of literacy' (Writing Poetry NLS, 2001) with an emphasis on form and an indiscriminate and arbitrary list of poetic forms to be covered, in Term 3, by each year group. In Year 4, for example, haiku, cinquains, syllabics, thin poems (sic), rhyming forms, prayers, epitaphs and free verse are amongst the poetic forms to be covered – a challenging and daunting list for even the most enthusiastic teacher working with nine-year-olds. Supported by anthologies and resources published by companies with an eye on the curriculum, many teachers were diligent in attempting to cover what was suggested by the NLS at fixed points in the school year. This may have ensured that teachers introduced children to a wide range of poetic forms but not necessarily with any *real sense of what makes poetry poetry* (Wilson, 2005: 230).

Progression in Poetry (2006), written to support the Primary National Strategy (2005), begins with a startling statement about poetry: *Like many art forms, poetry could be said to have little purpose…*. Undoubtedly, it was not the aim of the writer to confirm negative attitudes towards the arts in general and poetry in particular as the document goes on to assert that *every culture* has poetry as *an essential aspect of cultural inheritance*. Too late perhaps to rein back the idea that there is no purpose to either the arts or poetry but at least the arts, poetry and culture are mentioned together.

With the demise of the NLS, long lists of form vanished and *Progression in Poetry* pointed out that because *the mastery of many forms is highly skilled, young children may find themselves constrained by attempting demanding structures*. In place of 'demanding structures' *Progression in Poetry* recommends six 'simple forms' that it suggests children draw on for their own writing. These include 'short patterned poems for example haiku, cinquain, kennings', 'shape poems' and 'simple rhyming form, for example, rap'. The use of the term 'simple' seems to me problematic in that it presents a reductive view of form and, despite acknowledging poetry as a cultural inheritance, detaches it from any cultural context. In the real world beyond the classroom, where these forms are culturally embedded, none of them could be described as 'simple forms'. Presenting schooled versions of poetic forms as 'a coat hanger for ideas', as *Progression in Poetry* suggests they can be used, detaches poetry from any cultural roots the form may have. It also bypasses the most significant understandings that we need to bring to reading and writing poetry: form and content are inseparable and, whatever the form, *a poet's mission is to make words do more work than they normally do* (Jay-Z, 2010: 39).

Whilst the National Literacy Strategy and the Primary National Strategy may have ensured that poetry has a presence in primary classrooms that may not have been there previously, it could be argued that they have also acted as a perverse incentive. The Ofsted survey of poetry practice in English primary and secondary schools (2007) reported that provision for poetry was found to be 'weaker' than other aspects of English and noted the limitations of approaches that ask pupils to spot poetic devices rather than engaging with the poem or that focus on writing direct imitations of particular poems which, in many schools, was the only way in which poetry introduced. Kress (1999: 464) observed that the impact of literacy-based genre theory on the teaching of English may only be noticeable over time and noted that critiques of the approach foresaw young writers being *required to fit their writing to pre-existing schemata* which would turn their writing into a mechanical performance and encourage *stability to the point of stasis*. As the Ofsted survey indicates, less than a decade after the introduction of a genre-based approach to the teaching of literature, in many classrooms practices in both reading and writing poetry have been established that are limited in scope and narrow in intent.

Poetry thrived, however, in classrooms where teachers were enthusiastic about poetry and adopted a range of both formal and informal approaches. As a result, their pupils read a much wider range of poems and were able to talk knowledgeably about them. Although the report does not dwell on the observation, I think it is worth drawing attention to the recognition that what the report viewed as 'best practice' included *informal approaches* and *routinely reading with children without the need for constant study or written imitation* (2007: 11).

Just read

Myhill and Wilson (2013) suggests that one of the demands that poetry writing makes upon learners is that it, at some level, requires *a subversion or 'unlearning' of the normal rules of writing*. This is perhaps the case when what is 'normal' about poetry has not been fully realized. If, as Eisner (2002: 197) suggests, *getting smart within any domain requires, at the very least, being able to think with the medium*, then getting smart as writer of poetry depends to some degree on our experience of what poetry requires of us as a reader. It is in the reading of poetry that writing poetry has its roots and we need to be able to *illuminate the difference*, as Rosenblatt (1995: 42) states, between reading poetry and other forms of reading.

Poetry, as Christopher Reid (1998) points out, can do most of the things that prose can do. Like prose, poetry can tell stories, present arguments, express feelings and emotions, describe people, places or things, preserve experience and reflect on ideas. But it has, in addition, another important dimension. Poetry speaks to that part of our imagination that is susceptible to the patterning of sounds and the rhythms of language. When Auden and Garrett (1935: v) define poetry as *memorable speech* because of the way it can *move our emotions or excite our intellect*, they make clear that it is to the patterning of sound and the cadence of language that *we must surrender* when we read. Hearing poems read animates the feeling for syllable and rhythm that penetrates below the conscious levels of thought and allows us to experience the familiar feel of the pattern of language in poems where there may be strangeness and mystery in the words. Sharing poems through reading aloud is a way of lifting children over the threshold and into the poem.

As children become fluent, expert readers, reading becomes internalized and an almost automatic process that no longer requires the reader to voice or to subvocalize as they read (Wolff, 2008: 143). Reading becomes silent. However, when it comes to poetry we also need to take our measure from the needs of the art form and the quality of attention to the sound and the rhythm of language poetry requires from the reader differs from that of prose. In narrative, for example, voicing the language is not an inherent dimension of the text unless it is being read aloud to listeners. However, the connection between the voice and the text never diminishes in poetry. In reading a poem we have to become listener-readers because poetry needs to be heard to come into being and, like music or dance, is inseparable from its own performance of itself. Being able to read silently may be one of the markers of an experienced reader but not, however, when it comes to reading poetry.

Becoming an experienced and confident poetry reader depends on developing and extending the ability to read expressively and to hear and respond to what we experience as we read. Skilful readers of poetry know that, even if it is not voiced aloud, a poem has to be *lifted off the page* (Abbs, 1989: 73) and heard on the inner ear. In poetry, reading the words and listening to the words are simultaneous events.

When we speak of bringing a poem 'alive' what we are trying to do is make it shift from it being a silent text to becoming an experience that will create in the reader-listener *a mixture of sensations, feelings, images and ideas* (Rosenblatt, 1995: 33). If a poem is to become more than a collection of words, it has to be lifted off the page by a reader who is able to bring what Richards terms 'sensuous apprehension' to the reading (Richards, 1929: 13). This means that the reader has to be able to evoke meaning by responding to the pattern and tone of the language, having a feeling for syllable and rhythm and allowing the length of the lines and the phrasing to guide an elision of form and content. Reading poetry is a generative act and whether it's *Humpty Dumpty*, Shakespeare's *Sonnet 116*, or E.E. Cumming's *Buffalo Bill*, the game is the same: we read, not only with the voice, but with the eye, the ear and the imagination.

Reading poetry aloud can be a little intimidating for teachers especially if their previous experience has led them to believe that there is a special 'poetry voice'. Listening to the way poets read their work, on Poetry Archive, for example, can act as a template for our own reading and enable us to gain confidence. However, there is never one way of voicing a poem because reading poetry is an interpretative act on the part of the reader. If the reader doesn't inhabit what they are reading then the listeners can sense it; if they bring to the poem only their own personality then the listener hears that rather than the poem. If the reader is *really* reading, writes Pennac, and is as sympathetic to the listeners as they are to the poem then the poem *will open wide and the crowd who thought they were excluded will rush in after the reader* (2006: 172).

The way we use our voice in response to the text can influence the meanings that can arise and the experience we have of the poem and Abbs (1989: 73) suggests that a poem can have *as many meanings as the voice can render with artistic effect*.

We can recognize this when we think about music and the ways in which different performers bring their particular interpretation to the same song, giving it a different feel. For example, there are lines from the poems Mr Fawcett read that I enjoyed as a ten-year-old and which still resonate in my memory: *We were schooner rigged and rakish with a long and lissom hull/And we flew the pretty colours of the cross bones and the skull.* This is the opening of Masefield's *Ballad of John Silver* in which Silver tells the story of his life as a pirate. Imagine Long John Silver, the pirate captain from Robert Louis Stevenson's Treasure Island, as a braggadocio regaling would be pirates with his memories. Now imagine the lines as the interior thoughts of Silver looking back with longing at the adventures of his younger days. Listen to the lines with your inner ear spoken with these two different imaginative intentions behind them and notice the qualitative difference between them and how each way of reading creates a different evocation from the same lines.

Some poems lend themselves to quiet reflective voices. William Carlos William's *The Red Wheelbarrow* and Ian McMillan's *The Green Wheelbarrow*, for example, are both poems where the reader can feel as if they are overhearing the poet's private reflections. *This Is Just to Say*, also written by William Carlos William and composed as if it's a note, can elicit different interpretations from a reader who reads it as if they had written it after they had eaten the plums and one who reads the poem as if they had received it. Others come alive only when the rhythm and pattern of the language is given full attention such Carol Ann Duffy's *Peggy, Peggy Guggenheim* or Shel Silverstein's *Twistable Turnable Man*. Readers have to let their imaginative and perceptual energies reach out to the poem to become responsive *accomplices in releasing the possibilities* (Greene, 2000: 149).

When we are opening up the experience of poetry with children through reading aloud with them we want to make sure they know that what they're hearing when we read is an interpretation not a definitive reading. We need to enable them to discover for themselves that exploring and experimenting with the way we read a poem influences meanings we can release.

Go and open the door

I like what Dylan Thomas (in Herbert and Hollis, 2000: 116) has to say about poetry: *I read only the poems I like. This means of course that I have to read a lot of poems I don't like to find the ones I do, but, when I do then all I can say is 'Here they are!' and read them to myself for pleasure. Read the poems you like reading.* Dylan Thomas's advice is helpful but there are differences between what a poet is confident enough to do and children who are still discovering what they enjoy reading. It is, however, the place I think we want to get to with the children we teach: the confidence to make independent choices about what poems they find satisfying; the know-how to be a responsive accomplice in releasing possibilities when they read; the desire to read poetry for pleasure and the discovery that *the first good of poetry is that it is its own reward* (Heaney, 2004: 5).

But we also need to remember the gatekeeping role we have as teachers and that it can sometimes be easier to keep gates closed, sharing only a limited, and consequently limiting, range of poems than to open the gates and go out to explore the wide horizons of poetry. Reading to the class involves widening the horizons of poetry beyond the limitations of what children might be willing to or not yet capable of reading for themselves. In order to do so teachers have to be willing to stretch beyond choices with which they feel comfortable into unknown territory and to discover voices and styles of writing that are unfamiliar and that may challenge some of their own preconceptions about poetry. For any teacher who needs a map for the territory an anthology that hasn't been tailored to meet limited curriculum requirements, where they can discover poems that are surprising or challenging alongside those that instantly strike a chord is a good way to begin exploring.

Children can tolerate the uncertainty that unfamiliarity can bring especially if there is something in the poem that captures their imagination and, in the first instance, this often happens through the way the poem is read aloud. But there will always be poems that we find difficulty tuning into and no one can ever be blamed for not being able to respond immediately to something never before encountered.

George Steiner (1978) suggests that there are four aspects of difficulty that can leave the reader/listener with no immediate purchase on the poem and I have found these to be a helpful way of being aware of the resistances there might be to a poem, my own as well as those I teach. The difficulties Steiner identifies are 'contingent', where there are unfamiliar terms or historical references; 'modal', where it's a first encounter with a unfamiliar form; 'tactical', where the poet has deliberately played with poetic form; and 'ontological', where the poem may challenge previously held understandings of what constitutes poetry.

All of these categories are reminders that poetry has a presence across time and place, that form is culturally rooted and, as is the case with all art forms, that poetry reflects both constancy and change. Whilst it is important to resist the temptation to explain poems before reading, sometimes a poem can benefit from being considered in relation to Stein's categories and introduced in a way that helps to lift children over the threshold and into the poem. Enabling children to experience poetry as *meaningful against the experiences of their own lived lives* (Greene, 2000: 148) requires encounters with poems that engage their imaginative and perceptual energies. For example, hearing some boogie-woogie piano and being introduced to the period of the Black Renaissance in the United States during which Langston Hughes was writing can bring a different sensibility to Hughes's *Dream Boogie*, illuminating connection across time and space that are not at first obvious. Discovering how the idea at the heart of a poem links to familiar personal experience can be a way of connecting to unfamiliar forms. If, for example, you can imagine longing to be somewhere other than where you presently are or where you feel more at home, then two poems from very different poetic traditions will resonate with that experience: W.B. Yeats's 'The Lake Isle of Innisfree' and Grace Nichols's 'Like a Beacon'.

Bedding the ear

Poetry has its origins in situations where the voice is raised in rhythm. Fenton (2003: 23) points out that transmission is still in part oral and that when we learn nursery rhymes orally, for example, we are able to respond to rhyme, the beating of a rhythm, the fitting of word to pitch, which enables us to develop a tacit understanding of structure long before we can read. Although many children's first encounters with written poetry are at school, it will not be the first time they will have met forms of language that exist outside of the flow of everyday speech. In any classroom children will have rich and diverse experience of forms that have been acquired orally: songs; advertising jingles; rhymes and chants of the playground; football chants; nursery rhymes and lullabies; riddles, jokes and parodies; religious litanies and hymns and prayers. All of these have a commonality with written poetry in that they are language held within constraints of form and it is this feeling for form that children bring to the less familiar styles of poetry they meet in the classroom.

Heaney (1980: 47) writes of the way in which his early experiences of hearing secular and sacred forms and his delight in 'the verbal music' of, for example, the rhythmic pattern of the shipping forecast on the radio and litany of the Blessed Virgin, were ways of *bedding the ear with a kind of linguistic hard core* that he would one day build on. Heaney acknowledges that, although not 'consciously savoured' at the time, his retention of the rhythm and pattern of language heard in his childhood is significant in his development as a writer. Children who are familiar with the rhyme and rhythms of the playground often build on the patterns they hold unconsciously in their writing. For example, at a time when the most popular skipping rhyme was *Spanish girl, turn around/Spanish girl, touch the ground/Spanish girl, do the twist/Spanish girl, do the splits*. Christine, who was not a confident Year 3 writer, composed a poem addressing the tadpoles that were being studied using the pattern and cadences of the traditional rhyme she knows well and with which she feels at home: *Tadpole, tadpole,/how do you sleep?/Tadpole tadpole/how do you eat? ...*

Hearing poetry read – read well and read often – builds on the 'linguistic hard core' that is already embedded in the auditory imagination and extends the feeling for form on which writers depend. There are often echoes of what children have heard in the poems they chose to write independently where they recall, rework and experiment with poems that have caught their ears and their imagination. To take a brief example, in his poem 'The Whatifs', Shel Silverstein personifies the fears that torment him by crawling inside his head when he is trying to get to sleep. In her poem, eight-year-old Anni draws on the safety of an already experienced form and although she doesn't sustain the rhyme scheme throughout, the opening lines are a couplet: *Last week/when I was playing hide and seek*. In common with Silverstein, she uses a combination of the real and the surreal to write about her own experience of being beset by fears.

There are two other essential dimensions to poetry in addition to a feeling for form: *the conscious savouring of words* and an understanding that poetry brings *experience under the jurisdiction of form* (Heaney, 1980: 48). The experience of this as a reader is what the writer draws on. There is sense of eight-year-old Ben's understanding of the interconnectedness of all of these in his poem about Tricksy, the rabbit that spent a week as visitor in the classroom. The language reflects the rabbit's movement as she slides from his lap when he tries to hold her and the change of rhythm as he focuses on her nose: ... *she moves funny/ like honey/running down from a spoon./I'll miss her when she goes./The bit I'll really miss/is her nose/twitch/twitch/twitch* ...

Nurturing pleasure

Evidence in the 2007 Ofsted report indicates that informal approaches and reading poetry regularly to the class encourages children's enthusiasm, interest and expertise. As the structured spaces of the classroom become increasingly dominated by teaching and learning that is tailored to the production of measurable outcomes those places and times that offer the freedom for teachers to read to the class without the constraints of formal lessons can be elusive. But poetry can find a place in the marginal spaces of the classroom if it is threaded through the day: as a way of starting and finishing sessions, before going out for break, settling down after lunch or while the class is changing for PE, for example. When opportunities are created for the class to read to each other; to read for themselves alone to hear; to discuss the way poems are written; to explore how sound and meaning can chime with each other; to discover poems full of figurative language and others rich in colloquial speech and to make choices that resonate with their experience, then at the very least teachers will be nurturing reading for pleasure.

Creating classrooms where both teachers and children feel at home with poetry as readers is where writing begins. But teachers have no way of knowing what, if any, long-term impact the poetry they share in the classroom might have on children's lives or the ways in which it will stretch beyond the classroom into their futures. Mr Fawcett's Friday afternoon poetry reading lit a long, slow fuse on mine. It was not until I was visiting the British Museum as an adult, for example, and standing in front of the fine detailed alabaster carvings from Sennacherib's palace, built in the seventh century BCE, that Byron's poem 'The Destruction of Sennacherib' became more than a stirring narrative. And in a dovetailing with Masefield's 'Cargoes', the palace was at Nineveh – with its quinqueremes!

CHAPTER FOUR

Case Study I: Critical Reading and Student Engagement with Poetry

Daniel Xerri

Voices and choices

This chapter explores the significance of engaging students in the process of critical reading by providing them with the opportunity of choosing the poems they read and discuss in class. Focusing on my experience of teaching poetry as part of an A Level English course in Malta, this chapter underscores the need to capitalize on students' contributions.

The teaching of poetry in post-sixteen education is meant to help students develop the skill to read a variety of poems in a critical manner. Developing such a skill is sometimes a tortuous process that can lead teachers to adopt a pedagogy that emphasizes the modelling of a style of close reading, which arguably pushes students into the role of bystanders, thus sacrificing personal engagement. The teacher is at the centre of the arena and the students are meant to be learning by observing the master reader as he or she unravels the poem. The teacher might occasionally ask a question but 'When the whole class and the teacher tackle a poem together, what tends to happen is more like an oral comprehension test than a genuine discussion' (D'Arcy, 1978: 148). The students feel they have to provide the right answers to a set of questions that are not genuinely seeking new information but are there to test the kind of understanding the teacher is looking for. This means that the lesson ends up being dominated by teacher talk. McRae (1991) argues that 'Teacher input, to be assimilated and reproduced, invites static almost mechanical learning. Interaction, learner involvement, inductive learning, all contribute to making the process dynamic' (p. 8). The prevalence of such teacher input is a by-product of the act of teachers positioning themselves as 'gatekeepers' through whose 'offices' (Tweddle et al., 1997: 50) students read the poem. Hughes's (2009) description of her experiences at school probably resonates with those of many others, most certainly my own as a student of poetry:

> Our teachers encouraged us to find the specific meaning in the text, placed there by the author, whether intentionally or not. There was one meaning that could be uncovered and we were trained to do so. Often we didn't need to search for meaning at all because the 'correct' meaning was served up to us by the teacher; all we needed to do was listen and regurgitate the answers in our essays. (pp. 21–22)

Such pedagogy gives primacy to the teacher's role in the critical reading of poetry and risks underestimating the significance of student engagement, with the consequence that poetry ends up being perceived as something that can only be read within the confines of the classroom and only under the supervision of the teacher.

In light of the above, I find it hard to identify with Blocksidge (2000) when he asserts that 'Seminar conditions can be the norm from day one of the A-Level course and, in studying poetry, pupils can quickly grow used to the practice of questioning the poem, questioning each other and questioning me' (p. 105). My experience of the A Level poetry classroom is also at odds with the idea that students in post-sixteen education are used to a style of teaching 'based on a relatively intimate, interactive discussion group' (Amigoni and Sanders, 2003: 75). However, I do believe that this kind of pedagogy is highly desirable. The opportunity to interact and work in a group leads to growth (Bensey, 1991), develops metacognition and metadiscoursal skills (Hardman and Beverton, 1993, 1995) and facilitates understanding (Yazedjian and Kolkhorst, 2007). Students working in groups achieve more than individuals working alone and the process of achieving as a part of a group transfers to individual testing situations (Gabbert et al., 1986). In fact, it is also reported that group discussion has an impact on student's understanding of texts they are required to read and interpret as part of a test (Fall et al., 2000). When group processes are of high quality, all the students in a heterogeneous group of varying levels of achievement are bound to benefit (Wing-yi Cheng et al., 2008). Such a pedagogy is crucial because it values the students' voice as much as that of the teacher. Probst (2004) claims that 'If a class begins to work well, the students may accept the teacher as a participant in the same process of responding and thinking, able to contribute as another learner' (pp. 91–92). When the teacher seeks to create a democratic classroom environment in which students' opinions matter as much as those of the teacher, this will facilitate student engagement. A valid poetry teaching strategy is when the teacher 'helps them discuss their thoughts with other students, communicate ideas effectively and work productively with others' (Chambers and Gregory, 2006: 136). This kind of pedagogy values students' contributions and seeks to devise means by which they may flourish.

One kind of contribution that is sometimes entirely ignored consists of students' preferences as to what is read in class, which some teachers might see as their prerogative. It is true that even if as teachers we allow students to be involved in the choice of texts 'We cannot remove our authority. We are older and more experienced readers. But we can even the playing field, at least somewhat, by encountering poetry for the first time along with our students' (Connolly and Smith, 2003: 239). This is in line with the idea that 'students are more likely to be engaged if they have some choice about what they will study and the texts they will read' (Beach et al., 2006: 7–8). By being empowered to choose what they would like to read in class, students will be encouraged to stop seeing themselves as passive recipients of knowledge. Ultimately, the purpose of any poetry lesson should not just be that of helping students to pass their examination; what is more important is that it should inspire them to continue reading poetry for pleasure even after they finish their course. As Lambirth (2007) points out, 'If young people see poetry attached to hard graft and analysis, they will see no reason to incorporate it into their leisure time' (p. 14). Critical reading skills are of crucial significance but the development of such skills should not come at the expense of student engagement with poetry. That is why the pedagogy employed in the teaching of poetry at A Level should be sufficiently varied and cultivate ways of boosting students' voices and choices.

Context

I teach English at a post-sixteen college in Malta. My students enrol on a two-year course leading to an A Level English examination in which their knowledge and skills in relation to poetry are assessed in two separate components – a question on a set text and a question on an unseen poem. In the first year of their course, students attend a weekly one-hour lecture on the set text, which in the current syllabus (MATSEC, 2013) consists of an anthology of Wilfred Owen's war poems. Teachers are expected to cover a selection of twenty poems from this text in the first year. They also attend a weekly one-hour literary criticism seminar in which they are trained in how to critically read a selection of prose extracts and poems selected by the teacher. The emphasis of these seminars is primarily on poetry given that at the end of the first year, students sit for a department-administered test in which they are expected to write an essay on an unseen poem. In this test they also write an essay on the set text. In the second year, students do not attend any lectures on the set text but they continue attending weekly literary criticism seminars.

Pedagogic imitation

As already indicated, the emphasis of the poetry components in the A Level English syllabus in Malta is primarily on students' ability to read in a critical manner. The literary criticism seminars that students attend every single week over their two-year course are meant to be the chief means by which their critical reading skills are developed. In these seminars, students are expected to acquire a set of skills that they can use in tackling an unseen poem but which are also transferable to their handling of all the other literature components in the examination. According to Nicholls (2002), during a seminar, students should be given the opportunity to develop critical thinking and the ability to engage in argumentation; one of the teacher's roles during such a lesson is that of listening (p. 89). However, the main problem I experienced when I started teaching literary criticism was students' reluctance to actually take an active role in discussing the texts that I had chosen for them to read. They seemed to be quite content to sit and listen to me analysing the poem. Whenever I asked questions, very few students would hazard to offer an opinion and usually it was always the most eager students who initiated an unprompted response to the text. Despite the fact that they possessed a level of critical ability to independently come up with a reading of the poem, they seemed to rely on me to tell them how it should be read. It seemed as if the students' confidence in their own critical skills had never been adequately cultivated.

This situation led me to reflect on why students seemed so disinclined to participate in the kind of lively class discussions that I was after. I recalled my own experiences as an A Level student at the same school and remembered how one of the difficulties I had during literary criticism seminars was that of having to quickly make sense of an unfamiliar text that the teacher seemed to know inside out. My class used to be given a poem at the beginning of the lesson and a few minutes in which to read it and develop an interpretation. The teacher used to ask us questions and when we failed to come up with a suitable response or any response at all, he would start explaining the poem to us line-by-line, occasionally stopping to ask another question before giving up and moving on. As a student I felt I was being quizzed about something the teacher was very familiar with. I felt there was only one right answer and that I was expected to guess which one it was. This sometimes led to feelings of frustration and it made me see poetry as a cryptic genre. A poem had a hidden meaning and only the experienced reader sitting in front of the class had access to it. When I became a teacher I wanted to avoid spoiling my students' enjoyment of poetry by engaging in this kind of pedagogy; however, after the first few weeks I found myself imitating my own teachers.

Reflecting on my own experiences as a student, I realized that perhaps one of the main causes for the problem was the sense of inequality that existed in the seminar room. By choosing poems that I was familiar with, I was unwittingly acting as a gatekeeper to meaning and thus pushing students to depend on me for their understanding of the poem. Ironically, what were meant to be unseen poems were some of the poems I had read over and over again before taking them to class. The solution I thought of was that of trying to put myself in the students' shoes and read poems with them through a fresh perspective. This would entail asking students to choose the poems themselves, something I was not sure had been done before at my school.

Practices and attitudes

When I interviewed fifteen students and eight of my fellow poetry teachers about who selects the poems they read during the literary criticism seminars, they all declared that it is the teacher who is responsible for this. Half of my colleagues indicated that they had never asked students to choose any poems and another two claimed that they had either done it once or else that 'it hardly ever happens'. Two other teachers mentioned that they do encourage students to bring poems to class but both of them affirmed that first they vet the poems in terms of efficacy as teaching and exam-preparation resources. One of the teachers who had never asked students to choose poetry to read in class claimed that this 'would be a good idea, something which might work … I think they would be able to benefit from bringing their own poems'. According to him, in teaching literary criticism 'there is a clash between trying to encourage students to love the subject while at the same time, being the component which students find hardest in the examination, work towards building their skills'. For him and some other colleagues, the main challenge is the time needed to cover all that is expected by the syllabus.

Nine students declared that the fact that it is their teachers who choose the poems to be read in the seminars is 'a good thing', a few of them indicating that the teacher 'knows best'. Nonetheless, fourteen students suggested that they should have a say in the choice of poems, primarily because 'a lot more people would be interested in the lesson'. Being asked to look for poems to read in class would, for one particular student, be an opportunity to 'find the kind of poetry that I enjoy most'. For another student it would serve as 'a chance to express your own taste'. The very act of 'bringing it in class … actually shows that it means something to them and they're appreciating it'. Expressing the sentiments of most of her peers, one student explained that 'we would probably enjoy poetry more if we're given a chance of choosing poems'. The positive attitude of both my colleagues and students provided me with the reassurance to experiment with a different format for the poetry reading seminars.

Student-led reading seminars

When I invited a class of students to compile a small selection of poems to read in class, they initially found it strange because none of them had ever been asked to adopt such a proactive role. They had always associated text selection with the syllabus or with their teachers. I asked the students to form groups and to collaborate in finding published poems that interested them and which they wanted to share and discuss with their peers. Each month we devoted one of the literary criticism lessons to poems the students had selected. Over the course of a number of lessons, each group took the lead to present two of its chosen poems to the class and manage small group discussions based on them. Despite still being familiar with some of the poems that the students had chosen, I sought to minimize my interventions as much as possible during these discussions so that the students' contributions could actually take centre stage. I asked questions whenever I genuinely wanted to learn something but was very cautious about how I offered my opinion since I did not want to undermine the fundamental purpose of these seminars. I never censored anything the students wanted to discuss and they seemed to take the responsibility given to them seriously by avoiding poems that were intentionally offensive. Most students opted for strictly canonical poems that they found in poetry anthologies at home or at the library. However, some students trawled the Internet looking for contemporary poetry dealing with issues they considered relevant to their lives and interests. The fact that their peers were leading the seminar allowed the rest of the class to take a more active stance. The group that had chosen the poems were still privileged in actually having read (and researched) the texts in question, however, the other students did not feel in awe of them and hence were unafraid of contributing their own readings of each poem, especially when these conflicted with those of the students running the seminar.

The main advantages of these student-led seminars were those of heightening students' engagement and helping to boost their confidence as critical readers of poetry. As one particular student put it, 'Bringing in our own poems helped me see poetry as belonging to us all. It made me enjoy analysing poetry even though I still have to do it for the exam.' Ultimately, giving students the right to select some of the poems to be read in class proved to be beneficial even for the seminars I chose to run; most students gradually started to enjoy class discussions of poetry and were no longer reluctant to take part in them.

Conclusion

The belief that poetry is a difficult genre that requires the teacher to demonstrate how to analyse a poem so that students may be able to do the same in the examination might be one of the reasons for which poetry reading seminars consist of a high incidence of teacher talk (Xerri, 2013). By sharing the onus for the selection of poems with my students, I succeeded in not only curbing my own gatekeeping role but also in enhancing student engagement. It facilitated the creation of a more egalitarian classroom environment in which all those attending the seminar could actively engage in the critical reading of poetry. By being entitled to select the poems they wanted to share and discuss with their peers in class, students felt that their choices and opinions were being valued and this coaxed them into taking a more central role. My students were no longer just my audience but had finally become fellow readers of poetry who did not mind stepping onto the stage.

Student selection
of poems
ownership of
curriculum

CHAPTER FIVE

Case Study II: Not 'Puppets on a String' – Learning to Love Teaching Poetry

Andrew Lambirth

For one academic year my colleagues and I from a London University worked with five teachers from primary schools in South East London to develop the teaching of poetry in their classrooms and schools. We had known these teachers from some of our work with student teachers and from when some of them were students themselves. We had chosen them as we knew they were professionals that were keen to develop their practice. Three of the teachers were relatively new to the classroom and the other two had been teachers for longer than five years.

The four literacy team members from the university met with the five teachers for nine sessions over the academic year. Each session lasted for four hours. In addition, we met them for one-to-one interviews on the subject of the project on four separate occasions. The teachers and the academics together went to an international conference in Leicester to present on teaching poetry in primary schools.

This case study draws on the perceptions of being a teacher of poetry of one of those five teachers: I'm using the pseudonym Michael to refer to him. Michael was twenty-nine at the time and had been teaching for three years in a large primary school in a busy part of South East London near the River Thames. Michael told us that he enjoys working in his school and feels privileged to be with such able colleagues. He enjoys sport and plays football regularly. He is married with two young children and lives in London. Michael is a keen reader and he told us that he brings his enthusiasm for books and for reading into the classroom. However, at the start of the project he did not read poetry very often and would rarely choose to read it at home. In his interviews with the team, he was very open, honest and modest about his own abilities as a teacher. It emerged very quickly that Michael was a hard-working, thoughtful and effective primary school teacher.

The poetry project was funded and it enabled the five teachers to come out of school during weekday afternoons to come to the project sessions. At the start, we gave the teachers two published anthologies of poems written for children. Some of the poems from these books would be discussed alongside ways to introduce them to primary school children. The teachers were encouraged to go back into school to try out the ideas and report back to the group at the next session. The children's work would be brought in to discuss and analyse, and stories were shared about how the children had responded. In each session opportunities would be found for the teachers and the university team to write poems together. On one occasion the teachers were asked to write a poem at home and bring it in to share. By the end of the project the teachers had accumulated a large collection of teaching ideas, ways to plan for poetry, an anthology of poems written by them and their pupils and were ready and willing to disseminate their new enthusiasm to teachers in their own schools and elsewhere.

This case study will describe, with the help from the interviews we undertook with Michael, what assisted a teacher to give poetry a high profile in his classroom and to regularly introduce poems to be read and enjoyed.

Cutting the strings

Michael told us that before the project had begun, he felt that poetry was underused and rather neglected in his teaching. He explained this by arguing that as a fairly new teacher he often felt he 'was hanging in there, making stuff up as I went along'. Other teachers seemed to know what they were doing so well. Poetry was 'scary' for Michael.

> I felt intimidated by poetry and I had a misconception of what poetry was.

Michael was unclear about what poetry could be, what it looked like and what kind of effects it can have on its readers. This made teaching poetry a problem for him. As a new teacher lacking confidence, he would tend to be drawn to guidance that allowed him to know exactly what he 'should' do and what the outcomes would be. Prose seemed much more straightforward: 'where you've got to structure your piece of writing like this and it's got to work like that'. Michael would take comfort from what another participant on the project described as 'safe repertoires' of pedagogy, which had set outcomes that could easily be measured for quality. Michael's initial reaction to the poetry project reflected his perspectives:

> When I started this, after the first couple of sessions I wasn't going away very satisfied. It took me a while to get used to the pace of things. Concentrating for a while on a word or a sentence – I was thinking 'give me a unit plan', 'tell me what to do!' It took a while for me to settle and for me to get used to it.

Another participant on the project who had also been teaching less than three years had described how her school prescribed the pedagogy. They 'made me do things...like a puppet on a string' and that it was easy to become dependent on fixed methods and routines that were given to her to deliver. Michael felt he had more freedom than this in his school, but still relied a little too heavily on prescribed and safe approaches. Poetry offered a challenge because to him, it offered a freedom to readers and writers he was unaccustomed to and he was unsure about the outcomes and how to judge success.

Meeting new poems

The project provided Michael and his colleagues with ways to talk about the poems found in the anthologies we had provided. The teachers shared their favourites and chose the ones they wanted to use with their classes. This way the teachers brought unfamiliar poems into their schools. Often they were surprised by the children's responses to them and the maturity and insightfulness of their comments. One anthology used on the project was *Sensational* with poems chosen by Roger McGough. Another young male participant on the project had read Carlos William Carlos's 'The Red Wheel Barrow' and had been astonished by the interest and curiosity his class of six-year-olds had shown towards this poem. He reported how they wanted repeated readings of it and engaged in conversations about its possible meanings. Michael too welcomed the anthology:

> We looked at *Sensational* quite a lot and they really got the idea of the senses. *The Magic of the Brain* (Jenny Joseph) was powerful. Writing came from this. They liked the idea that a smell could bring back a memory. They could relate this back to the main fiction text we were using at other times. I think poetry can bring out a deep level of understanding of a literary kind – not just the things we are expected to teach, so not just similes and metaphors, but if you do it around a poem you can bring out so much more.

Michael used this poem in the early stages of the project. This poem will not be unknown to many teachers as it had been used as part of a scheme of work offered by the Primary National Strategy (2006). This possibly offered work around this poem a perceived greater legitimacy, but Michael makes the point that, because of the quality of the poem, children responded in ways that were surprising and went beyond his expectations. He went on:

> I have been surprised by the children on many occasions this year. They have shown an interest in poems that at first glance I would think they wouldn't enjoy or understand. It has shown me the value of exposing them to a wide range of poems and not being restrictive. The children also surprised me with the level of discussion that has come around poems.

In many ways it was clear that the poems used with the children fuelled the teachers' own enthusiasm for poetry. They enjoyed the responses to the poems from the children and recognized the intellectual benefits to reading and talking about poems in an open way.

Communities of readers of poetry

A striking feature of our work with Michael and the other teachers was how their confidence grew as they saw how the children responded so positively to the poems that the teachers read

> The thing I am most pleased with is the level of enthusiasm from the children. I hope I am correct in thinking that they do not find poetry intimidating or some lofty art form.

Michael reported that as he weaved poems into the daily life of the class through readings, performances and discussions, he enjoyed poetry alongside the children. He would read a poem every day and he told us how the pleasure was communal and rich. Interestingly and perhaps counter-intuitively, although he was reading poems outside of the classroom while looking for more poems to read with his class and to build into other parts of the curriculum, he did tell us that his reading of poems at home as a part of his leisure time, unconnected from school life, was still uncommon. The pleasure he found in poetry happened at and around school in his role as a teacher. The poems he enjoyed the most were the poems that the children debated, discussed and performed in school. His criteria for distinguishing what a good poem was, was how he believed the poem would be received by the children in his class.

Despite research (Bisplinghoff, 2002; Commeyras et al., 2003; Cremin et al., 2009; 'Dreher, 2003), which appears to indicate that teachers are better teachers of reading and writing if they have a personal, out-of-school interest in the literacy practices which form part of the curriculum in school, most of our teachers found their pleasure in poetry only in school. Of course, this does not suggest that the teachers did not enjoy poetry personally as well as professionally, but that they found pleasure in poetry as part of the community they formed with the children in school rather than in home communities and environments. The personal delight they found in poetry came from within the professional community in which they worked. They did not need to read poetry out of school to love it as people and professionals.

Conclusions

What all of us on this project, teachers and academics, found most interesting were the reports coming back from teachers about the aesthetic (Rosenblatt, 1978) nature of the readings of the poems by the children. This set in contrast the more efferent (Rosenblatt, 1978) readings of other texts the children were asked to read in school. Reading for the experience that reading provides in the single lived moment was brought to the fore. The children and the teachers were not asked to focus on what they could 'carry away' from that reading, but simply to enjoy what was happening to them there and then. The children wanted to hear the poems again and again and delighted in the experiences. This initially caused some anxiety for the teachers both in the project sessions and the classroom – Michael's frustration with reading poems in the sessions and not being given 'units of work' with which to walk away. It seemed that a unique aspect of pedagogy for poetry is the focus upon aesthetic readings and poetry's treatment as art. Rather like listening to music, readers of poetry enjoy the experience while it happens. Of course, that must be true of many kinds of texts, not just poetry. Yet, poets seem to revel in their ability to create work that allows these rich experiences to happen. So, poems help 'cut the strings' of approaches to literature that had more of a focus on efferent readings of texts. The teachers on the project found themselves having to approach the teaching of poems differently than they had with other forms of writing. Poems are special forms of art and the only way to work with them in school is to treat them that way.

Schooling and the utilitarian nature of many of its activities and goals has made poetry live on the peripheries, along with play and increasingly any form of arts education. This poetry development project allowed teachers more time to build up their confidence to use poetry in school and to enjoy poems amongst a community of people who loved reading them. As a result of this time, they saw and felt the power of the language arts on themselves and their children.

CHAPTER SIX

Commentary and Practical Implications: Righting the 'Wrong Kind of Orientation'

Andrew Lambirth

Speak again. *Said by which king? You may begin*
'Mrs Schofield's GCSE' by Carol Ann Duffy (2011), The Bees

In this chapter I will draw out what I believe to be the main issues that emerge from the four pieces in the Reading part of this book.

The authors in this part unanimously contend that in many cases the ways that poems have been introduced to children have had, what we may agree to call, the 'wrong kind of orientation'. This is an important theme across all four pieces in this part. Each of the authors demonstrates how poetry has often been made a central part of more instrumental approaches to schooling, as beautifully depicted in Carol Ann Duffy's poem 'Mrs Schofield's GCSE'. The authors give examples in each of their chapters. It seems to me that recruiting poems to become part of a preparation for tests and examinations is indicative of two fundamental misconceptions: a misconception about what education is for and a misunderstanding of what poetry is. I want to begin this chapter with a discussion of how an understanding that poetry is fundamentally and unchangeably an art form must determine how poems are presented to children in schools – or indeed anywhere else. I will then discuss the second issue found in the authors' work in this part, namely the concept of a community of poetry readers and how this concept and this reality is often challenged by the power differentials established in schools. Furthermore, I wish to be bold and propose two important principles for teaching poetry formed from what our authors in this part are telling us. These principles may appear rather extreme or idealistic in the present education climate, but I believe they do follow from what is being argued in this part of the book. Finally and consequently, I will discuss how schools can still be an appropriate environment for reading poetry.

Poetry is art

I do not intend – you will be glad to hear – to wrestle with the problem of finding a *true* definition and value of poetry in this chapter, but I am tempted to distil a brief and incomplete composite contribution to an understanding of what poems are from how the authors in this part write about them.

Some scholars have argued that a poem tells us, or should tell us, nothing (Ogdoen and Richards, 1926) – or at least nothing in the way that other forms of writing tell us something. McGuinn reminds us, through his own poem 'Auntie Jan' and Seamus Heaney's words, that poems should not be taken so seriously and we need to 'loosen up' when we are presented with one to read. I interpret this as saying that the knowledge that poems offer is not the same as the knowledge offered by other forms of written texts. Therefore, our approach to poems needs to be different. There need be no anxiety about meanings. We cannot often walk away from having read a poem with a knowledge or skill that we can adapt for some useful and practical task outside of reading poems. As McGuinn argues, poems demand to be read aesthetically and the ideas contemplated. However, unlike other texts, a poem offers more than a simple meaning or profound idea. If that is all it did, it could be put aside once those thoughts and ideas have been understood (Budd, 1995). Wittgenstein famously wrote: 'Do not forget that a poem, even though it is composed in the language of information, is not used in the language game of giving information' (1967: 28). Indeed, one could argue – as many have (for example Brooks, 1971) – that the real core of the meaning is not just the ideas themselves. So, paraphrasing a poem cannot hope to communicate the meaning of the poem, as the meaning is wrapped up and indistinguishable from the way it is articulated as a poem. The poem itself is the *only* medium that can communicate the whole meaning it offers (Neill, 2003).

This is true of other art forms too; for example, I have a pencil drawing of a tea pot and tea cup on my wall at home. The drawing is by Jacqueline Ritvi. In the image the subjects are sitting on a table with what appears to be a fireplace behind them. I am fond of this drawing and it moves me. Yet, it is only a drawing of a domestic scene. The main subjects are simply a tea pot and a tea cup. But they are not just a tea pot and tea cup, it is a drawing of these objects and the drawing with its fine execution of pencil shading and marks transforms that scene into (without trying to confuse the argument) poetry. The drawing is full of meaning that only that drawing can convey. No other medium of representation could present that meaning in the same way. Moreover, the drawing has no other purpose or utility other than to please and to move the observer.

I wish to propose that because of the nature of poems as art forms and how they operate as sources of particular aesthetic knowledge and understanding, they intrinsically do not fit into a utilitarian and instrumental model of schooling. Mr Fawcett's readings of poems, as described by Steele in her chapter, were read for no other reason than for pleasure. Quite frankly, there can be no other reason for reading poems than the pleasure of making meaning from them – whatever that meaning may be. Any other reasons or objectives for listening to poems, or music or viewing paintings for that matter will 'cast the shadow' that Steele describes across them. This is because reading poems cannot be approached in a way that seeks some outcome other than personal or shared pleasure. By pleasure, I mean the satisfactions that come from engagement with the language arts and that encourage us to come back for more. These satisfactions include everything from confronting the horrors brought about by tragedy and the human condition to the joys and delights found from language play and comedy. The pleasure found from poems can convince us of the righteousness of political causes or the validity of human feelings and desires; it is a profound pleasure that art and poetry can bring and in my view is one of the highest forms of experience we can enjoy.

Steele reminds us how The National Literacy Strategy (NLS) in England treated poems like any other text and by so doing increased the misunderstandings about what poems are for and what they can do. With the NLS, one could 'do' poetry in a unit of work just as one could 'do' instructional or explanatory texts. Poetry cannot be 'done' in this way without distorting the learner's perception of what one does with a poem. McGuinn relates the outcomes of that long shadow of schooling that has damaged the perceptions of poetry of many of the students he meets. Xerri, in his case study, looks for approaches that will allow his students to experience poems as much as possible for pleasure. He encourages them to choose poems they want to read. Michael, in my case study, was initially confused by how the poetry project he was attending was approaching poems for discussion. He wanted an objectives-led package of activities, which would lead to a clear tangible teaching outcome. Happily, as I describe in the case study, Michael begins to realize that if children are to enjoy poems aesthetically, they need to be introduced in ways that emphasize the moment of reading.

Principle 1 for the pedagogy of poetry: poems must never be taught for any extrinsic reason like tests and examinations and should only be introduced in schools for the pleasure of reading (or writing) them. There must be no other teaching and learning objective.

Communities of readers

The notion of establishing communities of readers amongst teachers and children has been studied by those seeking an important bond between participants in classrooms discussing literature (Cremin et al., 2009). The authors in this Reading part emphasize how important it is to establish more equal partnerships in endeavours to bring out the meanings in poems. Xerri describes school situations within which poems become the vehicle for preparation for an examination. Inevitably, power between the teacher and the student is established in ways which ensure that learning travels only one way – from teacher to student – and the lessons become mechanistic and the poems means to an end. The power relations here stress the devaluing of the role of the reader and the subjective response in favour of the text and the guiding role of the teacher (Dias and Hayhoe, 1988). McGuinn quotes his student declaring how the notes she wrote about a poem were not from her responses at all, but from the teacher's as these views were considered the most relevant and useful.

Yet, Xerri looked for ways to mediate these kinds of power differentials and constraints. He introduced choice into his lessons: the opportunity for students to choose the poems they were going to be read and discuss together. The teacher gives up a little of his power in trusting the students to present poems that may appeal to them. In doing so, the students learn something about each other through the choices of their peers and consequently the orientation of how poems are presented is changed a little. This is a small step towards a community and what Steele calls the 'nurturing of pleasure'. Steele describes how in primary schools poems can find a place in 'the marginal spaces of the classroom'. They can be 'threaded through the day' and in Xerri's case small concessions can allow pleasure to be nurtured in a community that is provided with the opportunity to communicate something through the sharing of poems chosen by the students.

A community of readers that includes teachers and children is also described in my case study. The teacher, Michael, does not read poems at home as part of his leisure activities. However, within the community of his classroom, he describes how much he (as a person and a teacher) enjoys poems. He takes delight in discussing fine poems written for children with the children themselves and relishes the children's reactions and meanings they make. In addition, the children note how the poems arouse the teacher's genuine curiosity and interest and they watch as the poems create a new awareness and understanding about the world for him. In these situations everyone becomes a model for a reader of poems for everyone else. The subjective nature of responding to art is celebrated through the pedagogy.

Principle 2 for the pedagogy of poetry: create a community of readers in your class. Introduce poems to your children as an equal. Choose poems

that arouse your own curiosity and brings you delight. Ask questions about poems to which you do not know the answer.

Schooling and poetry

Schools potentially offer a wonderful opportunity for introducing poems to children. They can create communities for discovering new understandings about the world through the medium of science and art. This book demonstrates what can be done to make poems special and meaningful in classrooms across the world. Yet, as we have read in this part, instrumental approaches to schooling can do a great deal of damage to perceptions of art and poetry too.

The much promoted and consistent need for countries to be able to compete in world markets can shape the curricula and the pedagogy in schools to be blatantly instrumental and utilitarian. This fact helps to explain the frustrations of teachers and inspectors about how poetry has been taught as described by McGuinn. Goodman (2014) has recently argued that today more than ever multinational corporations have increased their drive to reduce the influence of the democratic state in favour of the market in ways that I have argued (Lambirth, 2014) reflects the crisis in the economy all over the world. The hand of business in mass schooling influences the form of knowledge and skills which are to be valued. So, if schooling is to be driven by these market forces in the future (and this will be determined by whether the people of the developed world give their consent), one could almost argue for poems being removed from the curriculum altogether. We are only too aware of the damage that can be done to young people's perceptions of poetry if it is used only as a vehicle for examinations or is taught in ways that treats it like all other forms of texts.

I want to finish with a message of hope. Despite the constraints placed on teachers and the high levels of surveillance from managers and inspection regimes to ensure compliance to instrumental forms of education, teachers continue to possess a special kind of social power: everyday they meet and talk with children from different walks of life and influence them. The authors in this part and across the whole book demonstrate ways that ignite poetry in the hearts of their students. Steele describes how, if necessary, 'poetry can find a place in the marginal spaces of the classroom threaded through the day'. This nurturing of reading poems for pleasure provides the rich moments when poems can have the greatest effect on their readers – away from the hurly burly absurdity of teaching for tests. Indeed, it is in these moments the two principles for the pedagogy of poetry I have suggested in this chapter can be applied. Poems flourish in such circumstances. There is hope, and it begins here.

PART TWO

Writing Poetry

CHAPTER SEVEN

Inspiring Young People to Write Poems

Cliff Yates

I was talking to a group of Year 8 students in East Sussex recently, after reading them some poems in assembly, and one boy said: 'Oh I see, poems can be about anything.' This is exactly what I want students to realize, that they can write poems about anything, however ordinary and everyday, however strange and unbelievable. Poetry belongs to them: it's theirs, and anything is possible.

I always begin a day in school with a short poetry reading. As well as an opportunity to introduce myself and set the tone for the workshops, it's an opportunity to de-mystify poetry, to challenge and dispel any prejudices that students might have, for example that poems have to rhyme, or that they have to be difficult or, if they are difficult, that they can be enjoyed anyway; there are many ways in which a poem can be enjoyed and there's no right answer. Significantly, it often surprises students to meet someone who actually enjoys writing.

I want to give young people the experience of writing like writers. For this reason, my first workshop exercise is free writing. Free writing, sometimes going by other names, such as 'automatic writing' and 'writing practice', is to write without stopping for a few minutes, without regard to the outcome (Goldberg, 1986: 8; Sansom, 1994: 68; Sweeney and Williams, 1997: 9). Free writing introduces students to the way in which they will write throughout the workshop, in short, intense bursts. I tell students not to rhyme, that it doesn't have to be neat, and not to write to the edge of the page, so that it 'looks like a poem', which is a preliminary way of introducing them to the importance of line breaks, arguably the most fundamental skill in the craft of writing poetry (Yates, 2007: 15–18; Yates, 2009: 29).

With free writing, you can start off with one idea and find yourself somewhere else. Something happens during the writing. This, of course, is the way in which writers write: in such a way as to allow the process of writing to take the work in a new direction. It is a process of discovery: dynamic, exciting, surprising. There's a famous story about Balzac who was so surprised and moved by the death of one of the characters in the novel he was writing that he opened his window and shouted: 'Le Père Goriot est mort! Le Père Goriot est mort!' (Plimpton, 1986: 259). I tell students that if they are surprised by what they have written, it's a good sign that it's going well: as Robert Frost says: 'No surprise for the writer, no surprise for the reader' (Frost, 1960). Indeed, I'm constantly surprised what young people write during a workshop and have learnt from experience never to underestimate what they can do.

I introduce free writing as a 'warm-up', but in practice it can lead to remarkably complete poems. Calling it a warm-up helps take away the compulsion to 'get it right', which can inhibit students. I also say that no one will be forced to read back. If students think that they might be compelled to read out their work, they might play safe and write what they can get away with in front of their classmates. I don't want students to play safe, I want them to *feel* safe: to write about what they want, without fear; not to impress their friends, or to please me, but to please themselves. As Peter and Ann Sansom point out, free writing provides pressure without anxiety (Yates, 1999: 104). Students have only a few minutes to write something and therefore it doesn't matter how good or bad it is. They have permission to fail. Making art is a risky business.

Often the most difficult thing for students is knowing where to start. I provide opening lines such as 'The first time I...', 'I shouldn't say this but...' or 'This time last week...'. The opening line is a focus, even if this focus gets abandoned during the writing. The most important thing is to keep going, even if it doesn't make sense. A useful opener is 'I remember...', which originated with the artist Joe Brainard, whose autobiography consists of hundreds of brief paragraphs, each beginning with that phrase (Brainard, 2001). 'I remember' can be used as a structuring device as Brainard uses it; if the student runs out of material, they can repeat it and continue:

In a rush

I remember discovering the buzzing smells of summer,
dust gathering in illuminated shafts
through the gaps in the morning curtains.

I remember falling through clouds and
moist, dewy pansies. Rolls of dry grass
grazing my knees and staining my elbows, the

tips tingling the tops of my fingers as
I lay back into the worn hammock, head over the edge
so gravity reversed and I got pulled from the blue blanket of sky.

I remember you and I, balancing on the pond
bricks, uncontrollably spluttering out strawberry-tasting giggles
as Uncle Steve scooped us up before we fell in to

swim with the fish and breathe under water
like magic.

I remember one time you did fall, claiming that
in our bunk bed every night
you prayed so hard to become a mermaid
that surely by now you would have the power to
transform and grow a willowy tail.
I remember waiting for you
to rise triumphantly from the distorted, swaying weeds,
out of the tinged dirt glint
and shatter the unusually calm surface.

Agnès Lambert (Year 10)

'In a Rush' demonstrates how free writing can work: the poem seems to gather momentum, as if the writer discovers what she wants to say during the course of the writing. It's good to have Uncle Steve in the poem – I tell students to include the names of people and places in their poems; it adds authenticity and makes the poems completely their own. Here, Uncle Steve provides a down-to-earth contrast to the extraordinary image of the mermaid with the 'willowy tail' and helps make the ending curiously believable.

Because it often results in a complete poem, free writing demonstrates how a poem can be written quickly. It also demonstrates how little time in the timetable is needed to keep up the practice of creative writing. When I was teaching English, I had students writing poems throughout their secondary school career, even if it was just one poem every half term. Writing poems improves every aspect of writing, including writing in exams, because in a poem every word counts and this experience of working closely with language spills over into everything that students subsequently write.

Free writing adds immediacy and energy to students' poems so that their work has this quality even when it was written in different circumstances, like this poem:

James Bond

The moveable trolley rockets
down the privy
looking for
a restored Aston Martin
which was looking for
an old stately home.

1964 Fantasy Novel.
Live for the moment:
the glamour, the fame
the thrill
of when the dining
room table with 50
seated guests
galahants into
the kitchen.

William Kerley, Year 9 (Yates, 2001: 36)

'James Bond' was written as a result of the furniture game, which is one of the best ways I know to get students using metaphors: students think of a person and answer a series of questions, such as if this person were a piece of furniture/building/room/etc./what would they be? William wrote his answers to these questions quickly, in what was in effect a series of brief periods of free writing. He then re-ordered and linked his answers to form a narrative, adjusting line breaks to increase the sense of pace, for example interrupting 'dining/room table' and ending the first line with the verb 'rockets'. This vivid, dynamic and unpredictable poem effectively gives the impression that it was written in one sitting.

It is important to give students plenty of scope and freedom to find their own direction and to get engaged in writing on their own terms. In an adult workshop for example, no one is blamed for not being able to write a poem during a particular exercise: some exercises will work better than others, some simply won't work for you. It's the same, of course, with young people. For this reason, I always do at least three or four exercises during a workshop when I visit a school, and tell the students that not all of them will necessarily 'work': if they get one poem out of it, it will be a success. In practice they usually get at least two or three. When I was teaching English I always came at a poem from different directions, providing different 'ways in' to enable all the students to get a good start. I would play variations on the furniture game, for example, so that they had plenty of material to choose from, and I would share with students example poems by their contemporaries to demonstrate a variety of ways that they could use the material in order to create a different type of poem, with permission to surprise me by trying something new (Yates, 1999: 16–21). This meant that all the students would use the furniture game to write a poem, but the final poems could be strikingly different. It goes without saying that it's important to be able to give the students direction with how to develop their poems, so that they have as much space as possible to write something original.

For this reason, I see reading poetry as part of my job. The more I read, the more open I become to what is possible; I will be more able to recognize originality in students' work and I will be better equipped to help them develop first drafts into completed poems. If teachers have experience of reading a range of poetry, this is bound to increase their ability to see possible directions in the work of their students. For this reason, INSET sessions where teachers explore contemporary poetry would do an enormous amount to improve writing in schools. I also think it's important to introduce students to a variety of different types of poetry, to give them an idea of what is possible. I have, over the years, shared some particularly challenging poems with students, curious to see what they would make of it, by writers such as Maggie O'Sullivan and Tom Raworth, and been hugely impressed by their response. I like to stretch students and rarely use poems written for young people in the classroom; in my experience, students have no problem reading 'adult' poetry.

I also believe that ideally teachers should experience writing creatively for themselves: a free Arvon Foundation course as part of teacher training! When I started teaching, I felt uncomfortable getting students to write poems when I had no idea how to go about writing them myself. Eventually, after joining in a workshop with the late great Pete Morgan, I was off. Within a few months I had poems published in magazines. The experience of writing in that short workshop, that intensity of focus, was all I needed to give me the insight and the confidence to be able to start writing. This is why I'm so keen on workshops. Writing poems transformed the way in which I taught. I was teaching from the inside, like an art teacher showing students how to draw and paint, passing on a craft. Of course, it's possible to teach creative writing without having experienced it, but there's a world of difference. Enjoyment is contagious.

And writing, as I'm describing it here, is enjoyable. My students tended to see all writing, even essay writing in exam conditions, as an opportunity to be creative. I remember Tom, writing a persuasive essay as part of his mock GCSE English exam, laughing to himself so much at what he was writing that he could hardly carry on. I told him to enjoy himself but also to be sure to answer the question and do all he had to, to show the examiner that he knew what he was doing. I needn't have worried: he got an A* in English. Not everyone can get an A* of course, but everyone can enjoy writing.

The point about allowing first drafts to be untidy is crucial. Creating is about trying things out, going in new directions, taking risks, and students can't do that if they're being compelled to write neatly, which is more about getting it right first time. When I was teaching English, I gave my students writers' notebooks for first drafts, which could be as untidy as they liked; I wouldn't mark them, or read them without permission. This allowed students to write freely. Of course, in practice they often showed me their books, but the principle is fundamental: not only did it demonstrate that I respected their privacy, but also it encouraged them to take their writing seriously. Notebooks could be used for writing poems or stories outside English lessons. Occasionally, when I was setting poetry homework, a student would ask: 'Is it OK to hand in one that I wrote at home?' That was rewarding – to see young people writing independently, as part of their lives out of school.

I spend a lot of workshop time talking with young people, encouraging them to share ideas and stories, and listening. Valuing what students say is giving them permission to be themselves and to have confidence in their own voice. When students say something memorable, sometimes I get them to write it down, so that they can 'use it in a poem'. This takes students by surprise, but they soon get the message. It's making the connection between talking and writing: writing is talk that is written down. I know that this isn't the whole story, but it's a useful working principle for the poetry workshop in the classroom.

After free writing, subsequent workshop exercises mostly involve reading contemporary poems and using them as starting points for students' writing. One exercise that I strongly recommend, which enables students to access imaginary areas of experience (and in so doing, perhaps, to access complex ideas, attitudes and feelings) is to write from the point of view of an animal, object, person from history or a fictional character (Yates, 1999: 49–65; 79–91; 115–126). The following poem was written after reading Jo Shapcott's 'Tom and Jerry Visit England'; the idea was to write a poem from the point of view of a fictional character that is normally silent or near-silent, giving them a voice (Shapcott, 2000: 39; Yates, 1999: 123). The following poem ambitiously takes on what must surely be one of the most forgettable fictional characters of all time: Weed in the 1950s BBC children's programme, The Flower Pot Men:

Weed wants to travel

(for Bill and Ben)

On a normal day
you'd see my stalk quiver

towards the moss-free flowerpots
which I live behind.
But underneath there's the legful haze
of my crazy roots encountering
worms. The furious tingle
of spread-eagling round bricks
and buried stones, oval and sea-formed
in perfection – my treasure.
My ambition? To travel.
I want to laugh
my whispery name
down your drainpipe,
to echo and boom when you
turn on your taps.
To slowly drive my legs
through rich earth,
letting a hunch of gathered snails
clatter from my leaves.

Ruth Yates, Year 10 (Yates, 2001: 58)

'Weed Wants to Travel' imagines what it could feel like, physically, to send roots into the ground: 'The furious tingle/of spread-eagling round bricks/ and buried stones.' The variety of sounds is evocative, as if tuning into Weed's wavelength and gently increasing the volume: 'to laugh/my whispery name/ … /to echo and boom/ … / … snails/clatter from my leaves'. The use of 'My ambition?' as a structuring device is borrowed from Simon Armitage's 'Ten Pence Story', which the class had already used as a starting point for writing from an object's point of view – the fact that Ruth chose to borrow this phrase for this poem demonstrates how reading a variety of poems with young people can give them a repertoire of possibilities: ideas and devices which they can draw on for their own purposes (Armitage, 1989: 64; Yates, 1999: 112).

The workshop techniques and methods that I've discussed are derived from the practice of established writers. They enable young people to write like writers and to see themselves as writers. I use similar techniques working with adults, but with young people, as I have mentioned, I spend more time encouraging them to talk, and listening to what they have to say. I believe that if I can demonstrate the connection between talking and writing, students will see that writing poems is a mode of expression which, at the very least, is as intimate, immediate and powerful as their speaking voice, perhaps more. As Ted Hughes says, the important thing is 'not "How to write" but "How to say what you really mean"' (Hughes, 1967: 12). This is the point: to enable young people to discover for themselves what they really want to say, and then to say it.

Acknowledgements

This chapter draws on material in *Jumpstart Poetry in the Secondary School* (Yates, 1999), *The Poem as Process: Theory and Practice* (Yates, 2006), 'Flying, A Poetics' (Yates, 2009) and 'Writing Like Writers in the Classroom: Free Writing and Formal Constraint' (Yates, 2007).

I am indebted to Peter and Ann Sansom for the strategies around free writing as I have discussed them here (Yates, 1999: 102–106).

'In a Rush' by Agnès Lambert was highly commended in the Foyle Young Poets of the Year Awards 2008; 'James Bond' by William Kerley was selected for the *Times Educational Supplement* Young Poet feature on 22 May 1998 and was also published in *The TES Book of Young Poets* (Grogan, 1999); 'Weed Wants to Travel' by Ruth Yates was an overall winner of the Foyle Young Poets of the Year Awards, 2001. Their poems are reprinted here with their kind permission.

CHAPTER EIGHT

Teaching Poetry Based on Actual Writing Practices: Beyond Words

Mandy Coe

Poetry is all around us, moving effortlessly between public and private arenas. Whether adding to the stadium's roar or hushing babies at night, this democratic and creative art form crosses all cultural and national boundaries. For those of us who learn to love poetry, it guarantees a lifelong journey, each new poem demanding a re-evaluation of what poetry actually is. Sharing these pleasures with children and young people can be as simple as 'modelling' enjoyment in re-reading and relishing a poem's mystery (being comfortable outside an established 'right' or 'wrong' analysis). This sharing approach is less likely to meet with the defensive 'I don't get it' response – often driven by feelings of exclusion. Positive modelling gives children permission to engage with the puzzles and pleasures of poetry in a far more varied and interactive way. Indeed, most poems intentionally leave space for readers to develop their meanings, so the individual's subjective response is an act of creation in itself. This notion of reader as joint creator is an empowering one for young readers. By demonstrating that poetry is not a one-way process of production and consumption, children can learn that all art is deeply interactive. When classrooms creak under pressure to provide definitive answers, the child-sized possibilities of a poem bring a welcome chance to swap opinions, play, puzzle and guess.

Modelling can be surprisingly casual; librarians, carers or teaching staff sharing responses to a poem, or instances of a poem providing an emotional resonance. A memory I have from primary school illustrates the power of such modelling. Mr Bailey, a Year 5 teacher, walked into the classroom and pinned a poem to the wall. He didn't refer to it during lessons, but we could see he'd underlined sections and added a scattering of question marks. This piqued our interest. A few days later, it was ripped down. The next morning it reappeared, sellotaped and with the creases smoothed out. 'I was thinking about this poem on the way to school', he said, 'and I changed my mind.' Mr Bailey didn't teach the text. I don't remember the name of the poem and am not even sure if his modelling was consciously planned, but Mr Bailey subtly shared with his class his process of questioning and exploration, modelling a fluidity of response: the act of being consumed by a poem. He pinned the poem up, but didn't pin the poem down. The class observed … and absorbed. Mr Bailey, thank you.

Another step towards demystifying reading or writing poetry is to untangle it from its medium: the written word. Teaching poetry solely within English is a little like teaching visual art within science just because oil paints include chemicals. A poem begins within the writer's physical world: a view of sky, a whisper of footsteps, a shower of rain. These experiences/memories are interwoven with myth, history, biography and drama; drawn from subjects across the curriculum and beyond. Pen and paper – the gathering and re-ordering of subject-related words – should be presented as but one part of the process.

Confining poetry so firmly to an act of writing/text-production has an even greater impact on our young writers and their future as readers. When inspiration and innovation (the primary drivers of the craft) are sidelined, poetry is in danger of becoming, not a thing that *is*, but a thing that *does* – a linguistic game, a rule-bound activity with literacy-objectives. The primary demand of written text in literacy classrooms is clarity, whether in reports, arguments or stories. Functionalism distorts poetry. Associating poetry so closely with our expectations of texts in general is problematic. We start to see the very shape of a poem – its ambiguities, metaphors and layers of meaning – as eccentricities rather than craft.

The temptation to utilize the 'fun/novelty' aspects of poetry in order to meet the technical demands of a literacy curriculum so rooted in functionalism is almost irresistible. But if we persist, presenting poetry as something that springs from the substance of our lives, we can still create confident reader/writers who show a heightened awareness of the world; ensuring that an 'I don't get' it response is transformed into the desire to 'discover' it.

* * *

Activity: Connective Leaps

Here's an easy out-loud exercise to do in the morning, to wake up your class and find laughter in the art. It begs for surreal thinking, costs nothing and needs only the voice. This activity can be explored by the whole class, or within smaller groups.

Sample Poem:

Thanks
The rain is thankful for the cloud,
the cloud is thankful for the wind,
the wind is thankful for the bird,
the bird is thankful for the worm,
the worm is thankful for clay,
the clay is thankful for the rain,
the rain is thankful for the cloud.

Mandy Coe

How to:

- Set off with a start line, for example *The flea is thankful for the fox*.

- The next person along takes it up with *The fox is thankful for … chickens*.

- The next person may decide that *Chickens are thankful for jazz*, or *feathers*, or *eggshells* and so on, each new person adding a new line.

- Each day, pupils will get faster, braver and more surprising in their connective leaps. They will learn to move, not forever inward and smaller, as with those little wooden Russian dolls, but outwards, sideways, backwards, upwards.

- Any halting thoughts of 'Will I get this wrong?' or 'Will I sound daft' should be noted and accepted as a normal aspect of risk-taking and speculating aloud.

Development

The Ted Hughes poem, 'Amulet' (Hughes, 1978), is another poem based on connections, in this case those of scale and imagery. For this activity to cross curriculum subject boundaries, choose a start line such as *Volcanoes are thankful for heat* or *War is thankful for bullets*.

Sample poem:

Inside the Sea
Inside the sea there are waves
Inside the waves there is wet
Inside the wet there is smooth
Inside the smooth there are shells
Inside the shells there are waves
Inside the sea I feel the cold
Inside the cold I feel the air
Inside the air I feel the sea.

Amy (The Write Team, Bath)

In this example, using 'Amulet' as a model, this Year 8 writer makes connective leaps with both texture and sound. The repetition of 'Inside the ...' invokes an almost meditative tone, working both to support performance and to create patterns of typography on the page. She cleverly loops the subject full circle, so as to start and end with the word 'sea'.

* * *

Like many writers who guest-lecture in higher education I see budding novelists, script writers and poets arriving at university, frequently due to positive feedback given in school. These students then have to negotiate the gap between the writing cultures of school and university. Where schools provide ambitious stylistic models and aim to build vocabulary, creative writing degrees demand concision. Lecturers annotate creative work with 'overwritten' and overtly poetic language is scored out. The primary obstacle for many first year students is their belief that being a writer is all about writing down words – and lots of them. But unnecessary words are the biggest obstacle to allowing the reader to see, hear and feel without the intrusiveness of the authorial voice.

The following exercise is simple and instantly readdresses the balance between vocabularies (form) and questioning (content). In seminars and INSET, it is a light-bulb moment for teachers, as it models approaches to a subject that are counterintuitive but deeply effective. I recently presented this idea to a group of teaching staff. Here's what we did:

Activity: Building Word Banks

The group was invited to build a word bank in order to create a group poem. We chose the subject of rain. On a flip chart we listed the following words:

rain, cloud, water, drop, wet, splash, umbrella, raincoat, rainbow, cats and dogs, puddles, weather, wellington, acid, thunder, sky, cascading, shower, mist, drizzle, storm

How to

The participants are then asked to imagine two doors; one leading to a library containing a thesaurus and a range of rain-related word banks. The other door opens onto a monsoon. The door the group unanimously chose to open was the latter. Because they chose to write from reality, they were then told that the poem must be written using *none* of the words listed in the word bank.

The response to these most obvious, clichéd, words being off the table is interesting. Participants puff out their cheeks, throw down pencils and roll their eyes. 'This', they say, 'is impossible.' But then the questioning starts. Gentle prompts, such as what does rain really sound and smell like? Can you share one memory of rain? How does rain reflect light? How does rain feel on the skin? And the poem puts down its roots – not in words, but in life. Here is the piece they came up with.

Sample poem:

Old coats and moss,
dogs shaking off diamonds.
Traffic jams.
Wipers sigh.
The white noise of wind is in high trees
as the sky drums fingers on the roof.
All crowds are distant,
we dissolve.

By assuming a poem starts with pen and paper, we fail to value where it really begins: in real or imagined experiences made even more vivid by the writerly habit of close observation. This exercise allows words to assume their rightful place: not as building blocks, but as a medium of translation, chosen with care, not through word association. In order to share human experiences existing (in the main) beyond words, we need to be led by seeing and by *becoming* the subject; by the true writer's process of questions, questions, questions.

* * *

The importance of presenting creativity as a 'finding-your-way', risk-taking activity is summed up by educationalist, Ken Robinson, 'If you're not prepared to be wrong, you'll never come up with anything original' (Robinson, 2010). He is not alone in this thinking. Most champions of learner-centred pedagogy, such as Bell Hooks, Mick Waters and Paulo Freire, argue that creativity and critical thinking are at the heart of effective learning and a healthy sense of self. A closer reading of Robinson's quote allows for an even deeper insight. It seems – true to real writing practices – that reducing the *fear* of getting things 'wrong' means we can get even more things right.

The following activity suspends notions of right and wrong completely by inviting pupils to use 'visual translation' in order to explore typography (in this case, the following Chinese phrase, Shan Shui Qing, which roughly translates as 'love of mountains and rivers'). Language is infinitely variable, and UK schools are lucky to have such a diversity of mother tongues. One way to boost confidence is to explore abstract translation. You can also invite pupils who have other mother-tongues to share words for visual translation.

Any mother tongue speakers of this language will be in the privileged position of being actual translators; the rest of the group get to create new meanings.

Activity: Images and Symbols

Ask pupils to respond to the following phrase by describing any images or symbols they may see, such as swans floating past, or two men leaning against a wall. This way of looking can be quite liberating for pupils with dyslexia, as it celebrates alternative ways of perceiving text.

山水情

Development

Invite pupils to take the same approach to their own name written out in capital letters, exploring pictorial shapes and sounds.

Sample poem:

In My Name (MANDY)
In my name are mountains,
blue and white and high.
My name holds a thousand
miles of rock and sky.

In my name are valleys
climbed by Ma and Man
with a forked-top, walking-stick,
ready hold a thumb.

In my name is a yacht's sail,
the sound of the river Dee.
In my name is a world,
in my name is me.

Mandy Coe (from If You Could See Laughter)

* * *

A friend came across her son's secondary school set-text poetry anthology and was horrified to see he had used a biro to gouge out the eyes of the poet on the cover. 'It's nothing personal', he replied when challenged. 'Studying the poems drove me to it.' The majority of teachers and educators acknowledge the disaffection secondary pupils feel when faced with poetry – due to an imbalance between critical and creative writing. Asking pupils to study poems as set-text, without being given time to explore their own poetry, is like teaching pupils to cook without tasting the food. But if current government policies continue to transform schools from places of education to places of 'schooling', it is inevitable that children will experience reading and writing as a chore – thereby starving them of creative experience.

Promoting creative approaches to poetry in the classroom can do wonders. However, there is a difference between working with the education system to encourage creativity and the expectation that teachers should individually defend the right of pupils to experience creativity in the classroom. This sense of personal responsibility (fuelled by vocation) can and does occur when teachers are supported in their workplace through INSET, funding and outward-looking management. However, dismantling teaching education colleges, proposals of performance-related pay, tests and league tables make the threat of failure ever-present and personalized. Writers in education see first hand how common it is for teachers to feel undermined and exhausted. Through open letters to the education minister, a number of well-known authors have shared their concerns on the radical reduction of creative opportunities in our schools. In a recent article in the *Guardian*, educationalist Mick Waters goes so far as to argue the need for 'an education spring' (Waters, 2013). In talking about *Making Poetry Happen*, we have to acknowledge the fact that an education system based on standardization and anxiety is an education system calculated to kill creativity stone-dead.

Activity: Restricted Word Banks

As a direct contrast to the activity where word banks are off-limits, the following exercise offers limited word choice but infinite combinations. But the restrictions of workshops can be surprisingly liberating. As with all the activities outlined here, it is a 'start-up' only, and time should be given for poems to be developed and/or the original rules disregarded.

> escape red soft begin dark wolf heart glass fall touch forget remember once forever sleep stepping fingertips why window candle thunder fall quick ice silver water night dawn sunset reflected journey shadow blue spark memory city broken perfect call loud twisted streets midnight curved straight hurry secret laughter lands space everything air walk wall

Pupils can choose, in any order, any amount of words from this list. They can add their own words, change tense or transform singular to plural and so on. To encourage randomness, pick a word with eyes shut, then find a way to connect it to another.

> Sample poem:
> Midnight curves, midday is straight.
> Thunder falls and ice rises.
> The wolf is candle, the bird is sunlight.
> Laughter is loud but the heart is secret.
>
> Year 6 pupil, Young Writer's Science Day, Wallasey

This young writer plays with contrasts and the senses. The poem holds both movement and a metaphysical sense of play. As always, the challenge of writing such poems allows for invaluable insights, making reading poetry a far more interactive and critical experience. Peer editing will further develop this two-way interaction of reader/writer.

The resonance of the random words used to stimulate this poem is due, in some part, to their origin (they were drawn from the *Selected Works of Ted Hughes* (1995)). Ted Hughes, a poet deeply connected with myth, nature and landscape, was renowned for his common use of Old English rather than a Latin-based vocabulary. He wrote a number of books on poetry, and in emphasizing the 'liberating limitations' of workshops, he remarked that *These artificial limits create a crisis, which rouses the brain's resources: the compulsion towards haste overthrows the ordinary precautions, flings everything into top gear, and many things that are usually hidden find themselves rushed into the open'* (1967).

* * *

As Ted Hughes's observation suggests, when we move poetry from the clerical into the physical, barriers are broken down. All at once, the sun is a button; an ocean can be folded up and put in your pocket. For practising writers and children alike, realizing that we can be anywhere, create anything, through poetry gives us the ability to see the world with new eyes.

If, in addition to modelling by teachers and school librarians, we factor in teacher-writers and visiting authors, we already have a pretty powerful infrastructure capable of modelling true-to-life approaches to poetry. Of course, the real powerhouse is the energy generated by young people themselves, pursuing their interests through personal reading, reading awards, book clubs and reader/discussion groups. Organizations behind events such as the annual Poetry Society's Foyle Young Writer's Prize, the adult T.S. Eliot and Forward Poetry Prizes even provide online support for such groups.

This modelling infrastructure co-exists with and informs formal teaching (and vice versa). But there are compelling reasons to maintain a clear separation. Coleridge observed that 'Poetry gives the most pleasure when only generally and not perfectly understood' (in Wheeler, 1981). Indeed, many adults who are uncomfortable around poetry attribute their ambivalence to memories of school or college, where personal resonances were severed by too much objective dissection. Avoiding all aspects of 'teaching to the test' is unrealistic. But counterbalancing set-text requirements with examples of poetry's defiant ability, not only to see new worlds, but also to see the old world with new eyes, encourages children to feel confidence rather than discomfort in the state of 'almost, but-not-quite-knowing' that poetry evokes so well. Language is not an intermediate between us and the world, life comes to us directly through the senses. Young readers and writers need confirmation that poetry lives where they live, not just in words but in the world.

CHAPTER NINE

Case Study III: Becoming a Poetry School

Jennie Clark with Myra Barrs

I am an Advanced Skills teacher for the London Borough of Redbridge and for Churchfields Infants School in Redbridge, where I have been teaching for over twenty years. For me, a Key Stage 1 school is one of the most important places in the world. It is a place where children's imaginations are nurtured and where we can build on all children's previous experience and on their language skills. Young children are listening all the time and they love the music of words. They like repeating expressions they've heard; they like playing with words and having fun with language. All this is a hugely important part of their becoming literate.

Poetry is central to what we do at Churchfields. As a school we have a very strong music tradition, and poetry often comes into our musical activities and performances. Children get attuned to listening to the music of words. We often learn nonsense songs and songs in other languages, such as African songs – to us these songs are pure sound and we respond to their patterns. We invite children to bring in poetry in their own languages and it's remarkable to listen to the patterns and tunes in the poems – even when we don't really understand the languages they're written in, we can hear the poetry music.

I do an assembly every week and I always read a poem, often one that involves the children joining in – call-and-response poems or poems with refrains. I want children to experience the musical nature of poetry. Recently, I did a Year 1 lesson and I taught alliteration and onomatopoeia, but I taught these through actual poems, through reading the poems aloud together. It's no good teaching things like that in the abstract; they need to be approached through experiential learning.

We had a great time with a book by Agnes Lestrade called *Phileas's Fortune* (2010). It's a story about a country where words have to be bought – the rich have all the big important words. The main character, a little boy called Phileas, only has a few words that he's caught with his butterfly net – and he needs more so as to send a birthday message to a girl he loves. We set up a town where you have to buy words – we designed shop fronts for shops selling words, decided on the most important words to sell, and then brought the scene to life. It was a wonderful way of exploring the value and variety of words and of enabling children to think about how much you can express with just a few words, carefully arranged.

We teach philosophy – it may be the most powerful thing that we teach. It makes children think about and question everything. So when you read them poetry they do question and they can go very deeply into a poem. Last year we had a philosophy week and we used Anthony Browne's book *Through the Magic Mirror* (2010) as a central text for exploring questions of identity. The pictures in this book tell the story and they are surrealistic, you have to interpret what is happening. Some texts seem designed to get the mind thinking, like Chris Van Allsburg's *Chronicles of Harris Burdick* (1984). And many texts, especially poems, require you to think about and interpret what's being said – you have to look at what's behind the words. Children don't always get everything, but they get some of it.

All of our planning is linked to quality texts; they are our main curriculum resource. And whenever we plan, we assume that a poem will come out somewhere. I spend a lot of time researching texts – it's my hobby as well as my job. I like to find books that are worth spending time with and that are about important ideas and feelings. Tomi Ungerer's books are wonderful for that – they're so clever, they provoke so much thought. I specially love books by Sean Tan and Colin Thompson; children write powerful poetry in response to them. Some books I've discovered recently include *Fox* by Margaret Wild (2006), a story set in a burnt forest in the Australian desert. It's written as if with a burnt twig – it's a disturbing book and leads to searching discussions. John Light's *The Flower* (2006) is another favourite. It is a story of a boy who lives in grey urban future world with no flowers, and his discovery of some flower seeds. And *Henry's Freedom Box* (2007) is a story of slavery by Ellen Levine, about a slave who had himself posted in a crate to Philadelphia and freedom. One child's response to this book was 'It doesn't look like a poem but it sounds like a poem.' This Year 2 class and I did some shared writing after reading the book – what was it like for Henry inside the box?

> It's as dark as a dragon's cave,
> My throat is as dry as a desert,
> I feel stiff, cramped and my
> Head is burning hot.

I am petrified of the blackness,
It's worse than being in prison,
I am a mouse in a trap,
The rays of light give me strength,
I hope I reach freedom soon
Sweet freedom.

All of these books have a dark side but they all repay discussion, there's a lot to reflect on and the language, in all of them, is clear, strong and poetic.

Of course, poetry is an ideal resource to support literacy learning. It certainly helps with phonics – it draws attention to initial sounds and the beginnings of words, and we look at that when we discuss alliteration and make up poems in which everything begins with the same letter. It also draws attention to word patterns, and to the endings of words, through rhyme. In general, it attunes children to the sounds and structures of language; it makes them look at words and see how they are made up. And it's memorable, it gives you a whole store of texts to remember which become part of your reading repertoire. I can't think of a better way of learning about language.

Poetry helps with spelling in the same way, by making children aware of the sounds and shapes of words. It introduces children to new vocabulary and words that are interesting and unusual. Children love acquiring new words – we celebrate 'tasty words' here and look at how they are built up. And poetry can also be useful for teaching grammar. It can highlight sentence patterns or draw attention to descriptive language.

Above all, poetry supports reading and writing. Poems are ideal bite-size bits of reading that everybody can enjoy even if they haven't got much reading stamina yet. And if they're good poems, they can be read over and over again – wonderful reading practice for inexperienced readers. We use poetry for guided reading here – the children share poems, take turns, discuss and compare interpretations and responses. It's very important that children learn to read aloud well, and reading poems together gives them a chance to find their voice and read in public.

And as for writing – well, they love writing poetry and experimenting with language. We are constantly writing poetry. I never ask children to write poems without doing it myself. We find all kinds of ways into poetry writing – writing poems about food is a favourite; then you can make 'poetry menus' of the poems that have been written. Three Year 1 children wrote a poem about 'Slippery Spaghetti':

Wibbly wobbly
Iggly scribbly
Gooey and squelchy
Twisty twirly
Sticky and tickly
Tangly and squidgy.

And once we built a den in the playground made of bamboo. It was signposted 'The Monster's Den' and the children were told that the monster who lived in it loved poems, so they left poems for him there. A group of six reception children wrote:

I am an under-the-bed monster
I am the forest monster
Or reading a newspaper monster
Birthday monster
Gooey monster
I am a stinky monster.

We look carefully at things when we write about them. We asked children to look at the moon, and we learned about different parts of the moon and how it gets its light. A Year 2 boy wrote:

As silver as the Sea of Tranquility
As shiny as a mirror reflecting the Sun
Dark, dark moon
As she walks along she shines light on the Earth.

We continued this theme and looked at the relationship between the sun, the moon and the stars. Focusing on this huge subject prompted a group of children to write very exciting poems as they imagined space:

The glorious sun
Bursting like fireworks into space
Moon
Music of the stars
Burning in me
Destroying
Cracking the Earth
The sun speaks like shining stars

We published these and other poems in a book in the *We Are Writers!* series produced by Scholastic Ltd.

I feel that storytelling is very close to poetry and I am very interested in oral storytelling. I know the Grimm stories very well – I had a German mother and I grew up on Grimm. As part of one of our open afternoons for parents, I told both parents and children some of the original Grimms' Tales that I know so well – the Little Fir Tree, The Fisherman and his Wife and Baba Yaga. Even though people are so sophisticated now, they all like a storytelling session – it's such a powerful way of experiencing a story. It has always seemed to me very important to appreciate the oral roots of story and how close oral stories are to poetry. I'm currently looking at Anansi stories with the children and we're doing a lot of retelling and storytelling out of that.

Some of the biggest influences on my own teaching have been books – Michael Rosen's *Did I Hear You Write* and Brian Merrick's *Exploring Poetry* (1987). Last year I followed a Michael Rosen poetry course and it really enthused me. I did a big INSET meeting here about becoming a poetry school – every member of staff performed a poem. As a consequence of this initiative, we purchased a whole new collection of poetry books. I have kept this initiative alive by my regular weekly poetry assemblies and by bringing poetry into our staff meetings. The teachers here are very-well informed about the resources available for poetry now. They listen to poets reading their own work on the Poetry Archive website, and everybody takes part in our regular celebrations of poetry writing.

We have a Creative Week every half term for two classes at a time and parents are invited in on the Friday afternoon to share in the week's activities – it's a way of introducing them to our Creative Curriculum. We work with children, parents and grandparents all together, they all get involved. On one of these Fridays, the teachers performed Eric Carle's Spider and Fly for the children and their families and we went on to develop ideas from it in mixed-age groups. Some groups developed dramas round the story, and there were art activities, creating the spider's parlour. We made a huge spider's web and drew an amazing array of creatures that the spider had caught. The whole group created poems about the Spider's Pantry:

In the Spider's Pantry
In the spider's pantry is foul festering fly cheese
Yucky worm soup sloshes in the bowl
Gory gruesome bugs CRUNCH between the teeth
Old socks full of lacy wings
Slippery slug slime sliding down my throat....
Sticky smelly fly sausage sizzling in the pan
Clotted bloody fly juice makes me happy to be who I am!

All of this work was displayed in the hall and corridors and created a real sense of visual excitement – the display was all in black and white and the poems were pinned up on a many-branched Poetree.

That's the power of poetry. It gives people another way of expressing themselves. We need many forms of expression. As an adult I find that reading poetry helps me to deal with things emotionally – looking at paintings is like that too. I think that all teachers need to be nourished culturally, just as children need this. I enjoy working on things at my own level – recently I went to a course on Philosophy and Art at the Tate Gallery. I go to poetry readings sometimes – hearing Sharon Olds read was a recent memorable experience.

Children have to deal with all sorts of things in their lives and poetry gives them an opportunity to contemplate experience and to talk about it. Poems deal with so many important aspects of human experience. We talk a lot about emotional intelligence and poetry seems to me a wonderful way of developing that kind of empathy and sensitivity to other people and their feelings. When we discuss poems, we're often exploring the subtext – what is really going on in this situation? Or we're exploring our responses – how does this poem make you feel? How do you think it does that? I actually think that poetry is a way of becoming healthy; writing and reading poetry help to make a healthy, responsive, aware human being.

Just because we're teaching young children here, it's very important not to patronize them. Today, for instance, I was talking about refugee children with a class; we had been looking at an animated film about refugee experience. Such complex emotions are involved in this – the world has an impact on children's lives and we need to let them talk about the experiences that they are being exposed to on television, or nearer home.

My role in this school is to support the teachers and to make sure we're always developing as a group – including 'becoming a poetry school'. I try to share what I do myself and to get everyone involved. Good children's books and poetry are at the core of what we do. For us the main outcome of 'assessment for learning' should be that children develop their own sense of standards. Their progress is indicated by their enthusiasm, by the way they often choose to read poetry, and the way they always say 'YES!' when they're told we're going to write poems. We also see the impact of their poetry reading on their writing – on their readiness to experiment, their enjoyment of words, the way they begin to edit their own work. It's great when they say 'Can I read my poem?' – to do that they have to sit in the Poet's Chair.

We don't mark children's work; we think that can get in the way. We were quite open about that with the Ofsted team who came here recently. But they didn't pick us up on it. Instead they were impressed by the children's confidence – the way they perform texts, the way they talk about texts and question what they've read.

How would I describe my pedagogy? Well, I hope that any child I teach would recognize my absolute love of books and words. I try to open that world for them and give them access to a very wide range of texts. I hope I communicate my deep love of poetry; I think that kind of teaching by example is essential. The key thing for young children is that they should become really engaged in books and literacy and should want to use words to create their own texts. I have high expectations for our children and I think I communicate these expectations through the texts I introduce and the way I model how you can approach a piece of writing. But the most important influence on their writing will be what they have read, or had read to them. I read them quality books where the words are like poems. Great words create pictures in your head and feelings in your heart. But you have to try to understand how this works too, how words have this power to move you and allow you to see things.

CHAPTER TEN

Case Study IV: Why Poetry Matters in the Primary School

Sue Ellis and Amy Clifford

Poetry matters in the primary school. It provides children with a means of expression and a way to explore and make sense of their worlds – both their inner and outer worlds. And it plays a crucial role in literacy learning

Key Stage One

At Torriano Infants School in Camden Town, poetry, rhyme and song are core elements of the early years and Key Stage One curriculum. The school recognizes the significant role poetry plays in children's language and literacy development and prioritizes opportunities to build on young children's natural affinity with rhythm, rhyme and word play. It's well known that children can initiate and sustain language play from early on. George Szirtes (2013) describes this exhilarating feeling as 'The shaping of your mouth, lips, teeth and tongue in the enterprise of getting the sounds out' (Szirtes, 2013).

A memorable music

This school provides multiple and regular opportunities for songs and rhymes to be enjoyed as a key approach to fostering children's linguistic and literacy development. During the nursery year, children and their parents become familiar with a wide repertoire of songs. The school makes cards, songbooks and related props available for sharing at home and school. Parents introduce songs from their home cultures and languages and these are recorded, creating a richer store of material to draw on.

The school's emphasis on patterned language helps children to develop phonological awareness and to internalize the tunes and rhythms of language, which serve as an 'external facilitator of verbal memory' (Neisser, 1967). Poetry and rhyme can be seen as the true foundations of literacy since they introduce children to the patterned nature of written language.

Songs have a powerful presence across the school, supported by a music specialist who sustains everybody's interest and enthusiasm and teaches new songs to both staff and children. Through the many class-made big books and whiteboard versions of songs and rhymes which are used for shared reading, young children gain access to phonic knowledge in a pleasurable, contextualized way, learning to match the sounds they know to the print on the page.

They are also encouraged, using their growing knowledge of the features and structures of familiar songs, to make up their own songs, sometimes related to class topics. Children tune into the memorable music of language and make it their own.

The following poem, composed in shared writing, records children's observations of autumn. In the classroom where it was composed, their autumn poems were often sung to start the day during that term:

> *Five autumn leaves blowing on the branch,*
> *Five autumn leaves blowing on the branch,*
> *And if one autumn leaf should flutter to the ground*
> *There'd be four autumn leaves blowing on the branch.*
> *Four autumn leaves blowing on the branch....*

Nursery rhymes

Nursery rhymes also provide an important bridge between home and school. A variety of classic nursery rhyme collections are kept in each classroom. Children, parents and teachers become familiar with a wide range of nursery rhymes from the different cultural traditions represented within the school community.

These highly patterned poems often represent children's first experience of rhyme, story, and metaphor. Their familiar structures allow children to manipulate the form and create their own versions, inspired by poems like those in John Foster's *Twinkle, Twinkle Chocolate Bar* (2000) and poems by John Agard and Grace Nichols in *No Hickory No Dickory* (1995):

Three juicy pineapples
Three juicy pineapples
See how they wibble
See how they dribble
All over the wobbly bridge
The mother cut off their spikes with a carving knife
Did you ever see such a thing in your life
As three juicy pineapples?

Children's knowledge and enjoyment of poems and rhymes, from hearing them read aloud, gives them confidence to read these books independently. That poems are generally short, memorable and contained makes them particularly accessible to the very young, allowing children to build stamina as readers and writers.

Language play

There is a strong emphasis at Torriano Infants School on valuing and connecting with children's own experiences in the poetry they read and write. In a Year 1 class, children compose poetry using their names and interests as a starting point. Through experimenting and making careful word choices, they compose their own alliterative poems to sum up something meaningful about themselves:

Astonishing Annabelle
If you want help with batting and catching
Ask Annabelle.

Great, Grand Griffin
If you want to play draughts
Ask Griffin.

The simple structure provides an open and supportive framework for children's individual poems. When the poems are put together they are read aloud at circle time. This kind of shared experience encourages collaboration and the sense of a class identity.

Language play arises naturally out of group play activities. One nursery activity, stimulated by reading *How Do Dinosaurs Say Goodnight?* by Jane Yolen (2000), led to children making a dinosaur nest in the school grounds and filling it with home-made dinosaur eggs. The next morning, as they found and 'hatched' the eggs, the teacher scribed their excited comments. Later she presented their words as a spiral egg-shaped poem, to create a record of the event:

Dinosaur eggs

They're hard.
It's cold
They're too hard.
It feels so squishy.
I can scratch it.
It's really hard.

Exploring the world

Taking children out into their local surroundings and bringing their discoveries and observations back to school always provides a rich resource for poetry writing.

The reception class at Torriano Infants regularly visit nearby Hampstead Heath to explore the environment and collect natural materials. Back in the classroom they talk about their trip and make collages from their discoveries. They look at related books, such as *Leaf Man* by Lois Ehlert (2005) and artwork by Andy Goldsworthy. They examine and study the leaves, twigs, seeds and cases they have gathered as the teacher lists their comments and impressions in a piece of shared writing. Children can go on to compose group poems from the words and phrases used in shared writing. Often these are written on strips of paper that enable children to rearrange and shape their poems until they are satisfied:

Conker

The conker is ...
Sticky like glue
Hard like a rock
Smooth
It rolls like a ball ....

Other exercises in natural exploration are imaginary. In a Year 2 class, children imagined animals inhabiting a magical landscape. Two boys, both reluctant writers, collaborated on a joint poem, as if playing a game of tennis, batting ideas backwards and forwards. It began:

White is the loneliness of an elephant
Who has lost his family.
Grey is the shiny slug
Who quit being called a snail without a shell.
Silver is the freezing ice that covers the ocean

With seals that pound the ice.
Silver is a city of sharks under the sea.

A child who hardly spoke as a rule, wrote:

Blue are the eyes of a wolf
Howling in the graveyard.

Talking about poetry

Children were asked to reflect on what they'd learned from talking and writing their poems and said this:

Poems should give us pictures in our head
We need to think about the words we use, not just the first ones that come into our head
Colour can be an animal, a feeling, a place or a smell

Talk is at the core of children's developing understanding of poetry. Every time teachers work on a poem, they talk with children about its possible meanings, their feelings about it and any new or powerful words and phrases they have found in it. Children's talk is recorded in class poetry journals: teachers note down their comments, questions, likes and dislikes, drawing on the discussion framework in Aidan Chambers's book *Tell Me* (2011).

Poetry can be an ideal form for children talking about and exploring their feelings. Following on from a study of Picasso's Blue Period paintings, and their reading of *The Huge Bag of Worries* by Virginia Ironside (2011), children in Year 2 were invited to share their worries in group discussion. A simple suggested shape enabled them to write their individual anxieties as short poems, combining them into a group poem. They came to realize that other people had their own private fears.

I worry about
What if my dad doesn't come back
After an argument?
I'm scared.
What if a brick is thrown
Through our window?

I am afraid
Of going to sleep at bedtime.
What if I don't wake up?

Further development through shared reading and writing

At this school poetry is read aloud regularly so that children become very familiar with the well-chosen anthologies and rhyming picture books in their classrooms. Films of poets reading and performing their poetry, from poetry websites including *The Poetry Archive* and *Poetryline*, help to bring poets into the classroom. And poems are frequently the focus for shared and guided reading.

In shared reading, taking time to discuss (and sometimes perform) poetry – not rattling through a text – builds solid and meaningful poetic experiences. Discussing why a poet has deliberately chosen particular words to express subtleties, nuances and possibilities can be demonstrated explicitly.

Teachers at Torriano Infants use shared writing to help children to think like poets. It helps to make the writing process explicit for children and builds their confidence. Skilfully led, shared writing involves children in generating ideas, making choices and reflecting critically. Children are not so daunted when they come to write because they are used to putting down ideas, reflecting on them and revising them.

There's a freedom in poetry writing compared to other kinds of written forms – a licence to invent. Through poetry, children experience phrasing and vocabulary not encountered in ordinary spoken language, thus stretching their language beyond the everyday. A contextualized approach like this is more authentic and effective than choosing from a list of 'wow' words.

Shared writing and technology

By using smartboards for shared writing, it's possible to write a whole poem together and display it straight away on the classroom wall or in the class anthology. Children can have individual copies to take home – it's very satisfying to experience the whole process and be able to show the outcomes. Technology allows these outcomes to be shared much more widely, through school websites or blogs.

Teachers regularly use smartboards for shared and group writing, where the technology allows the class to make a whole poem together: gathering responses, composing, moving text around and shaping the poem on the page. Children use smart notebooks for playing, experimenting and creating their own poems. Low-technology alternatives for manipulating text by moving it around strips of paper or using dryboards work well too. Two reluctant-writer boys working together in this way became animated as they attempted to describe a beetle, finally deciding on:

A beetle fighting
Like a warrior going into battle.

Children can also create poems on 2Simple, adding images from their artwork to be displayed with their poems and including video of their poetry performances, uploaded onto the school website for parents to see. Poetry and poetryscapes are regularly uploaded onto Tapestry learning journals, enabling a group or class poem to appear in the journal for every participating child.

Performing poetry

Performance plays a crucial role in children's enjoyment and understanding of poetry. Many poems explicitly invite children to join in with call and response structures and choral refrains. Such experiences really engage children with poetry and often lead to them learning poems by heart.

Through performance children are also able to interpret poetry through expressions and actions, giving attention to the different facets of a poem. Children will often add sound effects and music and sometimes improvise costumes and props. Some poetry performances are recorded so that children can evaluate their work as an audience.

Performance makes a very satisfying climax to reading or writing poetry. The Key Stage One class teacher says, 'Performing a poem is producing something together. It's confidence boosting, especially for reading, using readers' theatre approaches. We use this as part of guided reading sessions in Key Stage One with children performing in groups independently at the end, using masks and props etc. This is really motivating.'

Key Stage Two

As children move into **Key Stage Two,** they draw on a wider experience of literature and more sophisticated content in developing their writing range. Still, the most authentic and powerful writing often stems from children's first-hand experiences. They write about what matters to them and what impacts on their lives and thoughts.

Poetry from Southwark schools

These poems provide windows into children's worlds and imaginations. Recurrent themes emerge: themselves, their friends and family, their school and neighbourhood, and wider, global concerns too, that affect them intellectually and emotionally. All this can be seen from the poems published in a set of poetry collections from Southwark schools: the *Southwark Poetry Anthologies*. Published over a twelve-year period, 2001–2013, the anthologies provided an important opportunity for children to give voice to their ideas and experiences through poetry writing. They also provided a sustained opportunity for teachers to think about how to foster poetry writing, sometimes in collaboration with storytellers and artists. This played a significant role in developing poetry of high quality.

Intervention and pedagogy

In his inaugural professorial lecture on children's poetry writing, Andrew Lambirth (2011) recognized the 'pivotal role skilful teaching plays in enabling children to articulate their ideas and to guide the shaping of them'. Lambirth agrees with Vygotsky that 'the teacher is indispensable and children need to be guided – children are not natural poets – they need to be introduced to the cultural tools that can be utilised to make them poets'. For Lambirth, 'the imagination and creativity becomes richer if a person's experiences are rich and they are encouraged to develop their creative capabilities. [They are] working with the tools that may be developed further in later life, but which at this age will only indicate that they are on the path to development'.

He cites Vygotsky (1930/2004), who argues that teachers have a key role in facilitating children's development as writers of poetry:

> *The right kind of education involves awakening in the child what already exists within them, helping them develop it.* (p. 51)

Acts of discovery

Michael Rosen (1997) shares this view in saying that one of the values of poetry is 'to enable the writer, through the act of writing, to discover something about herself'. The *Southwark Poetry Anthologies* include many examples where this act of discovery has occurred. For example, children often reveal something of themselves when they choose to write about the people they know best, and this can be seen in a poem a child wrote about his father, inspired by reading *Locomotion* by Jacqueline Woodson:

Daddy George

When I think of my dad,
I think of cocoa butter
and I think of his soothing voice
and the smell of cocoa butter cream.
Every time I smell that

I feel like I'm in a sea of pillows.
His smell is like the wind,
blowing the leaves in the air.
The smell dances up my nose,
tickling all my senses.
The smell of cocoa butter cream
sends me to a bed of clouds.

Kingsley Etuk, Year 6, John Donne Primary School

The poem is a series of memories and sensations recalled by a particular smell associated with a child's father. It is an imaginative piece where the writer captures, in several vivid images, his pleasure in thinking about his dad. It reveals the warmth of the relationship and shows the willingness of a Year 6 boy to use poetry to write an affective piece, drawing on strong emotional connections.

Children respond to the freedom poetry offers them to express their ideas succinctly, often without the constraint of a specified pattern or rhyme. It allows them to shape a poem in their own way. This poet takes an imaginative leap to see the familiar urban world around him from the unlikely perspective of a street litter bin:

The litter bin

Old, dirty, alone,
The street's eye
Gingerly glancing at him.
But he stays.

Burgers, coffee cups, rotten crisps
Swim freely in his stomach.
He remembered happiness,
But had forgotten how it worked.

Now, alone, outdoors.
Left to endure the freezing cold,
The only protection was the garbage around him.
But still he stays.

His stench kept everything away from him,
Everything but the foxes
Rummaging through his worn out belly.
But still he stays, he stays, he stays.

Luke Sinclair, Year 6, Dulwich Hamlet Junior School

Creating the litter bin as a character telling the story of his lonely life, the writer arouses sympathy through a series of bleak images. There is a rhythm within the verses and the echo running through each last line conveys the steadfast nature of the character. The poem shows a developing ability to control language and to create an effect on the reader.

Playing with ideas and language

Poetry provides a concentrated form for children to explore and play with ideas. A group of Year 3 children collaborated in writing a poem about 'what I want to become' and composed verses about an architect, teacher, lawyer and shopkeeper. In the final verse they focussed on the delights of being a poet:

A poet

To juggle words like sweets
To unwrap them and chew them
To bite them and inspect them
To toss them in the air and catch them
To make a poem like this one.

Group poem, Year 3, Peckham Park Primary
School/Harris Academy Primary School

In this verse children reflect on language and delight in the transformational effect of words. Words are seen as versatile objects, to be played with, studied and savoured. The conscious use of repetition creates a structure, a pattern and a pace, adding to the reader's pleasure in the ideas and language these young poets use to craft the poem.

There is a balance to be struck in the delicate but necessary process of enabling children to develop their craft as poets, whilst maintaining their individual voice. Enthusiastic and knowledgeable teachers play a pivotal role in this. Enabling children to tune in to the music of language and to create, shape and share their own memorable music through poetry writing involves ongoing dialogue and a genuine appreciation of what children have to say.

With thanks to the children and teachers at Torriano Infants School, Joe Rea and the children and teachers at Southwark Primary Schools.

CHAPTER ELEVEN

Case Study V: Making Poetry Happen in a Sixth Form Environment

Jane Bluett

Two years ago I conducted a survey with A Level English students about their experience of poetry at school. This was part of my contribution to the ESRC Poetry Matters seminar series, cited in Chapter 4 of *Making Poetry Matter*, by Gary Snapper (2013). I would like to return to this survey as a starting point for my consideration of how we might make poetry writing 'happen' in a sixth form environment.

Of the thirty-one students questioned, only eighteen recalled writing poetry at school. Most of these remembered writing poetry at *primary* school. Of those who had written poetry at secondary school, the responses to the question '*When did you write poetry?*' produced the following comments:

Only if needed as part of a lesson
Only at school
Telling the story of Romeo and Juliet but it wasn't a compulsory activity
We had to write a sonnet when we studied Romeo and Juliet in year 10
English Language GCSE coursework
For competitions
For the school magazine
I used to when I was interested in furthering my writing ability and critiquing other poetry effectively
For my parents to make them laugh

The first two responses are interesting because of the use of the word 'only'. This seems to suggest that the students were aware that poetry could be written in other contexts. The middle responses suggest an implied association of writing poetry with compulsion. Only the last two come close to demonstrating an understanding of writing poetry in a wider context – writing poetry to enhance linguistic understanding (as outlined by Deborah Myhill in Chapter 6 of *Making Poetry Matter* (2013)) and writing poetry for a purpose outside the academic context.

This is an indication of the experience that students bring with them of writing poetry when they arrive at sixth form college. Few will regard writing poetry as an essential part of their personal development; many will regard it as something they might be 'made' to do as a part of the English curriculum. How do we encourage an enjoyment and enthusiasm for writing poetry in such circumstances?

Students at sixth form level are very focused on their A Level courses. They are often reluctant to undertake activity that does not explicitly feed into their assessment outcomes. The A Level English specifications do offer students an opportunity to write poetry for coursework. This includes re-creative responses to Literature texts and writing original poetry for Language assessment. Neither option is compulsory and students taking these options are likely to be those who already have a keen interest in writing poetry. Students who don't are unlikely to be introduced to writing poetry in any constructive way, unless an individual teacher is determined to make time for this. Thus, although Literature students are compelled to read poetry, there is no such compulsion to write it. To write poetry well it is essential that you read poetry – but the converse does not seem to be true in current attitudes to teaching poetry at this level.

The 'Afterword' to 'Writing Poetry' in *Making Poetry Matter* cites Don Paterson's study of the sonnet form where he states that '[the sonnet] represents one of the most characteristic shapes human thought can take' (Paterson, 1999). It is here that I believe our thinking about the use of poetry at sixth form level might begin. The act of writing poetry is a process. It forces the poet to encapsulate and distil thought in order to communicate and suggest ideas to others. Writing poetry therefore can be a powerful tool in getting students to clarify and articulate their thinking. It allows students to grapple with abstractions in meaningful ways, necessitating language use that is both clear and appropriate. Why, therefore, write a 1500-word essay to explore an aspect of a novel when writing a sonnet could engage you in the same process with a far more specific focus on Language use?

But a quick survey of my colleagues assures me that the sonnet will not replace the essay as a means of assessment any time soon. Anthony Wilson's chapter 'Teachers' Metaphors of Teaching Poetry Writing' in *Making Poetry Matter* (2013) clearly demonstrates the fears and anxieties that teachers have when approaching the subject of poetry writing. In a recent conversation I had with a group of teachers who were keen to teach creative writing, one exclaimed that he didn't consider himself a writer because his own writing was 'rubbish'. When pressed, he admitted that this judgement came from comparing his work to the Literature that he taught.

Teachers as writers

Writing poetry must, I think, be uncoupled, in teachers' minds, from ideas of publication and from canonical baggage. Viewed as an enjoyable process and also as analytical, communicative activity, poetry becomes a means to an end as well as an end in itself. The more teachers can be encouraged to see themselves as practitioners of poetry the more opportunity there will be for students to *talk and think like poets* (Myhill op cit). Writing poetry is a powerful 'threshold' activity between the study of Literature and Language and should be widely regarded as such.

It is my belief that anyone hoping to write effective poetry needs to read poetry and have a genuine interest in the workings of Language. During my own PhD research (Bluett, 2012), I explored the relationship between the two by writing poems in response to canonical Literature (e.g. Shakespeare) and about Language concepts (e.g. accent, gendered Language). What I discovered was that, as a teacher of Literature, my poetry in response to Literature was stifled by my inner literary critic. In effect, I was writing as a critical reader. Specifically, this resulted in my including literary devices and techniques in my poetry because these are the features I encourage students to explore. In its worst form, this is feature spotting in reverse. It was only through putting Literature aside for a while and writing poetry that directly engaged with Language as subject that I managed to free my writing of this tendency.

A teacher really wanting to get students writing poetry has to balance two roles: first, that of someone who engages with poetry and the creative process and, second, that of a teacher with a responsibility for helping students develop their writing in the light of assessment criteria. I believe this can happen only when the teacher writes themselves and engages with the complexities of the process. In the same way that a teacher of A Level Literature feels little or no compulsion to be a published literary critic but *is* a practising one, a teacher engaged in encouraging the writing of poetry at this level should feel no compulsion to be published, but *must* practise.

In my sixth form college, I try to use writing poetry to encourage students to see it as an everyday process and not something to be regarded as the remote practice of an elite. I shall endeavour to illustrate this practice here through a consideration of examples of students' work.

Encapsulations

Very few students are scared of haiku. It is an attractive form that many will have experienced at primary school. But it can also be used very effectively to 'encapsulate' literary texts. Here are two haikus that summarize well-known A level texts:

> *Dead dad. Not what you*
> *need, Mother, when you're off at*
> *university.*

> *Nothing great about*
> *him. A dead man in a pool.*
> *No green lights. Daisy.*

The challenge here is to strip the texts down to their essential situations and thus demonstrate understanding. This exercise encourages students both to distil the essence of a text into a single image or description, and also to appreciate the extraordinary economy of form and expression represented by the haiku.

Maths and Physics

One cohort of students in my college take the International Baccalaureate and therefore combine several subjects. To demonstrate that poetry is a process that can be used to shape human thought in all disciplines, not just English, I have included the work of a student whose main academic interests lie elsewhere.

Sonja is an IB student whose first love is Maths. She has to take English as it is a compulsory part of the diploma. I had introduced the students to a range of poetic forms in preparation for their unseen poetry exam. We looked at Julia Copus's specular 'The Back Seat of my Mother's Car'. From the mid-point of the poem, every word contained up to that point must be used in reverse order. I challenged the students to write something similar. The strict patterning of the form obviously appealed to Sonja's mathematical mind and a week later she produced this:

$$\frac{d\,(x^2 + 12)}{dx}$$

Calculating, simplifying and integrating worlds, measuring and considering functions.
Falling, swirling, creating arcs, lengths, chords, curves, sectors, tangents, angles and perimeters.

Rearranging, rationalising, sequencing, combining, and translating points.
Mapping, merging, dividing, showing, concealing, assuming and proving.
The complex and simple forming limitless shapes and expressions.
Inequalities expressing clear infinite values.
Proving and processing arithmetic constants.
Sketching reflecting gathering numbers.
Redefining and replacing,
Differentiating,
Substituting,
Solving.

Solving,
Substituting,
Differentiating,
Redefining and replacing.
Sketching, reflecting, gathering numbers.
Proving and processing arithmetic constants.
Inequalities expressing clear infinite values.
The complex and simple forming limitless shapes and expressions.
Mapping, merging, dividing, showing, concealing, assuming and proving.
Rearranging, rationalising, sequencing, combining and translating points.
Falling, swirling, creating arcs, lengths, chords, curves, sectors, tangents, angles and perimeters.
Calculating, simplifying and integrating worlds. Measuring and considering functions.

This is as far from the typically confessional poetry of the average seventeen-year-old as you can get. When I asked Sonja about it, she made two significant observations: that the Language of maths was in itself poetic and that, when used in poetry, it took on irresistible connotations. Here was a student using poetry to explore the Language and meaning of the mathematical discipline.

Sonja also revealed that the title is not simply a random equation but refers to the number of lines and syllables she has used. The poem deservedly won a prize in the Nottingham Festival of Words and Sonja hasn't stopped writing since. I have always suggested that sonnets have a lot in common with the quadratic equation in terms of thought process but I had never suspected a student would seize the idea and develop it in such skilful and interesting ways.

Writing under constraint

Our sixth form college is fortunate enough to have a thriving enrichment programme. Students from many disciplines attend a creative writing workshop on Wednesday afternoons and it is here that some of the most imaginative poetry writing takes place. The workshop comprises one or two creative writing exercises and students can write in whatever form they choose. Again, a sharp focus on Language techniques is key. Giving students language constraints to work within produces surprising results. This poem was written in ten minutes; the students were allowed to use words of only one syllable.

Our House

On the night of the full moon,
I saw her smile at him.
Her eyes were bright, lips were full,
You should have heard her sing.
He was a dick. He should have died,
I hate him more and more.
One day soon I'll hunt him down
And hurt him so much more.
He took her there, in that place.
He did not ask her once.
I beat him up, took his balls;
The heart wants what it wants.
She loves me now, we laugh all day
In our stone-cold house.
I hope she does not find out.
He was a crap, fat, louse.

Cheyenne Meyer

It is useful to compare this to a couple of stanzas written by another student in the group at home. This is fairly typical, I would say, of the sort of poetry seventeen-year-old students write. There is an overreliance on the present continuous, the rhyme is forced and there are clichés and unhelpful abstractions. This results in confessional poetry that is obviously heartfelt but lacks form and impact. It is exactly the sort of poetry that I suspect teachers are wary about criticizing, purely on the grounds that it is heartfelt. There are good lines here, 'bullet-shaped words' for example, but they are undermined by the whole.

Darling, we had a good run
Now you're setting me free.
Thinking back,
to when I was your boat, you were my sea.
We floated away, so delicately.
Three whole words, eight letters to go.

Maybe if you were told
I wouldn't deceive, my heart, my soul.

No more thinking, no more waiting.
I'll get over you, wishing, wanting
I was yours for the taking
the dirt just settling.
We're heading for no-mans-land,
we're going hand in hand.
I'll steal your breath…
With bullet shaped words.

If we now consider again what Cheyenne wrote under two constraints – that of time and that of form – using only monosyllables – we can see that the result is much more effective and the represented emotion is just as real. Focusing on syllables and working quickly has produced a subtler use of rhyme. The punch of the monosyllables produces a tough and provocative tone but it is in the use of the verbs that the strength lies. Not a continuous present in sight.

Many of my students who write poetry are instinctively attached to rhyme, often believing that use of rhyme *is* poetry. Encouraging them to explore other lexical, grammatical and phonological devices is often the best way to remove their reliance on rhyme and show them that free verse can be just as patterned and powerful. They may return to rhyme in the drafting process but they will have understood that there are many more poetic tools at their disposal. Imposing a constraint gives them a focus and is an extremely efficient way of actually getting words on a page.

Poetry as academic discourse

The final question I asked my students when researching their previous experience of poetry was 'Why Does Poetry Matter?' I was delighted when one of my A Level Literature students replied in poetic form.

Poetry

Poetry:
Poetry brings comfort
And thus also strength
But all us readers wonder
Oh, where our poetry went.

With Yeats and Keats
It thrived, leaping
Through hands and families

And minds.
Alas now it's sleeping
Alone
On the library floor.

Beth Keetley

The poem appeared in the journal *English in Education* and Beth was thrilled. Her publication success obviously validated her writing and encouraged her to continue writing poetry.

The content of the poem raises two relevant issues. Firstly, this student was aware that poetry could be used for the purposes of academic discourse. I think we should encourage more of this kind of writing. If you want to explain the ways of God to man, write a poem, not an essay. In Jane Spiro's words, poetry should be used to 'combine personal and public messages' (Spiro, 2013). Secondly, students who are aware of this aspect of the poetic tradition are being ill served by the current curriculum, which signally fails to encourage them to choose alternative ways of expressing ideas and theories.

Talking and thinking like poets

At the time of writing, a new A Level in Creative Writing has just been introduced. Its advent has allowed teachers the freedom to really encourage students to 'think like poets' (Myhill). For the first time writers are being encouraged to develop their practice in a meaningful way that is supported by both timetable and curriculum. In A Level writing classes, students write. They take part in writing exercises, keep writing journals and openly explore and discuss their own writing processes. Key to this is the writing workshop where, very quickly, students are asked to share their work and offer constructive criticism.

The Creative Writing A Level foregrounds the need for teacher training in this area and initiatives such as the National Writing Project are already running 'Teachers as Writers' groups throughout the country. As teachers, we need to support students by offering them ways of developing their writing processes, and not simply by criticizing ineffective work. We can do this only if we think as poets and practice writing poetry, otherwise we have very little to offer. It is only through being a practising poet myself that I have come to understand the power of the writing workshop and how to give constructive feedback. My students, likewise, have quickly discovered that a workshop of their peers is a motivating and inspiring way of developing their work.

Conclusion

There are many ways to make poetry happen in the sixth form environment. To ensure that it does, we as teachers need to see writing poetry as a process that can be used in the curriculum to express thought, practice Language skills and respond to texts and ideas. Poetry can be a tool for learning as effective as reading, discussion and academic writing. Writing poetry does not have to be part of a 'poetry' lesson. It can be used to teach linguistic concepts, textual understanding, a sense of self and place and even Physics. Once we recognize the power of poetry writing as a way of knowing, we might be able to reclaim its central position in the curriculum.

> *Writing poetry is a way of striving to see as deeply as possible, as widely as possible, as accurately as possible.*
>
> James Berry (Berry, 2011: 14)

All poems are reproduced with the permission of the students.

CHAPTER TWELVE

Commentary and Practical Implications: A Flicker in the Mind

Myra Barrs

This book, *Making Poetry Happen*, and its predecessor, *Making Poetry Matter*, arose out of an ESRC seminar series entitled *Poetry Matters*. Writing workshops were a fundamental part of the seminar series – every seminar included a workshop, an opportunity to *write* poetry. That was just as it should be. Since the aim of the seminars was to study contemporary research and practice in teaching poetry, it was essential that, in the course of these investigations, participants should actually immerse themselves in the making of poetry.

So I thought myself. I was all in favour of experiential approaches to learning and looked forward to the first writing workshop, led by Cliff Yates. But the first half hour of that workshop was just misery for me. Somehow I couldn't get going. Cliff offered us various ways in, ways of jump-starting the poem-writing process, but they all seemed, for me, that morning, like empty exercises. I did attempt them – my notebook shows that I tried writing a poem that took off from my experiences early that morning – capturing the essence of those first morning hours, from breakfast to leaving the house and catching the train. But nothing was happening. I tried writing a funny poem about the frustrations of writing a poem – just as flat and heavy. All around me people were scribbling as if they really meant it; there was a feeling of energy and purpose. I decided that it wasn't my day, I might as well give up.

But then Cliff suggested that we could try writing a poem that started 'That was the day when…'. And something flickered in my mind. What happened specifically was that I immediately knew what day I was going to write about. I remembered everything about it, the whole situation was suddenly present to me, yet it was a day from twenty-five years before. I began to write the poem, with energy and purpose. Here's the first verse:

The frozen land

That was the day when
we were driving up into Bruce County
where you were going to lead a teachers' workshop
and the air was heavy with snow, already dark
over the frozen land and the road ahead.
You were talking too fast, it was hot in the car –
you were living in a rundown rooming house
just outside New York, on the edge of a rich suburb
where your new lover lived, and in the daytimes
you were meeting while her husband was at work….

In retrospect it was obvious why this particular incident should have occurred to me. We – my friend in the poem and I – had been driving to a small Canadian town where he was booked to give a teachers' workshop, a writing workshop. And in the context of the present workshop I remembered that heavy, dull day and the atmosphere between us in the car – and that became the feeling, the flicker in the mind, that started the poem.

Cliff Yates calls his chapter in this book 'Knowing where to start' and observes that this is one of the hardest things for students. In his workshops he aims to provide a range of possible openings:

> *In an adult workshop for example, no one is blamed for not being able to write a poem during a particular exercise: some exercises will work better than others, some simply won't work for you.*

That was certainly true for me. As a teacher I knew this process from the other side – I knew how to help children find a subject, find a first line, find a seed. Perhaps the key thing is that the *teacher* should 'know where to start' and know how to trust the creative process – the way the mind is always silently working away, even if nothing immediately seems to be happening. I now think that the reason why I started to write with such urgency in that workshop, once I had found my starting point, was because of the pent-up energy and frustration that had been accumulating in the half hour before. Nothing seemed to be working for me, yet my mind was working.

The poet-contributors to the Writing part of this book approach the teaching of poetry writing in a different way from the teacher-contributors.

The poets help students to 'know where to start' by presenting them with ways in, or with models, which will lead them to 'discover' a poem in the relatively short space of a workshop. Mandy Coe describes some of her openings as 'exercises' but at the same time is in no doubt that poems really begin 'in real or imagined experiences made even more vivid by the writerly habit of close observation'. She insists on creativity as a 'finding-your-way, risk-taking activity'. The poets' approaches are different from the teachers' partly because they have a limited amount of time in a school to make an impact and make something happen for the students.

The teachers are working in a different time-dimension. They place more emphasis on building the context for writing, and also on reading, on the slow development of a poetry habit. KS1 teacher Jennie Clark's chapter focuses on reading poetry:

> *Poems are ideal bite-size bits of reading that everybody can enjoy even if they haven't got much reading stamina yet. And if they're good poems they can be read over and over again – wonderful reading practice for inexperienced readers.*

But she also spends a lot of time reading 'quality texts', especially picture books, with children:

> *All of our planning is linked to quality texts; they are main curriculum resource. And whenever we plan we assume that a poem will come out somewhere.*

Some texts, she observes, 'seem designed to get the mind thinking' – and children often write powerful poetry in response to them. The language of the texts they are reading will also influence their poems.

As Vygotsky suggested, reading and writing are 'two halves of the same process; mastering written language' (Vygotsky, 1978). Reading poetry introduces students to new rhythms and patterns in written language. Readers take in and remember the tunes of literary texts, and as they do so, they begin to respond to different styles and move into new areas of language. This process is shown in action in the book *The Reader in the Writer* (Barrs and Cork, 2001). Though not a study of the teaching of poetry, it does demonstrate how pupils learn from the memorable language of powerful literary texts, picking up on their linguistic patterns and echoing their tunes.

Poetry, with its different ways of marking and emphasizing these patterns, through line breaks, verse shapes, repetition, rhyme, assonance and alliteration, rhythm and metre, and the layout of the poem on the page, provides students with an experience of a still wider range of literary styles and tunes. It helps to draw attention to these features of language and their role in enacting meaning. As Louise Rosenblatt expresses it, 'The aesthetic stance heightens awareness of the words as signs with particular visual and auditory characteristics *and* as symbols' (Rosenblatt, 1978: 29).

So, young writers try out these means of expression and learn from experienced writers of poetry how to shape their own writing and mark their own meanings. All writers are apprentices to the authors that they read. To write poetry, above all they need an abundant experience of hearing poetry read aloud and reading it for themselves.

The teachers in Torriano Infants School stress the role of reading in learning to write poetry, but place particular importance on song, where musical patterning underscores linguistic patterns. The teachers' practice also relies heavily on basing poetry writing on direct experiences. So, the classes visit Hampstead Heath and collect leaves, twigs, seeds and seedcases to take back to school, where they use them to make collages and poems. Young children in the nursery play with ice, or hatch home-made 'dinosaur eggs', found in the playground, and teachers write up their responses as poems. Older children discuss their feelings and secret worries and explore them in poetry:

> *I am afraid*
> *Of going to sleep at bedtime.*
> *What if I don't wake up?*

Despite some differences between the poets' and the teachers' approaches to teaching poetry writing, there is something essential that they have in common – they want students to get *excited* about writing; they know that a firing of energy and enthusiasm may be the start of a real poem.

Ian McMillan, in a *Guardian* article, remembers the 'best poetry lesson he ever had' when his junior school teacher took the class out into the yard on a freezing cold morning.

> *How cold is it? he asked and somebody said 'as cold as a fridge!' And we laughed and wrote it down.*

They walk round looking at a world changed by snow, and writing down what it is like. The teacher tells them what a poem can be: 'It doesn't have to rhyme, boys and girls, but it can if it wants to.' He reads them 'In the Bleak Midwinter' by Christina Rossetti

> *…and we talked about the earth being 'hard as iron' and the water being 'like a stone' and we had a look round to see if it was, and it was. We saw that we were part of a continuum and that all the poets who'd ever written were standing behind us as we wrote. And that didn't scare us: it inspired us.*

When they go back to class and write poems, Mr Meakin 'with his brow furrowed and his pencil in his mouth' writes too. Ian McMillan says that it was Mr Meakin's enthusiasm 'which bulldozed us into the arms of the muse' and is convinced that 'half the battle … is getting people excited about poetry' (McMillan, 2012).

Both the writers and teachers contributing to this part aim to get children excited about poetry. But some unconfident and inexperienced young people find it very difficult to see how they will be able to write a poem; unlike Ian McMillan's classmates, reading poets like Christina Rossetti doesn't inspire them – it scares them. Learning to write a poem, like many other kinds of learning, involves getting in at the deep end. It involves beginning to engage in the activity before you can actually do it, having the confidence to have a go.

In his book *Writing the Australian Crawl*, the American poet William Stafford uses an extended comparison to suggest how young writers – however inexperienced – can learn to write by having a go.

> *Just as any reasonable person who looks at water and passes a hand through it can see that it would not hold a person up; so it is the judgement of commonsense people that reliance on the weak material of students' experiences cannot possibly sustain a work of literature.* (Stafford, 1978)

But, says Stafford, swimmers know that it's OK to relax on the water, that it will buoy them up. And writers know that 'a succession of little strokes on the material nearest to them' will result in progress. As long as the process of writing is not analysed too much and made difficult by too heavy an insistence on technique, young writers can get started.

Stafford emphasizes 'the material nearest to them' – finding a subject that is close to you, that you know intimately, and that matters to you, is part of the trick of it. And observing your subject, reflecting on it, is what makes the poem grow. This is the 'writerly observation' that Mandy Coe talks about. It takes us straight back to one of the most acutely observant of poets, Matsuo Basho, who said

> *Go to the pine if you want to learn about the pine, or to the bamboo if you want to learn about the bamboo … Your poetry issues of its own accord when you and the object have become one …. (Basho, 2013)*

Similarly, the poet James Berry writes

> *When a poem works well it has different levels of reflection, it is a deep meditation … For me the most important thing about writing a poem is to try to explore the subject fully.* (Berry, 2011)

Writers need to write about what they know, and think, and feel. The KS2 boy who wrote about his father in one of the *Southwark Poetry Anthologies* quoted in Sue Ellis's article was writing about a subject close to him. His poem reminds us of how love dwells on every aspect of a loved one's physical presence, including their smell:

> *When I think of my dad,*
> *I think of cocoa butter*
> *and I think of his soothing voice*
> *and the smell of cocoa butter cream.*
> *Every time I smell that*
> *I feel like I'm in a sea of pillows ....*

Though this delightful poem is essentially a list, a succession of images, nothing about it suggests that the writer was using figurative language as an exercise. It is an expression of intimate feeling, a revelling.

A list makes a very accessible form for a poem. Inexperienced poets may need the kind of support that can be provided by helpful structures, what I often call 'open structures' – forms or structures which are supportive but not constraining. An example of this is Basho's preferred form, the haiku, with its deceptive simplicity. Making a haiku picture is a very satisfying experience. Other forms that do not constrain but support include poems with refrains, conversation poems or question and answer poems – and many more. Students often enjoy writing with the help of these kinds of patterned forms.

However, a few poems by older students suggest that some constraints can, paradoxically, provide a focus and be enabling. In Jane Bluett's chapter, Cheyenne's poem 'Our House' was produced under two constraints – students were allowed only ten minutes and were allowed to use only words of one syllable. Yet somehow Cheyenne, working within these parameters, created a poem with real energy and character. Within the same chapter, Sonja's tour de force of a 'specular' poem based on the language of maths is evidence that a very challenging poetic form can sometimes galvanize a writer rather than inhibit.

William Stafford, when asked when he realized that he wanted to become a poet, said that it was the wrong question.

> *You know, when we are kids we make up things, we write, and for me the puzzle is not that some people are still writing, the real question is why did the other people stop?* (Stafford, 1978)

Basho says that he once actually tried to give up poetry and remain silent:

> *but every time I did so a poetic sentiment would solicit my heart and something would flicker in my mind.* (Basho, 2013)

Writing poetry can't be taught in a half term 'unit'. It should be a more daily thing than that, a habit of mind, something you go on doing because it is pleasurable and engaging. You can do it wherever you are on any scrap of paper. All you need is a pen.

PART THREE

Speaking and Listening to Poetry

CHAPTER THIRTEEN

Poetry, Listening and Learning

Julie Blake

Introduction

This chapter argues for an understanding of poetry as a genre with an inherent orality, whether it is encountered in live readings, through audio recordings or on the printed page. This understanding has important consequences for poetry education, raising considerably the status of learning to listen to poems, of animating and inhabiting their human voices, aloud or in the mind's ear. It constructs poetry as a conversation in time and across time, which anyone can join. I will illustrate how with specific examples of activities I use in teacher workshops, free audio recordings available online and the opportunities available to students through the Poetry By Heart recitation contest.

The Oral Tradition

If listening is the Cinderella component of the English curriculum (Alexander, 2008), then *listening to poetry* must be the mice in the scullery wainscot component. As Education Director of the Poetry Archive (www.poetryarchive.org), the world's premier online collection of recordings of poets reading their own work, this presents something of a challenge. It is not that no one is listening to poetry: the Poetry Archive website has an average of 250,000 unique users enjoying approximately 1.5 million pages of recorded poetry *per month*. When I run workshops for teachers, however, listening to a poem is something to be done in the first one minute twelve seconds of the lesson before getting on with the main business of writing a point-example-explanation paragraph about the metaphor in line three.

It is not the case, however, that teachers are not interested in listening to poetry; far from it (otherwise why would they attend the workshops?), they are intrigued, there is a shadow-memory of something important. If it is a workshop with older teachers present, from a generation for whom an English degree was likely to have included the study of Old English, someone will nod sagely and say, 'ah yes, the Oral Tradition'. This allusion nods to a received idea of Anglo Saxon mead halls in which bards sang their stories, entertaining the king and his followers at feasts, transmitting in rhythmic verse their community's cultural achievements. These are mostly the beheading of monsters, but achievements all the same.

Both the mead halls and this 'Oral Tradition' are nice enough ideas if you happen to have enjoyed wrestling with the ninth-century Germanic case system of Old English, but the leap of faith from there to the jostling reality of the contemporary classroom is great. If, however, we leave aside the drinking horns and thrumming lyres, and focus instead on the central idea of an oral tradition – of something being spoken and heard, and *listened to* – then something different happens to our understanding of what poetry is, what it is doing in our lives. A poem becomes, in its very essence, a voice (or multiple voices) speaking to us, across time or within our own, in dialogue with other poets and poems, and in all the forms and varieties of language that allow for the richest and most fulfilling of conversations. If we listen to poetry, we have access to that conversation; if we also speak poetry, we start to join in.

In the next section, I will outline what joining the conversation is like as an experience. I will start with the experience of attentive, creative, imaginative listening, exploring two poems I often play the recordings of in workshops: Hilaire Belloc's 'Tarantella' and W.B. Yeats's 'The Lake Isle of Innisfree'. I want to illustrate some of the things that happen when listening to a poem becomes a central act of reading and understanding. I will describe some creative writing activities that flow from this and develop further the idea of voices and conversations. After that, I will explore audience and performance as key components of any act of listening to poetry, drawing on experiences of the Poetry By Heart recitation and remembering competition for schools/ colleges in England. I will conclude with some reflections on what this might mean for good poetry teaching.

'Do you remember an inn, Miranda?'

As the proud new owner of 'The Faber Book of Children's Verse' (Smith, 1963), my nine-year-old self delighted in the rhythm and wordplay of Hilaire Belloc's poem 'Tarantella'. It is most unlikely that anyone ever read it to me and I should not think for a second that I could have explained it; I just liked the sound of it and that was enough. As an adult sharing the poem aloud with children, I always read the first stanza with the same infectious exuberance, allowing that to almost completely override the 'Doom' of the second stanza.

I often play the Poetry Archive recording of this poem in teacher workshops. In this recording Belloc performs the poem in a highly mannered style. Gone is my simple Cockney delight in the rhyme of 'hadn't got a penny' and 'weren't paying any', to be replaced by singing – swirling and unaccompanied – with some lines sung against the dictates of the written form, repeated, forgotten and improvised. Here is a voice hard-edged in its Received Pronunciation, but with its authority cut across by the memory of hot nights in the High Pyrenees; a voice which struggles after authenticity in its rolled-r pronunciation of 'Aragon' only to undercut this the next second with an absurd rolling of the r-s in 'torrent'. It is a voice that both booms and whispers, asserts and cajoles; and though only a product of the quality of audio recording at the time, the constant background crackle heightens the sense of distress. My understanding of the poem gets darker each time I listen. I want to step nimbly aside from the slightly manic, slightly desperate speaker; I want to turn to Miranda and ask what she has to say. Does she remember? Does she want to remember? Is she even alive any more or did the 'fleas that tease' and the 'cheers and jeers of the young muleteers' kill her off a long time ago? It no longer sounds much like fun, but I am now ready to have the conversation.

Following this kind of listening (focused by discussion of who the speaker is, who the intended listener, what shifts of voice, tone and attitude, what intent and purpose) is often followed by a workshop activity which involves 'writing back' to the poem (Thieme, 2001), improvising, shaping and performing Miranda's reply. John Donne's 'The Flea' and Andrew Marvell's 'Coy Mistress' are also tried and tested poems for this approach. For extra challenge, you might have some students emulating the metre and rhyme scheme of these originals, or intercutting the two poems – established and newly minted – in performance.

A related approach is to explore other poems which write back' to the canon in this way, developing a conversation between different writers across time: for older students, Derek Walcott's 'Crusoe's Journal', Elizabeth Bishop's 'Crusoe in England' (recording available in the Poetry Archive) and A.D. Hope's 'Man Friday' develop a dialogue with Daniel Defoe – and each other – and with his novel *Robinson Crusoe*.

Simpler conversational pairings might include Wilfred Owen's 'Dulce et Decorum Est', written as a riposte to Jessie Pope's jingoistic output; Gillian Clarke's 'Miracle on St David's Day' in conversation with William Wordsworth's 'Daffodils'; John Agard's 'Toussaint L'Ouverture Acknowledges Wordsworth's Sonnet "To Toussaint L'Ouverture"' in conversation with William Wordsworth's 'To Toussaint L'Ouverture'; or for something longer, Coleridge's 'Rime of the Ancient Mariner' with

Nick Hayes's graphic novel of a poem, 'The Rime of the Modern Mariner'. The Bloodaxe anthologies 'Staying Alive' (Astley, 2002), 'Being Alive' (Astley, 2004) and 'Being Human' (Astley, 2011) are all very good for clusters of poems that talk to each other.

'I will arise and go now'

W.B. Yeats's poem 'The Lake Isle of Innisfree' is also much anthologized for children, apparently qualifying by virtue of its simple diction (give or take a few wattles and linnets), the lilting regularity of its rhythm and rhyme, and its folksy vision of oneness with bees and beans. It is also a poem I play with regularly in workshops. We might start by reading it silently, in the time-honoured classroom fashion, and then discussing in a general way what the poem is about, what it means. That does not take long: there never seems very much to say about *the poem* before we are resorting to things learned about its context in Yeats's biography. They are not uninteresting but they are a second order of learning. Listening and experimenting with the voice of the poem through speaking aloud attend to the first order of the poem itself.

In this part of a workshop, we often try different readings aloud: some are prepared by individuals, some by pairs, some by small groups; the same pairs or small groups prepare contrasting performances. Sometimes I present more specific challenges: how are you going to tackle that rhythmically awkward 'will' in the opening line 'I will arise and go now'? If we have time, we might pause and listen to the same line read by different performers of the poem, such as might be found in the Librivox collection of recordings by members of the general public (www.librivox.com). Some emphasize 'I' rather than 'will', placing the stresses of the trimeter on 'I', the second syllable of 'arise' and 'go'. Others emphasize the volition of the speaker, with the first stress on 'will'. What about 'go now'? Some performers stick with the trimeter and make 'now' an unstressed syllable, whilst others stress it to create a sense of urgency that fits semantically with the active verbs 'arise' and 'go'. A few questions about this single line are usually enough to sow seeds of doubt about the received idea of this as 'The Good Life' in verse.

By the time, then, that we have enjoyed everyone's performances of the poem, and the subtle and interesting variations between these, we have already developed playful, experimental ways of reading a poem, and of listening to these readings as a way of exploring different interpretations and perspectives. I then like to test everyone's critical tolerance to the extreme by playing the Poetry Archive recording of W.B. Yeats performing the poem himself. From its vaguely pompous 'When I was a lad' narratizing of the poem's genesis to the strangely unnecessary explication of noon as a 'purple glow', the introduction generally stuns people to silence, even before Yeats begins his incantatory (if not hallucinatory) intonation of the poem. Our ideas about the poem are almost always so starkly at odds with the poet's reading of it. This contrast makes a much more challenging point about poetry's essence: that at its core, there is something ineffable, something not quite fathomable, the something that listening to the poem invites us to attend to more closely.

James Berry's recording in the Poetry Archive of his short simple poem 'Seashell' works a similar kind of transformative magic, though usually in a less disturbing way than Yeats's reading. I often collapse the poem to a word list and start the workshop with teachers exploring the words and using them to write their own short simple poems. Sometimes I am laissez-faire about it; sometimes teachers have to use all of the words, no fewer and no more. We read our poems aloud and enjoy them, of course, then spend some time listening again to our favourites and exploring similarities and differences. Then we listen to James Berry reading his poem, and there is something about his voice – its warmth, its richness, its humour – that makes the poem so much more than the sum of its word list. The understanding of poetry that this generates – that meaning is inseparable from its articulation in human voice – is not something you can learn by glossary-led feature spotting.

Poetry By Heart

This bridging between listening and speaking, creative writing and creative reading is made manifest in a particularly powerful way when students have the opportunity to truly inhabit a poem's voice, through learning and performing it by heart. To this end, in 2013 Andrew Motion and I, under the auspices of the Poetry Archive, established Poetry By Heart, a recitation and remembering contest for pupils in years 10–13 in England. Poetry By Heart is a challenge and a dare, and an invitation to join the poetry conversation. Pupils learn two poems by heart – from a special online anthology – and then perform them for a school/college audience. The best pupil from each school/college progresses to a county round; the county winners compete in regional semi-finals, and the winners of these go through to a grand final.

What we saw throughout the competition was young people taking poems into their hearts, moving far beyond the matter of learning the words in the right order, and bringing them back out of themselves to share them with an audience. Pupils talked about a new enjoyment of poetry – of being able to 'feel' how language and form work through the act of preparing it for performance. Recitation is the word we have for this but it is more than that: it is an embodiment, a creative interpretation, a making corporeal the voice of the poem, in a way that is empowering for the speaker. Kaiti Soultana, Poetry By Heart national champion 2013, said 'what we gained by offering ourselves as orators of the poems was more than just the memory of the poem itself. What I gained was far more remarkable; I discovered the importance of poetry to human beings, and how this importance has spanned generations'. This is a key understanding but the speaker also gains a more primal power, the power to hold an audience spellbound. At the finals, parents and judges alike shed tears and in classroom piloting the most jostling class stopped and listened, pin-dropped, as the quiet girl they had barely noticed recited Byron's 'The destruction of Sennacherib'. In every case, the poem heard is both a treasure and a gift.

Returning to the oral tradition

The line of argument I am taking here is influenced by Ruth Finnegan's anthropological consideration of oral forms of literature in many cultures (Finnegan, 2005) and Joy Alexander's detailed re-reading of Coleridge's 'Rime of the Ancient Mariner' (Alexander, 2013). Alexander follows Finnegan in thinking about our (best) encounters with literature as a powerful experience of 'immediacy, in the temporal moment' (Finnegan, 2005: 176). The wedding guest is, even against his will and the other demands on his time, compelled to listen to the Ancient Mariner's story, and reels away afterwards, his world view at least temporarily changed by the experience (Alexander, 2013: 117). In the Ancient Mariner's oral, story-telling culture, this happens through a spell-binding performance. Encountered in performance (read aloud or enacted in some way), the poem is likely to have the same powerful effect on listeners, but when you see the poem in print you also have to pay attention to the third voice of the poem: the cold, analytical voice of the marginal note-maker disrupting the narrative's moment (Alexander, 2013: 12).

In Alexander's analysis, the poem is (amongst other things) an argument about different kinds of reading and experiencing literature. In Coleridge, immediacy and intensity rule, however disturbing the effect, but Finnegan argues for a more nuanced understanding, one in which oral and written forms of literature are closely related. In this view, written literature that derives from 'The Oral Tradition', such as poetry, retains as a central quality its need for 'performance and declamation aloud and to an audience' (Finnegan, 2005: 169). No matter that the reading of written poetry may most often be manifested in silence, the very essence of the form requires an 'en-performancing' of the text, re-enactment in voice (Finnegan, 2005: 176).

In this argument, the written text is no more a flat linguistic inscription than a reading aloud of it is merely an utterance of words: both are multisensory, multidimensional, multimodal and material. Citing Kress (2003) and Street (2003), Finnegan points us to the important idea that the written text of a poem is a multimodal script for spoken interaction (even if that stays inside our head). It invites us to attend to and try out the voice(s) as our own, using all the cues in the written form – layout, spacing and punctuation as well as prosodic and acoustic cues, and human voice variations – to guide our reading when we do not have the poet there to do it for us.

The implication is that the more effectively we 'en-performance' a poem, the closer we get to the intensity and immediacy of a fulfilling encounter with literature. That is something most English teachers would wish for their students as a self-evident good. However, I would follow Alexander in arguing that the more effectively we teach students to 'en-performance' poems, the more richly we allow them to explore meaning and form. Learning to listen to the voice(s) of a poem is not contrary to successful examination performance but perhaps more likely to secure it at higher levels. In the process, it may equip students to enjoy poetry throughout their lives.

Conclusion

I want to conclude by addressing two commonplaces which get in the way of good poetry teaching. First, it is a commonplace to hear it claimed that young people have an antipathy to poetry because it is not 'relevant'. This chapter shows that if we understand poetry as voice, and a poem as an invitation to join a conversation, then there is nothing irrelevant about it. We might well need to encourage young people to listen to voices of people they are unfamiliar with, outside the immediate circle of their everyday lives, but that is a different issue and one that is important anyway.

Second, it is a commonplace, in response to anxiety about teaching poetry, to regard student production of digital animations of poems with images, text and music as an appropriate task to help students understand what poetry is. This task may serve reasonable purposes in relation to understanding digital media, and getting 'the buggers' to sit down (Cowley, 2010), but in relation to poetry I am arguing for a more considered understanding of its multimodal potential: one that works not by digital transduction but by listening to and embodiment of the multimodal affordances of the poem itself in the human voice and performance.

Resources recommended

Librivox www.librivox.com

National Association of Writers in Education www.nawe.co.uk

Poetry By Heart www.poetrybyheart.org.uk

The Poetry Archive www.poetryarchive.org

The Poetry Society www.poetrysociety.org.uk

CHAPTER FOURTEEN

Rhyme Workshops

Andy Craven-Griffiths

Introduction

In this chapter I will be looking at how various types of rhyme can be practised through a variety of activities in one workshop day. I begin, just as I do in workshops, by discussing simple, full rhyme and couplets, moving through to half rhyme, accent-dependent rhyme and more complicated rhyme schemes. Throughout, I will discuss the benefits of each activity and type of rhyme. These include opening up a larger vocabulary, pupils' increased ownership of their writing, development of a more comprehensive understanding of rhyme and a greater ability to manipulate it rather than be constricted by it.

Although the basic structure of the activities and the workshop day remains the same, the content is always adapted both qualitatively and quantitatively for the varying ages, levels of ability and numbers of pupils that I am working with on a particular day. During the course of the chapter, I shall mention some methods of adaptation.

My background in writing, performing and workshopping

I began writing and performing poetry at the age of nineteen. Open mic performances lead to paid gigs, firstly at poetry nights, literary events and then at music festivals such as Leeds, Reading and Latitude. At Glastonbury in 2005, I won the poetry slam. After graduating with a degree in English and Philosophy, I began six months' shadowing the Birmingham Poet Laureate Dreadlockalien in his slam workshops. I have used the team structure and competitive format learnt from Dreadlockalien. We have developed and shared various exercises over the years since then. Since 2008, I have worked freelance in schools across England. In 2012, I was a lead poet on *Shake the Dust*, the largest UK Youth Slam Poetry project to date.

Since 2007, I have also been writing and performing with my band, *Middleman*. There is a natural crossover between our music and slam poetry in terms of a particular interest in rhyme, syllabics and rhythm. I think a good understanding of rhyme is especially important in slam poetry because it is an oral art form. It is sound-focussed, and the way that sound is presented and controlled is down to the speaker. The better we understand rhyme, the less constrained we may be by its apparent limitations and the more flexibly and inventively we can use it. This includes choosing where not to use it. In my poem 'Horse Shoes', this understanding allows me to form composite rhymes (primary/spy on me), to use rhythm to *make* closer rhymes from distant half rhymes (bus pass/ mum's house) and to abandon rhyme altogether where I want something to stand out (Oi Horses!).

Slam poetry workshop overview

My large-scale engagement slam poetry workshops are designed for groups of 50–100 pupils of any age from 8 to18. They work in teams of 6–8 in a large hall/theatre space. Throughout the day, teachers keep pupils on task and help them to work through various writing games and performance activities as directed from the front. Pupils hone skills they will use to create a final team poem. The day culminates in a mutually supportive team poetry slam in which the teachers become judges and give teams scores out of ten. During the day bonus points can be accumulated for good work, for winning at games and for being the first team to be ready/quiet for the next task.

The two most distinctive elements of the slam poetry format are:

1. It is a competitive format.
2. It is spoken word, to be performed and heard, rather than read.

In general terms, the competitive element encourages more spontaneity and less concern that something is 'good enough' to write down. Teams focus on beating other teams and are restricted by time limits. The oral format means that pupils are truly writing in their own voices, which in turn may help them to say what they want to say, rather than what they think poets are supposed to say.

Table 14.1 outlines the types of rhyme I will discuss and examples of activities used to practice each of them.

Table 14.1 Types of rhyme.

Type of rhyme	Games/activities
Full rhyme	Rhyme battles
Half rhyme (including accent-dependent rhymes)	Nothing rhymes with orange
Composite rhyme	Countdown/Building blocks
Assonance	Animal sound raps
Multiple/Internal rhymes	'Just a minute'

Full rhyme: Rhyme battles

All teams are given words to rhyme with. The given words must have plenty of full rhymes. The three I like to use are 'education', 'inspire' and 'create'. Younger pupils (aged 8–11) are given three minutes to write rhyme lists. Older pupils may have one minute. Two teams take it in turns to suggest a rhyming word for the starting word. The rhymes have to be full rhymes, so, for example, they cannot have 'cake' or 'face' for 'create'.

There are three rules in the battle:

1. No repetition
2. No nonsense words (names are optional)
3. No hesitation (If the team cannot give a new rhyme, I count down 3...2...1. If the team cannot give a new rhyme before 0, then the other team wins the battle)

If the starting word is 'inspire', the rhymes might run 'fire/liar/choir/deep fat fryer' and so on. Homophones are allowed if the team using the second homophone can give both definitions (for example, for tyre and tire, or higher and hire).

Difficulty can be increased in levels:

1. Single words from lists
2. Single words without referring to lists
3. Sentences ending in rhyming words from their lists. For example 'I go to school to get my education/I looked at the window, it was covered in condensation/We need teamwork, we need cooperation'.

4. Rhyming sentences without reference to lists.

5. Single words for new starter words given on the spot, such as 'write' or 'scope'.

6. Rhyming sentences for new starter words. For example: 'Words pour out cause I like to write/I'm scared of the dark so I don't like the night'.

Throughout *Rhyme Battles*, the competitive element, especially the time limit, forces pupils to come up with rhymes they did not have in their lists. This does not mean there is no focus on quality, only that something decent is written rather than something brilliant *not being* written. One polysyllabic word normally triggers a switch from 'mate, late, great' to 'medicate, celebrate, eradicate'. Pupils will often use words they have heard, but cannot accurately define (postulate, reverberate, exacerbate). This means they move beyond their regular and most accessible vocabulary. Teachers can supply or clarify definitions if other pupils cannot. More points can be given for polysyllabic words if desired. It is often good to end with a pupils-versus-teachers battle.

Half Rhymes: Nothing rhymes with orange

Me versus pupils

This game is about generating half rhymes by trying to find something that other people cannot rhyme with. I begin by giving an example and, if any team can rhyme with it, their team wins a point. So I might say, 'I've got words that are juicy as an orange' and a team might reply with

'For breakfast I like a lot of honey in my porridge.'

Then it is the teams' turn to give a starting sentence. If any team can say something that I cannot rhyme with, their team gets a point. If another team *can* rhyme with it, that team also gets a point.

Pupils versus pupils

Teams are paired up: A with B, C with D and so on. Each team decides on three words they think are difficult to rhyme with. They choose one of these words for their opponents to attempt to find rhymes for. Team A might have been given 'purple', 'orange' and 'silver' and team B have 'month', 'citrus' and 'circus'. One of these words is then allocated and each team is asked to write a rhyme list for it. For example, Team A choose 'month' for Team B and Team B choose 'purple' for team A.

The battle, at simplest, may then run 'purple/month/gurgle/hunt/gerbil/ dunce...'. Difficulty can be increased in the same way with *Rhyme Battles*. At difficulty level three (just mentioned), full sentences, we may get: 'I mix blue and red paint to get purple/I've got rhymes for each day of the month/ etc.'

There is, of course, an element of subjectivity in this. I act as the adjudicator if there are disagreements.

As well as the words already mentioned, lots of pupils' names may be difficult to rhyme with. Otherwise, there are various lists of non-rhyming words online, such as http://latestdud.hubpages.com/hub/Words-With-No-Rhyming-Words.

Pupils move away from the restriction of focussing only on full rhymes by practising rhyming with what sounds right to them. They will rarely be stuck for a (half) rhyme. They may use close half rhymes with a simple exchange of fricatives or plosives such as save/face or shabby/happy. They may substitute more distant consonant sounds (panda/bangra), or add consonant sounds (you/hooves). Pupils may use more distant half rhymes that substitute non-identical vowel sounds (Germany/Birmingham).

Accent dependent rhymes

Spoken rhymes are often accent dependent. I try to encourage ownership of rhyme by pointing out when rhymes work in pupils' own voices, in their accents, but not necessarily in other peoples'. For example,

> People feed birds, but the best goats can hope for is grass,
> they eat tin cans, jumpers, trousers and pants.
> *Birds versus goats animal rap battle* (thirteen-year-old pupil, Washwood Heath, Birmingham, UK).

Further south in the United Kingdom, the longer '*ah*' sound in grass, like the one in 'can't', would not rhyme with the short '*A*' sound in 'pants', like the one in 'can'. Similarly, 'grass' and 'start' rhyme in London (gr*ah*ss/st*ah*rt) but not in Birmingham (gr*A*ss/st*ah*rt). With a Hull accent we can rhyme 'from' and 'home' quite closely (from/h*er*m), but not in a Leicester accent (from/ho*a*m).

Accent may turn half rhymes into full rhymes (for example 'out'/'mouth' in some Irish accents), or make half rhymes from non-rhymes, as with this Francophone nine-year-old's use of 'done' and 'alone':

> 'To travel in time to correct the wrong things I'd (d*on*)
> Also the time when I was (al*on*)'.
> *If I had Wishes* (Geneve, nine, St Michael's Primary, Bath, UK).

Composite rhymes: 'Countdown'/Building blocks

'Countdown'

Both of these games are good for practising composite rhyme, where rhyme is spread over more than one word. In 'Countdown', a line from a nursery rhyme, song, poem or a made-up sentence, is written up on the board. Teams are given one minute to write a new line with as many corresponding rhyming syllables as possible. With 8–11-year-olds it is often best to allow nonsense sentences. So,

> 'I … love … mu … sic … and … feel … like … part … of … it … blow … ing … a … rasp … ber … ry'

might become

> 'Pie … dove … use … it … hand … wheel … might … star … ted … big … sno … wy … hay … has … to … be'.

Teams score one point for each syllable that rhymes with its corresponding syllable in the starting sentence. We can increase the difficulty of the game by stipulating that the line has to make sense:

> 'I just lose it, and see the harder kid's going to batter me.'

This would score 15/16 as the only syllable that is not at least a half rhyme is 'the', which replaces 'like'.

At all levels, pupils can write rhyme lists for each syllable as shown in Table 14.2 below:

Table 14.2 Countdown syllables.

I	love	mu	sic	and	feel
try	dove	new	nick	sand	steel
cry	bluff	true	thick	band	wheel
sly	does	few	trick	land	eel
why	must	crew	stink	can	meal
pie	trust	stew	bit	man	real
fly	cuff	flew	mix	fan	seal

They can then mix and match from their lists to try to make something that makes sense.

> From the starter 'I … love … mu … sic … and … '
> they might say: 'Why … trust … new … tricks … man … '

Building blocks

The Building blocks activity works with units of rhymes (either full rhymes or half rhymes). It starts with two-syllable units, for example 'X-Box'. Teams are given one minute to write a rhyme list of two syllable units to get them started:

'X-box, neck locks, red socks, less foxed, stress stops, legs cocked, text box, mess cops, Greg's tops'.

Teams have another minute to write as long a sentence as they can, using repetitions of the same two-syllable rhyme, with no more than two non-rhyming, 'connecting syllables' in between the rhyming blocks. Rhyming blocks are shown in bold below:

'When the **net's off** my **head drops** till I **get lost** on my **X-Box** and the **stress stops**.'

Once the example block has been used, teams can choose their own two-syllable blocks for another couple of two-minute rounds. The game can be extended, and the difficulty increased, by using three-syllable blocks; then four-syllable blocks and so on. It can be made easier by allowing more 'connecting syllables' between consecutive blocks.

Working with polysyllabic units of rhyme gives pupils the chance to practise at finding rhymes other than like-for-like, single word rhymes. This means they will have more choice and make less obvious rhymes:

'You get a giant sore throat you can't cure with **cough syrup**
we're a team for our queen, you're on your own, why **not give up**?'
Ants versus giraffes (thirteen-year-old pupil, Washwood, Birmingham, UK)

Assonance: Animal sound raps

As pupils develop their understanding of half rhyme and composite rhyme, the focus will increasingly be on vowel sounds and less on consonants. I make this focus explicit with an 'Animal-sound raps' activity. Each team chooses an animal along with the animal's onomatopoeic sound. They write a short poem in the voice of their animal, using their vowel sound as frequently and densely as possible, before performing it and accentuating the sound each time it is used. Cows will have 'oo' from 'moo', dogs 'u' from 'woof', lions the 'oar' from 'roar', snakes the 'i' from 'hiss' and so on. So a lion might roar:

'I **roar** till my voice is **hoarse** and blood **pours** from my **paws**,
drawn from my pray by **force** and, of **course**, I want **more**.'

This activity facilitates a move away from couplets and stricter rhyme schemes towards greater flexibility and use of more syncopated rhythms.

Multiple/Internal rhymes

Ad-libs

Until now, most pupils will have been writing in couplets, with a regular 4/4 rhythm, whereby the rhymes fall at the end of the lines. The regular rhythm causes us to anticipate the couplet rhyme. A quick game to demonstrate this is *Ad-Libs*. Pupils are asked to write couplets and miss out the last word. Everyone else is asked to shout out the missing word. The rhythm should help them to hear where the rhyme falls, and the context, what the word it is:

> At school some teachers thought I was a menace,
> But I did well, especially in sports like…

We can use rhythm to make half-rhymes sound closer to full rhymes:

> 'You know those girls who like to paint their skin **orange**
> with fake tan and stand around pretending they're **foreign**'.
>
> (John Berkavitch: 'A Short List of the People I Hate'.)

Because slam poetry is an oral format, we can manipulate how rhyme is heard (or not heard) by shifting emphasis and by altering rhythms:

> 'Merry Christmas! Turkey's are always so *tasty*
> We bring the family together so they're cel*ebrating* (not c*el*ebrating)'.
>
> *Beavers versus slugs* (thirteen-year-old pupil,
> Washwood Heath, Birmingham, UK)

It is useful to know how to do this so that we can add to the range of rhymes we can make and learn to avoid obvious and clichéd rhymes/rhyme schemes.

'Just a minute': Internal rhymes

This game (suitable eleven-year-olds upwards) works very much like the BBC Radio 4 programme of the same name. As well as helping pupils to practice integrating rhyme more subtly into their work, it is a good way of generating a volume of content quickly. Parts can then be refined and improved. Each team picks a subject they think they could talk about for a minute. Teams are given three minutes to speed-write as much as they can on the chosen subject, using a starting sound of their choice. If the subject is football, the word might be 'goal'. They must maintain the 'oal' sound as much as possible, just as in the 'Animal-sound raps activity'. Teams are then chosen to come to the front and battle to see who can keep talking longest on their subject whilst including the rhyme. There are four rules:

1. No repetition
2. No nonsense words
3. No hesitation
4. No deviation

When one person in a team cannot continue, any other team member can take over. When teams run out of pre-written content within the minute, they must freestyle. Rounds are timed and whichever team can maintain the rhyming for the longest wins the battle. The game can be repeated using two sounds from two key words, for instance 'goal' and 'post'. Then three sounds.

At the highest level (with sixteen-year-olds upwards), teams can be given a starting sound and be allowed to change rhymes throughout, as long as some rhyme is always obvious. By this point, teams are essentially group-freestyling and we have rhyming at its most malleable:

It's **20-to-10**, sat in front of my **keyboard eating plenty just when** my brother walks **in**, with a new addition to his collection of scars – his **chin**. I laugh out loud and he rips up the **sheet** I was originally **writing** on – what a **cheek!** I stop my **smiling** and say, 'speak'. Then he tells me a story and it's **peak** to **hear** my brother was a **deer** in head**lights**, full of **fear** while they **jeer** with their **peers**, yellow teeth **bared**, unknowingly **share** that they haven't changed their under**wear. Tears** in his **eyes** when he **finds** out his friend's telling **lies**. But it's true how **life's** a **surprise**. Not everyone lives, but we all **die**. He's feeling **used, mad, shy**, spent, angry and **confused**. Anything I say is **bad** and of no **use** cause I can't reach into his **mind** and pull out the **abuse. I try** to be **kind** but I **might** as well be **cruel**. We both know he has to face them after **school**.

Free-writing for 'Just a Minute' (Jasmine Morrison, age fourteen, Stockland Green, Birmingham, UK).

Even when omitting some of the seemingly deliberate assonant half rhymes, the following complex rhyme scheme can be seen:

AB-BA-CC-BD-BD-BB-EE-DE-EE-FF-FE-GG-GG-GG-HI-GH-IH-GH-
GG-GJ-J

A 20-to-10, plenty just when
B keyboard, eating, Sheet, cheek, speak, peak
C in, chin
D writing, smiling, headlights
E Hear, deer, fear, jeer, peers, tears
F bared, shared, underwear,
G eyes, finds, lies, life's, surprise, die, shy, mind, try, kind, might
H used, confused, use, abuse
I mad, bad
J cruel, school.

After some practice, pupils become more adept at creating their own rhyme schemes in more studied pieces. This is shown in the following excerpt:

'I opened an **eye**, a **bright light blind**ing my **sight**,
I thought about the **shoulda, woulda, coulda** mum would **spit**,
I hardly **breathe** and **briefly see** the **needle** pierce **chin**,
I **squint** and **wait** for **pain**, but I can't **feel** any**thing**'.
(Jasmine Morrison, age fourteen, Stockland Green, Birmingham, UK)

Conclusion

By the end of these rhyme workshops, young poets will have practised full rhyme in *Rhyme Battles*. The oral format reduces their worries about spelling, and speeds up the creative process. The competitive element will have opened up slightly less obvious parts of their vocabulary. It will have increased their confidence to try things out and to improve and edit their ideas, rather than feeling they have to produce something perfect first time.

Practising both half rhyme and composite rhyme will have widened their rhyming parameters, demonstrating the flexibility and variety of units of rhyme. Pupils will have begun to appreciate what sounds right in their own voices, rather than what looks right on paper, thus promoting greater ownership of language. Practice in using internal rhyme, rolling rhyme or 'jazz' rhyme schemes will have demonstrated the importance of delivery and rhythm in *making*, or masking, rhymes. Rhyme will be less of a restriction and more of a malleable, and often surprising, mode of creativity. Pupils will have a rhyme toolbox from which they can select tools to enhance their poetry writing, and performance, in the future.

CHAPTER FIFTEEN

Slam Poetry

Joelle Taylor

Introduction

I have learnt many things from this experience – that poetry isn't just words, it's about experiencing how you feel in words.

SLAM WORKSHOP PARTICIPANT

This chapter is about slam poetry and the transformative effect of spoken word on the lives of young people throughout the United Kingdom. It will look at the social and cultural effects of slam in schools, at workshop structures, the impact of live events and use of new technology in linking artists and students together.

For those still unfamiliar with what slam is, it is the competitive art of spoken word, performance poetry, rapping, emceeing (with beat box) delivered live to a dynamic and voluble audience and a panel of judges selected from the profession. It is the ultimate expression of interactive art where the audience is as important as the performer.

In essence it is a celebration of free speech.

In 2000, I won one of the first adult UK slam championships. As a spoken word artist it became clear to me through that event that slam was a force that would change the way we as a cultural community thought about poetry and the way it was presented. It also became clear that slam was something that could be used to engage young people from the most disadvantaged backgrounds. It would give them a space in which to speak, to learn and a platform from which their voices might be heard and finally understood. It is perhaps difficult to imagine now how revolutionary and radical the concept of a youth poetry slam (for 18 years and under) was when it was first introduced to the United Kingdom. A decade later, slam is now used nationwide as a way of engaging young people and of – ironically – improving their self-confidence.

Slam workshops

Slams are simple to run within a school or inter-school. From primary to university, they can be used to help students explore issues that affect them as well as those that would support curriculum study. For example, a poem can be written that ties in with the History syllabus, and involves research. The chosen topic of the slam can easily be linked to different school study areas. There are a few well-known slams across the country, but this chapter will focus on the longest running solo youth slam, SLAMbassadors UK.

SLAMbassadors UK began as the Respect Slam in 2001. It was a London-wide poetry slam funded by the Mayor of London as a tool to use in the fight against racism in the capital. It grew very quickly to tackle other kinds of prejudice and issues that affect the younger generation through poetry, such as cultural stereotypes, misogyny in all its incarnations, knife crime and gang culture and misrepresentations of youth as a whole. Within a few years it had expanded beyond the boundaries of the city and is now a national project.

SLAMbassadors UK targets those schools or areas throughout the United Kingdom where literacy is at a low average level or where high levels of economic deprivation prevail. The typical profile of a SLAMbassador – a poet who has entered the championship – is radically different to the literary norm. They might be the children of low-income families, secondary or academy educated, with very little access to or interest in cultural activities. They might be new arrivals to the United Kingdom (including refugee or asylum seeker heritage) or those with lower literacy attainment than would be expected of their privileged counterparts. We often target schools with a high proportion of students receiving free school meals.

SLAMbassadors is aimed directly and unswervingly towards those that do not have other access points into the world of poetry. This has meant that we have also historically been used by schools as a way of reaching those students who are disengaged from the education system. We have found that those students without resources or linguistic expertise often have the more powerful content, the strongest stories to tell within their poems. They use the project as a way of defining their experiences, or explaining them to themselves. Poetry can be an incredible therapeutic tool, and, when used well, can prise words out of mouths long silent. Mouths are scars that begin to speak. The theme of identity also encourages a kind of poetic excavation, this unearthing of the truths in their lives. It can lead poets to discover themselves. For example,

- What makes you, you?

- Is there a particular experience that you believe has defined you?

- Is it the colour of your skin or the response to that colour in the media or on the way home from school?

- Is it your gender? What is a woman? What indeed is a man?

- How does your faith define you?

- What was the last view you had of your home country?

Workshop structure

When I designed the SLAMbassadors workshops, there was no precedent; this is why they have been successful perhaps – because we, the poet coaches, taught ourselves. We have been influenced by our own poetry and experiences of years on the stage, before crowded theatres or at the backs of bars. We know how to get people to listen. We know that poetry has to be immediate in that environment, that a poem must be understood in a visceral, physical way. We understand that poetry in this case is not a private experience between a reader and a page but a most public one. Another difference is that we only focus on our own poetry and design our sessions around them, using them as templates for the students to work from.

The workshops take place over two days and focus on a small group. Day One begins with a performance. This is often the students' first introduction to an artist and can have a profound effect on them. For many it is their first experience of a live poet, and the first time they recognize how dynamic and arresting poetry can be – and how *visual*. Through the day we look at different techniques used within poetry to create a piece that is moving, convincing, authentic and cinematic. While different artists use different exercises to inspire, a prime focus is on poetic device and stimulus sources.

As well as exploring metaphor and simile, we use photographs to inspire new writing and to embed a sense of the cinematic in what is written. The same photograph can be viewed in a hundred different ways, and each student's job is to find the story that resonates with them. For example, is it in the image itself or in the imagining of who the photographer might be? What is the subject looking at just out of frame? Music can also be used as stimulus. This can lead to questions like: what was the musician feeling as she wrote this? What was she just about to do? Walking down the street and observing the people you pass is equally as informative and inspiring. Reading a mark on the ground will tell you much. In short, the students develop the awareness that there are stories and poems everywhere.

It is important to make use of all the skills in the workshop group. For example, beat box can be an incredible aid to literacy. It can draw a young artist into a room (s)he may feel disengaged from. When a class features a beat boxer, I know that others in that environment will use them to develop their work into a form drawn from music. They might make the poem bounce, make it sing or feel connected to its rhythm. There are thousands of examples of beat box on YouTube, including tutorials that you could play to your class on the smart-board.

Slam's definition of what constitutes 'poetry' is wider than most, and includes free verse, emcee bars, rap lyrics and flash poetry prose (see Glossary for definitions). It also embraces the use of the voice in all of its forms – speaking, singing and beat boxing being the most obvious and popular. This necessitates the use of Poet Mentors who are not only proficient in these forms but are also actively and currently producing work in them at a high level and have valuable experience and advice to offer. They are chosen from both the professional sphere and the SLAMbassador alumni. It is not uncommon when using these techniques with participants for us to discover a rap artist who later becomes a master in free verse poetry and goes on to publish work that draws on this influence. An example of one such artist is Kayo Chingonyi who began as a rapper in the Rise Slam and whose collection *Some Bright Elegance* was published by Salt in 2012. All forms are treated with the same level of respect and supported in their development during the workshops.

Day Two focuses on performance and investigating how a poem is different when it is written for the stage, for the skin. A spoken word piece often will not work as well or at all on the page – they truly exist only when they are performed. And so mentors and students edit the pieces according to how they are spoken; new words are found, others are lost. Once the poems are rehearsed, we film the young poets performing them for entry to the national slam. Whilst entry into the slam is an imperative of the project, it is not essential to the workshops taking place. However, I would suggest that a performance element is vital to fully engaging the student. While process is always more important than product, 'the gig' helps to reinforce unity in the group and to give a focus point to work towards.

The main reference point for the students in terms of performances is the poet coach themselves. They watch and learn to develop a way of speaking the poems with their bodies as well as their mouths. The focus is on re-living the writing of the poem onstage, and re-creating the original emotions. It is about believing what they have written. There are no special hand gestures, or any other ham theatrical devices. We do however look at breathing techniques, concentration exercises and posture – as well as microphone technique – but nothing substitutes for believing the poem. For examples on performances given by slam poets and spoken word artists, please see the links at the end of this chapter.

It is difficult to describe the energetic effect of a person sharing a poem about their lives with the rest of the group. It has an almost alchemical outcome when one person tells the truth about their life that sparks a response in other poems across the room. People begin to understand each other a little better; people begin to understand themselves. Over the course of two days, relationships between students, as well as that between student and teacher, begin to change. There is a sense at the end that we are all now listening to each other.

Supporting teachers

To support the workshops, I also lead in-service training (INSET) sessions for teachers in schools, and these are crucial for teachers to be able to adopt the skills that we use in workshops. There is no reason that a teacher cannot continue and develop the work begun by the artist, bringing in their own ideas and practices. One of our aims is to recognize the creativity of the teaching staff themselves, and so they take on the role of students in workshops rather than overseers. This creates a stronger sense of artistic community in the school, and serves as a creative release for staff.

When a person has been silenced and censored within the context of their own lives though, we should not be surprised that when they are offered the opportunity to speak they do so at the tops of their voices. Sometimes the school has placed a student in my workshop because they already know that the child has something they need to articulate. In other workshops the poems have disclosed abusive domestic situations or worrying expressions of self-harm. It is a sensitive area, which is why it is vital to have child protection training. It is also important for the poet to have someone to talk to. We are not made of stone and as the referral pile on a social worker's desk increases, the weight is also felt on our chests.

Technology

Technology ages rapidly and so it is perhaps difficult now to see the astounding impact that YouTube and social media had upon the development of SLAMbassadors – and on slam as a whole. In real terms it took us from a small live space to the infinite virtual arena allowing us to find more young poets and to – crucially – create an easily accessible archive of the work that remains long after the last audience member has left the theatre, an archive not only of poetry but also of languages and dialects, of ideas and images. It has enabled us to expand our outreach beyond London and the main cities of the United Kingdom towards the rural areas, including those places that have no direct access to contemporary spoken word. It turns the classroom into the slam arena. More importantly than that, it turns the private space of each student into a slam arena. New poets can record themselves performing, or create more aesthetically interesting poetry films, and upload them directly to the Poetry Society's YouTube page.

While we have one emphasis on working in formal and informal education environments, the other focus is on encouraging independent entries. These poets get little direct help from us although there are many exercises listed on the Poetry Society's Young Poets Network site, and suggestions on the slam blog cited later in the chapter. In spite of this, we get a substantial number each year. It is fascinating and encouraging to see a film that refers to another previously uploaded or that echoes the form or central image of another poem. I recognize the cadence of Hollie McNish, the delivery of Dizraeli, the revivalism of Kate Tempest or the imagery of my own poem 'Last Poet Standing' in many of the films. (Links to these are mentioned later in the chapter.)

The live event experience

Nothing can compete with the live event experience, certainly for a spoken word artist. The stage is as much a part of the script for the slam poet as the words themselves. We must constantly be aware of the semantics of performance, of writing a piece that will be instantly effective and understood and of knowing not only our words but also what script the body will be speaking. At traditional poetry readings, it is not uncommon for the featured poet to ask the audience to refrain from applause until the end of their sets; in slam the applause and screams of the audience becomes a part of the poem. Authors need to wait up to a year or two to discover what their readership thinks and feels about their new works. The slam poet gets to know immediately whether they have been successful or not. In spite of this, I have yet to hear of slam experience which has not been positive for the artist.

A core difference between SLAMbassadors and other youth slams is perhaps that we treat each slam as we would an adult event. That means we do not have team poems, synchronized movements or penalties for going over a time limit. In slam events, marks are awarded on Writing Technique, Performance and Originality, often with points deducted for time breaches. Winners are selected after a lengthy discussion on whether it is believed that they fit the profile of a spoken word artist. We look for one poet. One voice. One potential career in spoken word.

Continued mentoring

The point of the slam event is to inspire continued creation of original poetry and spoken word. It is not the full stop, but a comma. What happens next is always more important than what has just happened on one stage in one town in one part of the world. Continued intensive mentorship is at the core of the SLAMbassador programme, for all participants and not just the winners. At first, we simply offered the winners a set period of mentoring. This period organically developed into months, which have now become years, possibly because the mentors continue to provide opportunities for poets they like, whatever the age. The original participants on the project now work as mentors to young artists seeking their own lost words. What we were all still missing however was a space in which we could continue to network with both established and emerging artists in a flexible environment that would allow for workshops, gigs and rehearsal space. To meet this, the Poetry Society has collaborated with the Poetry Café in London to allow those poets who have evolved from the programme to use their space. Once a month we now have the SLAMbassadors sessions – a space for master classes, passing on workshop facilitation skills, collaborations between disparate artists, publishing, filming and performance. Each piece from the sessions is filmed and uploaded to a playlist on YouTube. It is a space to begin from.

The microphone is not only an instrument to amplify the voice but also a baton in an infinite relay race across generations. With this in mind, a vital part of the mentoring is focussed on the passing on of workshop facilitation skills. It is important not only for young poets' development and the ability to support themselves financially, but also to the continuation of the project. Those that were once found, go on to find others. This is achieved in two ways: firstly by creating a touring team of winners who shadow me in workshops and perform to the classes as well as touring to events across the United Kingdom; and secondly by leading specific master classes in which direct workshop facilitation skills are explored.

Conclusion

Slam offers a vital approach to understanding and creating literature and poetry. It has expanded beyond the rules of poetry, beyond the rules of slam itself, to become something living that is different in every venue. And it is crucial that this difference, this left-field nature, is recognized and respected. It can be used in any educational setting to help evolve an understanding of an issue, to find a creative entry point into the curriculum, to unlock lips so that dusty stories can fall out, to create solid artistic communities within schools and beyond. To conclude, I would like to set the record straight:

Slam is not a form but an event. It is not a noun but a verb. Slam is a doing word.

Resources recommended

Links to further information about slam:
www.poetrysociety.org.uk
http://slam.poetrysociety.org.uk
www.youngpoetsnetwork.org.uk
www.youtube/poetrysociety/slambassadorsessions
www.hammerandtongue.co.uk
www.applesandsnakes.org

Links to spoken and slam performances

(Each of the artists can be found by entering their names into YouTube.)
Hollie McNish: http://www.youtube.com/watch?v=bJX5XHnONTI
Kate Tempest: http://www.youtube.com/watch?v=i_auc2Z67OM
Dizraeli at Shake the Dust: http://www.youtube.com/watch?v=aEq_9mQMlkk
George the Poet: http://www.youtube.com/watch?v=cbtcuiwHvOs
Joelle Taylor: http://www.youtube.com/watch?v=GasEftVfyLI

UK slam teams

Leeds Young Authors: www.leedsyoungauthors.org.uk
Manchester: www.youngidentity.org
UK Group Slam: www.shakethedust.co.uk

CHAPTER SIXTEEN

Case Study VI: How English Teachers Use Slam Poetry in a Secondary School Setting

Christopher Parton

Introduction

In 2012, I participated in an ESRC-funded *Poetry Matters* workshop led by Joelle Taylor, the founder and Artistic Director of SLAMbassadors UK. The session's emphasis on the interplay of creativity and spoken language not only resonated with my own creative writing interests but also with my English department's increasing development of and interest in classroom oracy.

Over the course of an afternoon, the group explored and experimented with a range of creative stimuli and writing techniques in order to produce and perform our own slam-style poems. Joelle introduced and modelled several strategies for drafting out and producing poems collectively for performance, including a consideration of beat boxing and a variety of stimuli including character, image and random lines of poetry.

Since the ESRC workshop, I have worked with a colleague, who is the literacy coordinator at my school, Blessed Robert Sutton, to organize an annual week-long 'Robert Sutton Slam'. During the Slam, groups of approximately sixty, Year 8 Key Stage 3 pupils (aged 13–14) from a range of abilities are taken off their regular English timetable to participate in some of the activities first introduced by Joelle Taylor.

The following case study examines the employment, results and pedagogical implications of some of these methods in a secondary school context. In particular, it discusses three key areas. Firstly, because of the Slam workshop's lively and interactive emphasis, I investigate exactly what kind of talk is facilitated by the Slam activities, its relation to pupils' creative writing and what kind of affective or cognitive development it promotes. Secondly, I discuss the role these activities play in further developing pupils' critical literacy. And finally, I aim to determine the relationship between these activities and educational play.

The study draws on my experience of and involvement in the workshops at Blessed Robert Sutton since 2012; pupils' own writing; recordings of and discussions with pupils and a reflective questionnaire that all pupils from the 2013 Slam completed after they had participated in the classroom activities.

How the Slams work

In the school workshops, the literacy coordinator and I focus on what we and the children have come to term (affectionately if not a little clumsily) the 'relay' poem and the 'body parts poem'. With the former, pupils randomly choose a line of poetry using a technique that Joelle Taylor playfully refers to as 'bibliomancy'. Essentially, pupils are presented with a book of poetry and asked to select a page and line number at random. They use this as their first line and each member of the group writes a subsequent line until the time is up.

Beginning the poem in this way creates a sense of mystery and anticipation whilst also providing a reassuringly collective starting point for those more easily intimidated by the blank page. The first line therefore acts as a scaffold which focuses the young writers on particular images, ideas, feelings and even textures and rhythms which they can develop throughout the course of their writing.

With regard to the 'body parts poem', pupils mind-map different ideas for personas to base their poem on (e.g. celebrity, prisoner, victim of crime, politician). This mind-mapping is modelled initially on an interactive whiteboard before providing groups further opportunity to explore their ideas.

The aim is to stimulate creativity with simile and metaphor. Pupils list various body parts (i.e. eyes, tongue, hands) and then each writes a line of the poem describing this body part metaphorically as though they are the character that they have chosen. Below is an example from a group that worked with the idea of a prisoner:

My head is a surveillance cell.

Slam at school – classroom talk

When we have discussed poetry with the pupils involved in the Robert Sutton Slam and asked them to reflect on their experiences, fear of writing collaboratively is a recurring theme. In particular, pupils have a strong sense of anxiety surrounding differences of opinions and ideas and how to negotiate these. Therefore, pupils' own reflections on creative writing often contain statements such as the following:

I was worried that … we would have different ideas.

The problem that we could have faced was the whole group disagreeing and not working well together.

I was worried about people having different ideas and people arguing about this.

Considering the amount of group learning that takes place in my English lessons, I have found this dread of 'disputational talk' (Mercer, 2000: 97) surprising. One tentative explanation might be a continuing lack of explicit teaching of roles, ground rules and discourse strategies identified as important some time ago by the National Oracy Project (Corden, 2004). However, subsequent questioning of pupils also underlines how little experience pupils have outside of the classroom of writing creatively with others. Indeed, if writing does take place outside of school, it is very much a case of writing alone or almost exclusively with mothers/female carers. Taken together, these statements can hardly be considered conducive to creative openness and the sharing of ideas and learning. Yet the latter is characteristic of the liveliness of much performance poetry.

The conviviality and fiercely supportive atmosphere of UK Slam is, then, something that we have been keen to replicate. Initially this was more a case of simply creating enjoyment and staying true to the format introduced by Joelle. However, our early feedback also showed how this way of working might also be useful in expurgating the kinds of mutual distrust inhibitive of good quality talk. Sessions are, as a result, noisy affairs with an abundance of discussion, cheering and stomping. Our aim is to use the activities to create a learning environment which enables pupils to develop cognitively, improve their drafting skills together and hopefully obtain positive experiences of the kind of creative collaboration which pupils' own feedback suggests they lack.

Dymoke (2003) has identified a number of ways teachers can encourage dialogue and so create such an environment. She stresses the need to provide space for reflection, share work in progress with other readers, use questions and prompts, break processes into stages and allow for flexibility, negotiation and autonomy.

The activities chosen for the Slams ('relay' and 'body parts' poems) are ideally suited to facilitate many of these strategies. Both poems are very much about sharing work in progress. They are collective efforts with each member of the group contributing lines, reviewing and building on the work of others and offering helpful suggestions where necessary.

Even those students who fear disagreement in group work recognize the value of the interdependence encouraged by both the 'relay' and 'body parts' poems. Pupils have commented that 'writing a poem by yourself can be hard' and that they 'might have struggled without' the opportunity to share and review ideas. Indeed, we have been keen to stress this aspect of the drafting process. Although with both poems there is a clear expectation that pupils write a line each, we actively encourage the classes to critique and support the writing of the other members of their groups. Our hope in doing so is to provide greater opportunity for talk and to help more confident students support their less able peers. Similarly, we also extend the time period during which pupils are to write their lines and drafts. This ensures a greater quantity and depth of written material, whilst also providing greater scope for the less confident to build their confidence and expertise with the task. In this sense, we have tried to strike a balance between the kind of lively individual risk taking that more experienced writers might find easy and maximizing the opportunity for peer–peer collaboration and interdependency which are vital for well-structured group work (Corden, 2004).

During the drafting of one group's relay poem, one pupil wanted to use the line 'thinks he has a talent' to describe an out of work and washed up performer. Their stimulus had been a random line chosen from an unseen poem (Simon Armitage's 'Clown Punk'). Through their poem and discussion of suggested lines such as the one above, the group had evidently embraced the autonomy given to them and begun to create a whole character and diegesis. Patterns of classroom talk such as the following emerged:

A: Thinks he has a talent.
B: Yeah, but if he has a talent…
C: Yeah, because his talent…

Speaker A's contribution here clearly shows how the lines of the poems themselves become 'part of the flow of speech within a lesson' (Gordon, 2010: 48), but with B and C it is possible to identify pupils adopting the roles of initiators and supporters and therefore engaging in the cognitive processes of introducing hypotheses and extending/describing ideas, respectively. Classroom talk is, then, enriched by this activity. Discussion is not merely constituted of Initiation Response Feedback (I-R-F) but is a means for pupils to create meaning, effects and ideas.

Slam at school – critical literacy

But if the two Robert Sutton Slams have been about facilitating exploratory talk, then they have been equally about critical literacy and culturally relevant pedagogy. For instance, pupils mind-mapped a range of personas for their 'body parts' poems and some, though by no means all, belonged to marginalized groups such as criminals or refugees. Writing/speaking from and thinking within these different perspectives raises critical consciousness and helps achieve an 'understanding of where others are "coming from" and why' (Lopez, 2011: 89).

Here it is the emphasis on metaphor, a device that has the idea of movement at its very core, which facilitates this kind of 'border crossing' or 'implicit understanding' of others (Duncan-Andrade and Morrell, 2008: 52). Joelle Taylor pointed out the importance, when attempting metaphorical thought, of getting pupils to think of comparisons from within the context of the persona. This is something we have stressed at Robert Sutton and experience shows that teacher intervention is vital in prompting pupils to consider the places occupied by past experiences of and feelings felt by their chosen personas. The result is the difference between pupils writing, say, 'the farmer's face is lined like a zebra' and 'the farmer's face is a furrowed field'.

Crucially, the teacher's role is to help immerse pupils within the diegesis. When reflecting on the process of creation, pupils have themselves identified the value of, as they see it, 'trying to understand the person' that they are writing about so as to 'put yourself in that situation'. For these pupils, considering 'what it would be like' to be that person is how the poem begins to take shape.

The following is a draft of such a 'body parts poem' written by a group of five pupils who ranged from National Curriculum level four to level six:

I am a refugee
My head is a messed up battlefield
My wounds are tattoos permanently scarred on me
My shoulders are hard battle shields
The souls of my feet are as cracked as the ground beneath me
My eyes are sniper bullets waiting to slaughter and spot the enemy

Another set of pupils, this time working with the persona of an imprisoned criminal, described the scars on his face 'as the tally of my days'.

Norman Fairclough (1989: 33) has examined the way that discourse within institutions can serve to reinforce and perpetuate what he calls the 'hidden agendas' and ideologies of 'diffuse aspects of social structures'. Indeed, in recent years many classrooms in English schools have seen cohorts become increasingly diverse as a result of globalization. Blessed Robert

Sutton is no exception. Although a small school with around 600 pupils on roll, it has a significant number of different ethnicities and nationalities with languages spoken ranging from Lithuanian to Tagalog. The refugee poem above demonstrates how classrooms can be critical spaces, allowing pupils to respond sensitively to the experiences of marginalized groups.

Poetry as performance – 'Playing the Text'

Performance is a type of text processing which is generally undervalued in many classrooms (Mackey, 2004). However, it is difficult to conceive of any kind of Slam poetry without the play of performance. The bodily immersion in the text required by Slam provides pupils with an opportunity to develop what Nicholson (2004: 174) has called 'dramatic literacies' by exploring the ways in which 'aural, visual and kinaesthetic signifiers ... work together' (Nicholson, 2004: 177).

During the Robert Sutton Slam, teachers emphasize the importance and value of performance from the outset, so that pupils are aware of expected outcomes and know specifically what they are working towards. The Slams are noisy, lively affairs which are recorded specially by Key Stage 4 Media Studies students to give the experience further prestige.

Since the Slams started in 2012, pupils have adopted an interesting range of dramatic approaches to the performance of their poems. They have experimented aurally by reciting their poems as songs or, in one case, a shanty. They have used an array of mimes and kinaesthetic symbols and played around with timings, intonation, echoes and pitch. Learning is, therefore, differentiated, inclusive and takes place via a plurality of 'sensory channels' (Nicholson, 2004: 179).

There is, in addition, an interpretative element to these performances. On the one hand, the kind of imagined experience (Neelands, 1992) involved represents an extension and deepening of the pupils' 'border crossing' (Duncan-Andrade and Morrell, 2008: 52) into other worlds referred to above. On the other hand, it demonstrates a critical interrogation of language itself. Pupils who wrote the following lines, for instance, skilfully employed intonation, pitch and pause to tease out suspense and what they felt to be the dramatic quality of their poem.

> *His hunched over posture and dragging eyes* [hunching, stooping and scowling at audience]
> *What secrets* [pause] *are within lies* [whispered]
> *His imagination soars* [pause accompanied by raised arms] *making it up as he goes*
> *With coffee in his hand* [pause] *and frost on his toes*

Interestingly, however, parts of this suspense style reading did descend into playful parody at times, particularly when read by boys. This is a reminder that performance as play has the potential to 'subjunctivize reality' and keep 'meaning open' (Bruner, 1986: 26). The humorous dimension of the poem just mentioned was never explicit in the written draft but was only teased out through the orchestration and enactment of the performance. In this way, new meanings can be created and alternative linguistic nuances explored. It is essentially another stage of the drafting process which helps children do what they often find extremely difficult, 'release their attachment to their first drafts' (Dymoke, 2003: 32).

The boys mentioned earlier, who subverted the sobriety of the poem they were reciting, were not ruining the poem in any way but, perhaps in a manner they were more comfortable with, using performance to change their perceptions about a particular text and perhaps even poetry as a genre. Indeed, if we consider that poetry is often gendered in such a way to alienate young boys, and that our own pupil feedback suggests that on the few occasions when writing creatively outside of school takes place, it is more likely to be modelled by female carers, the kind of 'taking ownership' exhibited by the boys above is a promising sign of the potential slam has for attracting boys to the genre.

Conclusion

This case study has examined the classroom impact of Slam style poetry workshops in relation to oracy, critical literacy and performance. With regard to the former, it has highlighted the continuing importance of talk in facilitating learning (Majors et al., 2010); it has promoted exploratory language use and has allowed pupils to take on roles, generate ideas and create new meanings. Indeed, without this dialogic variety, it is difficult to imagine how the exercises could so successfully allow pupils to develop in the latter two areas. The critical literacy of pupils, who are interrogating cultural identities and engaging in differentiated and highly creative play characteristic of the performance, is both underpinned and orchestrated by meaningful high-quality talk.

Despite (and in some senses because of) these positive results, the slam-style poetry workshops at Blessed Robert Sutton remain a continuing work in progress with much scope for further development. Although individual pupil reflection is very much embedded within the workshops and has been useful in the formulation of this study, it is clear to me that it could still be developed further. By using such reflection, along with group drafts and performances, pupils could continue to hone their creative writing over subsequent lessons. The workshops would become integrated more fully into writing schemes of work and no longer stand alone as activities carried out over several lessons.

In reading through the pupils' writing again for the purposes of this study, I am struck by just how much potential for development there is even after a workshop has finished. Given very little to start with – just a stimulus line or an idea of a character – the Year 8 pupils can create something both complex and beautiful. They can, in the words of a poem they wrote called 'The Magician', 'speak things of new'.

The Magician

My hands are feathers fluttering
My mind is an artist creating everything
My face is explosive – like my magic
My eyes sparkle like the flashing lights
My mouth is a trapdoor full of secrets
My voice is soft like the bunny in my hat
My lips to you speak things of new
My magic an illusion, my magic a lie
The lights are of time to say goodbye.

CHAPTER SEVENTEEN

Case Study VII: Gothic Poetry

Brenda Ainsley

Introduction

I was delighted to be involved in the ESRC *Poetry Matters* series of seminars and to take back some of the ideas to develop my teaching of poetry. The lessons explored in this case study were conducted with two Year 8 classes (of 13–14-year-olds) over a three-week period at Kibworth High School. Kibworth is a rural school in south Leicestershire for 11–14-year-olds. I trialled approaches from the *Poetry Matters* slam poetry workshop, led by Joelle Taylor, in my classroom. In addition, during this period, we were lucky to have Ash Dickinson, a visiting poet, in school. His presence gave me confidence to try out some of Joelle's ideas and work with smaller groups of students, with an additional adult in the classroom. All of the lessons were integrated within a unit on Gothic Writing, which contained strong elements of speaking and listening. These were both tools for learning and outcomes, as performed poetry.

The scheme of work

The starting point was a discussion about what might be meant by 'Gothic'. As Taylor reminded us, stimulus material of many different kinds is really important. I provided students with strong and evocative images of the genre, such as spooky castles and churchyards (all accessed through Google). I used questioning to encourage them to think 'outside the frame' as to what the surrounding story was. They made rough notes about this and were given the opportunity to share their ideas with a partner. I provided a word bank of 'Gothic and interesting vocabulary' gleaned from 'The Castle of Otranto' by Horace Walpole:

I encouraged (Figure 17.1) them to use some of these words and to experiment with writing. I timed this writing exercise, as I wanted the students to distil their ideas and to develop a concentrated and intense style of poetry in which every word counted. I took part in this exercise too, modelling the writing process on the whiteboard and showing them that I too was experimenting and crafting my writing. I wanted to demonstrate that it wasn't about right and wrong answers and that poetry is a subjective art form – and fun to do.

For further stimulation, we turned to 'The Red Room' by H.G. Wells. I shared a list of unfamiliar – yet key – words from the text. Students were given the task of finding out definitions of these words for homework. They came to the next lesson ready to discuss these with a partner and to extend their definitions and understanding of the words. We read the text together and had a discussion about the story and its Gothic elements.

When planning these lessons, I was intrigued to discover the 'Goth-o-matic' Poetry Generator: http://www.deadlounge.com/poetry/. I was impressed with this resource as an interactive and potentially engaging

Some Gothic and interesting vocabulary

Mystery: diabolical, enchantment, ghost, goblins, haunted, infernal, magic, magician, miracle, omens, prophecy, secret, sorcerer, spectre, spirits, vision.

Fear, Terror, or Sorrow: afflicted, affliction, agony, apprehensive, commiseration, concern, despair, dismal, dismay, dread, fearing, frantic, frightened, grief, hopeless, miserable, mournfully, panic, sadly, scared, shrieks, sympathy, tears, terrible, terrified, unhappy, wretched.

Surprise: alarm, amazement, astonished, shocking, thunderstruck, wonder.

Haste: breathless, flight, frantic, hastened, impatience, running, sudden.

Anger: enraged, furious, fury, rage, raving, resentment, temper, wrath.

Darkness: dark, dismal, shaded, black, night.

FIGURE 17.1 *Some Gothic and interesting vocabulary.*

way of helping students to achieve a high level of success in writing in a specific genre. I modelled the use of the Generator on the whiteboard, to show how a really Gothic feel could be generated with carefully chosen words and phrases. I took suggestions for words from the class and then chose two students to experiment 'live' with the Poetry Generator. They came out to the front and experimented with the words offered by the Generator, with advice from other members of the class.

This was a highly participative session with lots of talk and plenty of ideas suggested from the floor. Other students worked in pairs. Some used computers, while others used hard copies. Their homework was to try out this tool independently, print out any poems they generated and bring them to the next lesson. Students who were unable to access a computer or printer at home were able to use one in school at lunchtimes. If I were to use this activity again, I would book a computer room.

During the next lesson, initially students worked collaboratively on their poems which were work in progress (some were printouts of poems composed on computer); some went on to produce a joint effort, while some ended up writing their own. I then asked them to reflect on the writing process and on how they felt about the end product.

I hoped that this tool would be an effective and interactive way of enabling students to experiment with less familiar words. Also, I wanted them to arrive at considered choices by working in pairs.

Here are some examples of their work:

Denial

Slender beams of accusation enter this darkened chamber, as I kneel,
Always a slave, always a slave.
Frozen here, waiting.
Tortured forms wrought in panes of glass
Loom as dust dances in the air forming an image in my mind,
    penetrating my naked flesh.
Blood on a deathless face.
I raise my head, now embracing this uncaring limbo.

Lori

Lori reflected that he had enjoyed the writing process, particularly playing with and attempting to subvert the genre and form. He had experimented with what he considered to be the 'most awkward words'.

With the same title, here is another example, in which it is possible to spot the similarities and differences that are a result of using a tool such as the 'Goth-o-matic':

Denial

Slender beams of accusation
enter this darkened prison

as I kneel, always a slave,
always a slave, frozen here waiting.

Tortured forms wrought in
panes of glass loom as
dust dances in the air,
forming an image in my mind,
penetrating my naked flesh.
Pain on a child's face.
I raise my head, now kneeling
before this uncaring Limbo.

Matt

Matt said that the experience of writing this poem was a 'creative and mindful activity'. He said that he had enjoyed working in pairs and deciding on phrases to use. Matt reflected that the most challenging point was when they both set about writing their individual poems.

A God that is yours
Slender beams of moonlight enter
the darkened church as I
kneel,
always alone, always in prayer,
frozen here, waiting.
Tortured forms wrought in panes
of glass loom as dust dances
in the air,
forming an image in my
mind,
sparing not my shamed soul.
Terror on a mirror's face.
I raise my head,
now kneeling before this
uncaring heaven.

Sophie and Lily

Sophie reflected that they enjoyed choosing words that 'we thought sounded good'. She also said that working with a partner meant less pressure, because they could both suggest good ideas. She went on to say that the hardest part was 'selecting the perfect words'.

Although we had discussed the importance of poem titles, I felt that the title chosen by both Lori and Matt was not especially well linked to the content of their poems; Sophie and Lily's title seems more appropriate, with references in the poem to the 'shamed soul' and, in the final line, to 'uncaring heaven'. Lori organized his poem so that 'Loom' was used at the start of a (long) line, drawing attention to itself; Matt uses this word midline, thereby changing the impact. The Goth-o-matic tool enabled these young people to experiment with words they probably would not have chosen themselves and also to play with line breaks and layout.

I was interested to hear students' views about the activity, especially the paired work. I was very pleased with the animated response that I had witnessed and how well they had all worked together in pairs and groups. One student said that the 'Goth-o-matic meant that you didn't get stuck with using the same ideas'. He felt he had written something that was – for him – a departure from the norm. It seemed to me that my students were becoming confident about the Gothic genre and were developing a real interest in communicating their ideas.

I was pleased with outcomes such as these, as students had produced convincing Gothic poetry and experimented with vocabulary they probably would not have otherwise used. Their comments showed that they valued working in pairs and generally enjoyed the experience of writing together in this way.

Visiting poet

As part of this suite of lessons, I was delighted to welcome Ash Dickinson, our visiting poet, into school for the first time. We ran a series of sessions throughout the day for all of Year 8, following an assembly which 'set the scene'.

The workshops took place in the school library (a colourful, airy and stimulating environment) that provided a good space in which to talk and work together. Two sets of my own students worked with Dickinson. It was really interesting to watch their reactions to and interactions with him. Dickinson took the students through a process, introducing and revising selected poetic forms, including haiku and quatrain. Students worked together confidently, applying themselves enthusiastically to the tasks set. As anticipated, several students 'shone'. I have consistently found, over the years, that a visiting poet brings out something hitherto unseen in some students – often underachieving boys. I felt that the workshop went particularly well as it built upon the poetry work they had been doing and wasn't an isolated event. The session with Dickinson enabled two boys in particular to make some thoughtful contributions and to eventually be chosen to perform their work. Equally, it was gratifying to see the contribution of a girl who had recently been a winner in an external poetry competition; it came as no surprise that her work was soon recognized by other students as being worthy of attention.

I had discussed with Dickinson the Poetry Matters seminars and my intention to take students towards a 'slam'. Joelle Taylor had enthused me about SLAMbassadors UK, the national youth slam championships which were administered by the Poetry Society and led by her. There is

lot of useful information on the website http://www.poetrysociety.org.uk/
content/competitions/rise/toolkit/.

As agreed with Dickinson in advance, the session culminated in a mini
slam competition. (This was a simplified version of 'slam', as time was at
a premium.) The slam was new territory for my students, so the process
was carefully explained, including the importance of audience reaction, who
would be voting (a teaching assistant, the librarian and me) and how to
make it more of a *performance* and less of a reading. The criteria for judging
were quality of the poem, quality of reading and audience reaction. The
students were provided with a thematic framework for writing about the
seaside and holidays. Based on a six-line poem, they were encouraged to
include

Line 1: a noun (e.g. sand)

Line 2: a feeling (e.g. happy)

Line 3: a colour (e.g. blue)

Line 4: a bird or animal (e.g. seagull)

Line 5: an item from a suitcase (e.g. sun cream)

Line 6: another feeling (e.g. relaxed)

The writing started. I was happy that they were all engaged on the task and
encouraging each other. There was a low 'buzz' of spontaneous group talk in
the room. All the adults in the room dipped in and out of groups, listening
to lines, suggesting words, if anyone was stuck.

Having been familiarized with the structure and expectations, students
moved on to writing the final poem for the slam performance. This time
they were using their own ideas and not necessarily sticking with the seaside
theme. Suggestions were made by Dickinson, for example a sports or news
event.

Students worked in groups of about six and nominated the best poets
to come to the front to perform. Poems were performed and voting took
place, giving rise to a range of winners – both the predictable and the less so.
I was delighted that several 'underachieving' students (boys and girls) were
chosen by their peers to perform. I felt that this achieved something of the
spirit of slam as Taylor had described it to us: empowering and enabling.
Also, typical of a slam, this was all very much 'in the moment', so there are
no examples of students' work to include here. This clearly has implications
in terms of assessment: there was no lasting record. I could have addressed
this by filming their responses, but was aware that the very act of doing this
would have had an effect – it would have altered (even possibly destroyed)
the very empowerment that a slam should provide. I was not concerned that
there was no assessment of this particular outcome; there are many other
opportunities for assessment.

Again, I was interested to gauge student reaction so the next lesson started with a discussion about the visit from Ash Dickinson. Comments included 'It was a different way of approaching writing', 'It gave you a structure' and 'It was an easy way to write, when there were some words given'. As expected, students valued having someone different – a visiting expert – in the classroom. They really enjoyed the visitor's own poems and his performance of them. Dickinson was an excellent role model as a young male and students commented on his energy – I felt that this was reflected in their work and their performances.

Gothic slam!

Following on from the slam workshop, I ran a 'Theme Slam' with all performances conforming to the theme of Gothic. This tied in with my Gothic theme, but I also felt it would enable my young poets to feel increasingly confident about what they were setting out to do. It was important to set *some* parameters, but within that framework to empower and enable students to write and perform confidently – and independently of the teacher.

Using an approach modelled by Taylor, I gave students ideas for six lines of poetry; these could be incorporated in any order. I started with my own poem, composed on the whiteboard. Again, I did this 'live', demonstrating something of the writing process. I wanted to show my students that the process of writing is rarely simple and that the poet needs to review and amend their work. I went out to the front and modelled a 'warts and all' attempt at my own short poem. This led to a discussion about the process, after which the students were given the framework that Taylor had used:

I come from ....
And ...
And ...

I come from ....
And ...
And ...

Students were able to create an honest response, writing confidently about aspects of their own lives and experiences. This seemed to me to be close to the heart of slam. I did not want this to be an isolating process and encouraged students to talk with a partner about their work and also about the *process* of writing. This led to lively discussion and was more productive than 'Is this a "good" poem?' I stressed the importance of the concept of 'honesty' and whether they thought they had been true to themselves. I then gave students time to go back to their own work and to improve it. The first step was to give them all time to learn their poem and to consider the performance, as they had done with Dickinson. I then placed the students into groups of four and they performed their poems to the others in the group. The students then selected the best poem/performance from their group so that these students could perform to the class. On reflection, the students could have used more time to practise their performances; ideally this would be set as homework. I think it is a challenge for anyone to learn and perform their poem convincingly, especially if they are a Year 8 student in front of their peers!

Reinforcing the Gothic theme and using the same six-line format, I offered students a framework from which to develop their poem, this time about someone else:

Her eyes are...
Her skin is...
Her teeth are...
Her hand(s)...
Her arm...
Her voice...

For this poem, I encouraged students to consider the title they would give to their poem. Here are some examples:

Haunted Man

His eyes are darkness, beyond repair,
His skin is as rough as his heart.
His teeth are broken, like his mind,
His hands are shaking with agony.
His arms are linked to the madness he beholds
His voice is the voice of grief and the only voice he understands.

Jed

Elizabeth

Her eyes are dark and haunted,
Her skin is as pale as snow.
Her teeth are sharp and pointed,
Her hands are as cold as death.
Her arms are bare and withered,
Her voice is as lost as her soul.

Emily-Grace

In these final poems, there are echoes of the vocabulary from 'The Castle of Otranto', 'The Red Room' and the Goth-o-matic. These poems demonstrate confident use of these words and a growing understanding of the Gothic genre.

Outcomes

As the culmination of all the activity, I felt that these poems exemplify the progress that all the students made. Within two weeks they had become familiar with the Gothic genre and had experimented with a range of forms and approaches to writing. The classroom had been alive with purposeful talk and students had experienced a 'real' poet and a slam competition.

I felt that this scheme of lessons provided a positive learning experience. The next element in the scheme of work was to analyse 'Havisham' by Carol Ann Duffy. They went on to approach this with confidence – reading as writers. I thought that the lessons were successful in terms of the poetry outcomes and also in the use of speaking and listening as a tool for learning. Oral responses from students indicated that they had enjoyed these lessons as much as I had; I will definitely use these approaches again in the future.

I am grateful to the students who have given permission for their poetry to be included here.

CHAPTER EIGHTEEN

Commentary and Practical Implications: Inside the Poem's Engine Room

Sue Dymoke

In an editorial for *Modern Poetry in Translation*, Sasha Dugdale asserts the need for readers and writers of poetry to find 'new springs to drink at, new ways of reading and hearing poetry' (2013: 2). Her suggestion seems very applicable for teachers and students who need to discover new ways of speaking and listening to poetry through active engagement with its multimodal nature. The contributors in this part were all involved in the ESRC *Poetry Matters* seminars either as presenters or as participants. They reflect on and offer exciting, practical approaches which revitalize poetry listening, speaking and performance. Their contributions show how poetry can become a vital part of young people's lives in the long term rather than remain as a two-dimensional relic that has been anatomically dissected and scarred with annotations. I want to draw out some of the critical and unifying issues that their work raises before moving on to consider practical implications and some suggestions for further developments.

Critical issues

Listening and thinking

In their 'Afterword' for *Making Poetry Matter*, Myra Barrs and Morag Styles write:

poetry teaching should create change – change in awareness, changes in sensibility, changes in our sense of language and changes in our thinking. (2013: 195)

Through listening to poetry, thinking about how images and sounds take shape in their heads and savouring the sound of the words spoken aloud, young people can discover so much about how language works. The chapters are united by their deep attentiveness to language. This permeates the heart of the *Poetry By Heart* activities described by Julie Blake. It is explored in detail in Andy Craven-Griffiths's carefully structured workshops on the sounds of different rhyming structures and nuances of accent and dialect. Craven-Griffiths shows how intense listening can lead young people to have a greater dexterity with the language and, therefore, a better understanding of poetry's 'toolbox'. Listening to the voices of those who have never previously been able to articulate their stories is central to the modus operandi of Joelle Taylor's slam workshops and aspects of all three chapters are synthesized in the drafting and performance that takes place in Christopher Parton's and Brenda Ainsley's classrooms. Parton suggests how, in future iterations of his slam workshops, he wants to develop further opportunities for student reflection to support their redrafting processes. Matt, one of Ainsley's students, comments on the 'creative and mindful activity' which led to the writing of his poem. His choice of phrase neatly summarizes the importance of cognition within the creative process.

Embodying poetry through performance

A strong thread weaving this part together focuses on the different ways that poetry can be embodied through performance. Taylor writes of 'believing the poem' in terms of reliving a poem on stage, staying faithful to the experience itself and bringing it alive for the audience to share. Learning poems by heart – whether these poems are the students' own or those written by others – can enable young people to get inside a poem's engine room and experience at first hand how language propels a poem forward. In doing so, they move beyond recitation, learning to inhabit poetry and developing a greater holistic and metalinguistic understanding of how poetry works. In this way, their experience switches on the 'live circuit' (Rosenblatt 1978: 14) of the poem.

Collaboration

When students are writing a piece for performance, they can engage fully with collaborative processes in writing the poem and exploring how it can be enacted. They learn to interact with others as they experiment and redraft on the hoof. This was very evident to me earlier this year when I observed a small mixed group of 11–18-year-olds prepare their pieces for a Spoken Word Café public performance. An eighteen-year-old was rehearsing her piece (from memory). When she had finished, other students offered both praise and criticism of specific words or lines which had changed or been added since they first heard the poem. One boy commented on a section of the poem that was new to him and another that he thought had been edited out. Students gave new suggestions about word choices and how some words might be spoken or supported with actions. The young woman then re-ran parts of the poem reworking some of the lines to try out new ideas. Nobody had a written copy of the poem to refer to but they all seemed to know the poem and, even more significantly, to feel that they had a stake in its development for performance. I have seen at first hand how afterschool slam workshops can provide fertile critical spaces for young people of varied ages and from diverse backgrounds within a school community to collaborate on new work and to combine/'mash up' poems written by different members of their group. Writing and performance therefore enables them to explore varied perspectives on themes such as identity, history, challenges and aspirations and, through poetry, to find both the common ground and the contrasts in their lives.

Confidence

Confidence is a key issue in much of the above. This is the case for students who must be given the opportunity to loosen the curriculum shackles and make informed choices about what they have heard or how they might make others listen. It is also the case for teachers who, we hope, will be inspired by the examples presented here to see how it is possible to bring new poetry practices into their classrooms. There is a need for teachers to seize opportunities to experiment with and model less conventional approaches to poetry study, to replace language analysis acronyms such as Point Evidence Explanation (PEE) with acute listening and deep immersion in language at work in poetry. Both Craven-Griffiths and Parton strive to give students greater ownership of language so that they 'move into what sounds right in their own voices'. Many of the activities described are enabling students to become increasingly confident, critical listeners and performers who feel able to open, what Parton's students describe as, the 'trapdoor full of secrets'. They are doing so in classrooms that seek to nurture a growing fascination with the sounds of the vast lexicon of language at their disposal. They are experiencing structured and flexible workshop strategies, pair and group work and deep interaction with the technical aspects of poetry. None of the approaches are offered as a quick fix: the rewards will only be reaped through sustained use of activities within a supportive environment in which students and teachers are trusted to take creative risks.

Practical implications

Making time for listening

From the examples in this part, it is evident that attentive listening is paramount. Curriculum documents and assessment structures frequently undervalue this skill. The pressure of time within a standard 50–60 minute lesson means that, too often, listening activities are squeezed until they become rushed or token events at the beginnings and ends of lessons – the quick reading of the poem by the teacher or the hurried plenary presentation. Undoubtedly, it should be a much higher priority than has conventionally been the case: placing listening at the centre of learning so that everyone in the classroom experiences different readings or class performances of a poem is a highly effective way of reinforcing the existence and importance of contrasting interpretations. Challenging students to join what Blake calls 'the poetry conversation' by learning a poem by heart might sound scary but this activity can be shaped in accessible ways that are appropriate for a particular class. For example, students might build up to learning a whole poem by being given the choice to learn a particular stanza or a line that they like. They might be given the chance to work in a small group discussing and perhaps scripting out the way they will perform the poem together. Alternatively, they might choose to learn a poem they have written themselves.

Poems that talk to poems

Blake's suggestion to investigate poems that 'talk to' earlier works is also a useful strategy. My favourite sources for pairs of poems are the anthologies *Answering Back* (Duffy, 2007) and *Conversation Pieces* (Brown and Schechter, 2007). The approach could be refined further so that students learn to:

- talk back to a poem with one they have created themselves either in a group or individually;

- devise a mash up of lines from several different published poems which are thematically linked;

- collapse linked poems into a list of words or phrases and create a bank of overlapping sounds, rhymes and rhythms which can be used as the source for creating a third 'hybrid' poem;

- use role play to bring characters or poets who express contrasting views together for a conversation that develops from key lines in each of the poems. (Such as an encounter between the persuasive speaker of Andrew Marvell's poem 'To His Coy Mistress' and the speaker of Lady Mary Wortley Montagu's 'The Lover: A Ballad' or a discussion between William Carlos Williams and Ian McMillan about their poems 'The Red Wheelbarrow' and 'The Green Wheelbarrow'.)

Whatever activities are used, quality time spent listening to a poem's engine will ensure that tentative discussions about meanings can be informed by each student's experiences of a poem's sounds and silences. Although such activities are rarely considered assessment-worthy in themselves, they enable students to carry the 'memorable speech' (Auden, 1935: v) of the poem with them in their heads in readiness not only for end-of-year examinations but also for their rest of their lives.

Working with poets

All students need to gain first-hand experience of poets as living creative people from diverse backgrounds who love working with words. This is especially the case for those who have had little opportunity to meet writers and for whom poetry is not a regular part of their lives. Forward-thinking schools in areas of high socio-economic deprivation in the United Kingdom are using Pupil Premium funding to support or match-fund innovative literacy initiatives such as timetabled poetry slam workshops, after school poetry cafés and other creative events led by spoken word artists. Other opportunities for sustained poet–student contact include school residencies and, in the United Kingdom, Arvon Foundation courses for school groups. If a visit is to be truly successful and have a lasting impact, then it needs to be much more than a present opened on a special day and then forgotten about ever after. The students need to be very well prepared for it beforehand. The poet/spoken word artist should be properly briefed about the students and adequately paid. The poet's and students' own words should take centre stage but, wherever possible, everyone attending a workshop should also participate fully in the activities (including any writing). In addition, as Ainsley demonstrates, a workshop experience should fit coherently within a scheme of work. Links should be made with previous poetry activities and workshop approaches should be embedded securely within future poetry teaching, serving as a reference point for students.

Using digital resources

A key implication concerns the use of digital resources to bring other poets' voices into the classroom and ensure that students' voices can be heard. Developments in mobile phone and tablet technology have made high-quality recording much more widely available to many young people in their own social spaces. With permission, ephemeral lesson and public events can also be recorded for future use as models to inspire other classes. Students' recordings (including those shared by Janine Certo and Andrey Rosowsky) provided a rich vein discussion during the ESRC *Poetry Matters* seminars. In his presentation 'Heavenly Singing: Multilingual Verse and Song', Rosowsky (2011) vividly explored how young people can engage with, rework and record poetry and song in their traditional languages and in transliterated forms. In doing so, they are able to share their voices on the global digital stage.

A plethora of digital sources (both websites and apps) have been published over the last few years. Sadly, their quality remains very variable. Some appear to endorse the myth that poetry is a two-dimensional genre in which words might occasionally be supported by visuals. However, the very best sources fully exploit the affordances that digital technology can offer. They enable students to listen to, record and interact with a variety of voices, performances, perspectives and manuscripts. Such sources include the previously mentioned *Poetry By Heart* and *Poetry Archive* as well as the websites *Poets.org* and the *New Zealand Electronic Poetry Centre*, and apps like *The Wasteland* and *Shakespeare's Sonnets*. YouTube gives many people the option to hear and upload live performances by experienced and new performers. Clearly there are important safeguarding issues to consider. All schools have rules about how web links and mobile phones can be used in classrooms: advanced planning and appropriate downloading will be crucial to safe and successful use. Nevertheless, it is essential for teachers to acknowledge that very many young people are confident 'prod-users' (Bruns, 2006) of digital texts outside school. Wherever practicable, critical spaces need to be opened up in classrooms for their voices to be shared, listened to, recorded and critiqued.

Public performance and competition

All the chapters describe lively workshop experiences in which the classrooms can become performance arenas. Many of these experiences demand audience interaction. In some cases the performance involves a competitive element. The expectations for how such performances should be managed clearly need to be agreed in advance and reinforced so that students are well supported in their endeavours and, in turn, listen attentively to other performers. Some might argue that poetry should not be competitive but the writers in this part show that the competitive edge of a 'rhyme-off' or the group performance at a spoken word event can give *all* students a chance to work collaboratively and inclusively.

When handled carefully, the intense workshop atmosphere can become a hothouse for creative expression. Students can push each other on to combine and use words in dynamic new ways that will take them (and their audiences) by surprise. Undoubtedly, performances can present particular challenges for young people and their teachers in terms of public presentation of painful personal/community events. The students may well feel that they have been helped to find their voices and are ready to share their experiences in a controlled way (of their own making) for the first time. There is no denying that some colleagues may perceive such public events differently. It is important to debate these tensions sensitively and to be aware of the power that poetry can unleash within students. The inspiring film *We Are Poets* vividly portrays the extremes to which energetic commitment to poetry can be taken. It tells the story of a group of 13–19-year-olds from Leeds Young Authors who are chosen to represent the United Kingdom at the Brave New Voices World Poetry Slam in Washington D.C. It could provide the starting point for a discussion among teachers and/or senior students about just what can be achieved through poetry.

Conclusion

We Are Poets and the many practical examples discussed in this part illustrate a key message from the *Poetry Matters* seminars that 'poetry can potentially exhilarate children and develop their confidence' (Certo, 2013: 115). In 'What Is Poetry?' Adisa writes, 'Poetry is written on paper, but poetry doesn't live there' (Hoyles and Hoyles, 2002: 128). To leave poetry on the page in a classroom is to sound its death knell: poetry is an organic, enriching form of communication that has a place in everyday life. Poetry taps into all our senses. It is constantly renewing and reinventing itself to afford us transformative ways to view the world and to express ourselves. It needs to be spoken. It needs to be heard.

Resources recommended

Guidance on workshop opportunities

Coe, M and Sprackland, J. (2005) *Our Thoughts Are Bees*: *Writers Working with Schools*. Southport: Wordplay Press.

http://www.arvon.org/schoolsandgroups/

http://www.firststory.org.uk/writers-schools/

http://www.nawe.co.uk/writing-in-education/writers-in-schools.html

http://www.nawe.co.uk/DB/current-wie-edition/editions/writing-on-location.html

Websites and Apps

Shakespeare's Sonnets (2012) *The Arden Shakespeare*, Faber and Faber Ltd, Illuminations and Touch Press Ltd.

The Wasteland (2013) Touch Press Ltd and Faber and Faber Ltd.

http://www.nzepc.auckland.ac.nz/

www.poets.org/

Films

Ramseyer-Bache, A. and Lucchesi, D. (dirs) *We Are Poets*. Distributed by Dogwoof Popup Cinema. For details go to: http://wearepoets.co.uk/about/ (Accessed 06/03/2014)

PART FOUR

Transformative Poetry Cultures

CHAPTER NINETEEN

Building Children's and Teachers' Interest and Confidence in Poetry

Jenny Vernon

Introduction

This chapter draws on the experience of teaching a professional development course held each year between September 2008 and July 2013: *Poetry Right Now*. Whilst it was open to educators across all phases, the majority of participants were from the Early Years and Primary sectors. The course, one day per term, was the offspring of a previous, very successful course for teachers led by Michael Rosen and Myra Barrs: *A Year in Poetry* (CLPE, 1997). Having been a participant on that course, I was delighted when Michael agreed to lead workshops on this new programme, a decade later.

Our intention was to offer teachers a holistic and enjoyable approach to the teaching of poetry, to move away from the constraints of 'doing' poetry in discrete time and genre blocks, as advocated by the National Literacy Strategy (DfEE, 1998). We wanted to show how, through incorporating poetry into the everyday curriculum, teachers and children could become enthusiastic readers, writers and performers of poetry.

Ofsted's report on poetry teaching in England notes that the most engaging poetry lessons are characterized by active teaching methods, enthusiastic teaching and well-chosen activities which lead to pupils demonstrating sophistication and self-expression (Ofsted, 2007: 3).

The specific aims of the course were to:

- develop teachers' confidence and enjoyment in teaching poetry
- explore practical ways of engaging children with poetry
- consider the role of poetry in the curriculum
- share ideas, developments and discoveries

Participants were given a learning journal to record a personal research question, subsequent observations and examples of work throughout the year, both during the INSET sessions and in school. They were asked to complete a brief personal poetry history and a poetry attitude survey of their class at the beginning and end of the course, as well as choosing two case study children. In addition to an anthology of poetry related articles, they received a poetry book at the end of each INSET day to share with their children and report back on, in the following session. We also gave them a new poem to peruse each day, before the session started, and invited them to bring poems of their own choice to share with the group. They were encouraged to share developments in their classrooms by bringing in examples of children's poetry performances and composition. This proved a very powerful way of disseminating ideas, especially for teachers of the same key stage or year group. At the end of the year teachers gave a short ten-minute presentation.

Poetry histories

Teachers came with a range of previous experiences of and attitudes towards poetry on the first day of the course. Some were poetry lovers who wanted to learn how to share their passion with their children. Others were panicked at the thought of teaching poetry and wanted a fail-safe formula for delivering this part of the curriculum.

To gain a sense of their various expectations, we began by encouraging the participants to share their personal poetry histories. Many couldn't remember poetry lessons from primary school but remembered studying WW1 poets in secondary school. One teacher only remembered copying out poems for handwriting practice from primary school. We asked them to write on a sticky note something, general or specific, that they would like to know about poetry. Their questions were very illuminating.

Some wanted to know:

- What is poetry?
- Does it have to rhyme?
- What different forms of poetry exist?
- Why do we teach poetry?

- Why so many inhibitions about poetry?
- How to make it relevant to children?
- How to find inspiration?
- Why do I find it hard?

Many wanted recommendations of what to teach while others wanted to know how to support specific groups of children such as children with English as an Additional Language, reluctant boys or the school as a whole.

One of the most frequent concerns was how to teach poetry writing. Teachers reported that, although children enjoyed reading poetry, it was difficult to get them to write. They wanted starting points: ideas for making poetry writing engaging and fun. The Early Years teachers in particular wanted to know how to make poetry relevant for younger children.

This discussion served to help teachers begin to formulate their personal research questions and for us to shape the content of the workshops.

What poetry can do

Michael set the scene by musing on the nature of poetry and what it has to offer. He stressed its potential for involving every child in the class, its portable qualities: how it 'puts chunks of language in children's ears'. Poetry suggests (connotes) as well as tells (denotes). It is about unlocking these connotations. Poetry doesn't neatly tie up all the ends, often leaving questions unanswered. A poem can slow things down. For example, a narrative scene can be frozen and closely examined as in the tense moments of a drama or opera. New possibilities can be opened up through experimenting and playing with language: 'Nonsense becomes new sense.' Figurative language can invite children to make comparisons of unlike things: one thing standing for another. It can make familiar things unfamiliar and vice versa. Above all, poetry offers great talking points, as long as all the questions are open ended and we don't know the answers before asking. These points were developed in the subsequent workshops.

A poetry-friendly environment

An environment which celebrates poetry acts as a fertile backdrop in which a love of poetry can flourish. It is key to effective poetry teaching and learning. Together we drew up a list of ways this might be achieved:

- Share poetry – read aloud a wide range of poetry regularly
- Encourage children to choose poems to read aloud to the class or illustrate and record for the listening area

- Create a poetry box, a poetry corner, a poetry shelf, dressing up box
- Pin up an enlarged version of a poem of the week and invite children to add comments in their own time
- Make links to different areas of the curriculum through poetry
- Choose a poet as the focus for an author study
- Invite poets into school to perform their poetry and talk about their work
- Encourage children to work together with a partner to create a poetry poster
- Respond to poetry through music, dance and drama
- Prepare class or group performances to share with another class

Referring to this list, the first task was for teachers to make an inventory of their own poetry environment and to consider how it could be developed. They noted this 'to do' list in their learning journals and were encouraged to bring before and after images to the following session.

Routes into poetry

The many routes into poetry, which we explored over the subsequent sessions, were underpinned by a philosophy of collaboration, inclusion and enjoyment, within the context of a poetry-rich environment. The workshop activities were premised on Aidan Chamber's genuine enquiry approach: *Tell Me* (1993). They were designed to engage children with all aspects of poetry: reading, responding, performing and composing. Teachers were able to trial this wide range of activities at first hand, all the time considering how they might adapt them for their own classrooms.

The Poetry Show

The first workshop was Michael's *Poetry Show*, which acted as an excellent ice breaker. It demonstrated how easily mixed ability groups can become meaningfully engaged in an enjoyable poetry activity. Groups were invited to choose one poem from a selection of poetry and rhyming picture books piled on each table, and were given ten minutes to prepare a performance for the rest of the group. After briefly agreeing on a group interpretation of the poem, each text was brought alive through choral reading and dramatization.

Popular choices and subsequent highly entertaining performances included 'Supply Teacher' by Alan Ahlberg, *Slinky Malinky* by Lynley

Dodd, 'My embarrassing Dad' by Lindsay MacRae and 'The Leader' by Roger McGough. We discussed the inclusive nature of reading and responding to poetry in this way and how, through careful grouping and matching tasks to the strengths of individual children, the whole class can access it. Here is an example, taking the well-known nursery rhyme 'Hey Diddle Diddle':

Unison: Hey diddle, diddle
A: Hey diddle, diddle
B: The cat and the fiddle
C & D: The fiddle, the fiddle, the fiddle
A: The cow jumped over the moon
C & D: The moon, the moon, the moon
B: The little dog laughed
C & D: Woof woof, woof woof
A: To see such fun
C & D: Funny funny, funny funny
A & B: And the dog ran away with the spoon
Unison: The spoon, the spoon, the spoon (fading away)

As each group was invited to come to the front, they were given a rousing, variety show introduction, which added to the excitement of the performance and enhanced a sense of achievement for each individual.

The Angler's Song – secret strings

Throughout the course we explored several individual poems, including Jackie Kay's evocative and mysterious 'The Angler's Song' from her collection *Red Cherry Red* (2007). Teachers shared their initial responses to the poem using the Aidan Chambers's *Tell Me* approach: what does it remind you of; are there any puzzles, memorable or unusual words and phrases? After sharing these, we drew up a list of questions for the narrator of the poem, although these could have been directed at anyone or anything in the poem, for example the seabed. This developed into a hot-seating activity with teachers taking turns to be interviewed as the 'I' in the poem, which in turn provided the material for a new poem.

Are you happy?
Well, what do you think?
I make no promises. I offer nothing, not even light.
You say you have nothing to offer but is that true?
I make no promises. I offer nothing, not even light.
Why do you stay in a place that has no food, no easy prey, and it's freezing cold?

I make no promises. I offer nothing, not even light.
You say you don't lie, but how do I know?
I make no promises. I offer nothing, not even light.
BUT
I will give myself up to you.
I will give myself up to you.

Already familiar with the poem, Michael then asked the teachers to identify what he calls 'secret strings': the themes and patterns which lend cohesion to a poem and form the basis of textual analysis. They drew pencil lines between recurring words, phrases, letters and themes, thereby revealing previously unnoticed connections and links. Similes and metaphors became apparent in context rather than as separate features to be identified, as did examples of symbolism and juxtaposition of ideas. Through this close reading and discussion, many levels of meaning emerged, a reminder that there is no one 'correct' interpretation of a poem.

Red Cherry Red includes a CD of Jackie reading the poems and a synopsis of their genesis. The dot on the 'i' came when we played Jackie reading 'The Angler's Song' in her beautiful, mellifluous voice.

Starting with everyday experiences

We wanted to illustrate how children's everyday experiences can be taken as starting points for poetry writing. In groups of four or five, teachers were asked to think of a place they knew well and, closing their eyes, list what they could hear, see, smell and notice the thoughts going through their heads. After drawing up a list of these phrases, they were asked to agree on a sequence and choose one particular line to use as a refrain.

At the Cinema

Tall heads in front
3D glasses never fit
shuffling feet
'That's my seat!'

Popcorn buckets
slurping straws
rustling wrappers
'That's my seat!'

Grumpy ushers
torches flashing
sea of heads

'That's my seat!'
'I need the toilet'
'SSHH!'
'That's my seat!'

At the Supermarket

Stacks of baskets
Oh mine's stuck!
Supervisor to aisle 4
No frills, own brand
Wonky trolley, bag for life.

Special offer, two for one
Fresh bread, deli delicious
Frozen aisle, always chilly
Tempting lollies, 'no you can't!'
Wonky trolley, bag for life.

Baskets only, 10 items or less
Sorry, I'm closing.
Supervisor to checkout 4!
Have a nice day!
Wonky trolley, bag for life.

Examining a moment of high drama – writing from within a story

Examining a dramatic moment from a well-known story is another potentially rich route into poetry. Teachers were asked to interview, then identify with, a particular character or object in the scene, such as the part in Hansel and Gretel where the children discover that the bread trail has disappeared and find themselves abandoned in the forest. They noted down their responses, including internal monologues: asking 'What if?', speculating what might happen next, noting their hopes and fears. Individual lines were written in marker pen on A2 strips of paper. The strips were laid on the floor and moved around, with lines being edited, repeated or added, until the group agreed on a final sequence.

Lost

It's getting dark.
What's that noise?
Is that a shadow?

The cold air is pricking my face.
We've nothing to eat.
What are we going to do?
Will we have to sleep here?
Why did they go?
We're alone.
We're all alone.
I'm frightened.

Shaking up the world as we know it

Michael explained that poetry can challenge and surprise us, and shake up the world as we know it. He demonstrated this by exploring the first line of William Blake's 'The Garden of Love': 'I went to the garden of love.' He asked what might be found in such a garden, and what other such gardens there might be. In groups teachers pooled their ideas and described visits to their own gardens.

I went to the garden of pins

I went to the garden of pins
and hurt my toes among the tweeds

Needle-trees and button trunks
with hundreds of spiny eyes

I caught my limbs in binding thread
it wrapped itself around me tight

And pins, pins, pins in my sides.

Poetry can show us the world from a different perspective, for example from that of an inanimate object:

What am I?

Yes!
Released at last from that dark,
airless commuter bag.
Check out my genuine leather case,
my sleek format.
Not flash
like an iPad.
A discrete dispenser
of literature.

Outcomes

The teachers came together on day three to share their personal poetry journeys, presenting an aspect of the course which had been particularly significant for them. These included case studies, poetry work developed with their classes and stories of their own development as teachers and readers of poetry.

Several common themes emerged. Many remarked on how their own increased enthusiasm and confidence had rubbed off on their children who now enjoyed reading and performing poetry much more: 'Because I have been enthused by poetry, the children have too.' The enjoyment of listening to poetry also featured in their analysis: 'Children were asking to hear poems read aloud every day and loved just listening to them without having to analyse them.'

Early Years colleagues who had wondered about the relevance of poetry for younger children now realized the value of the nursery rhymes, songs and rhyming picture books, which they already shared with their children, as part of the long continuum of what constitutes poetry. They noted how learning songs, nursery rhymes and poems by heart for performance helped children in the early stages of reading, and that this love of particular poems provided them with a bank of familiar words which they felt confident to use in their emergent writing.

Several teachers remarked on the impact of the social and emotional aspects of working with poetry. They noticed that working with poetry in a collaborative climate nurtured confidence in the whole class, beyond the content of the subject matter: 'Performing poetry has given my class a sense of pride and has created a safe and trusting environment…The class anthology is one of the most popular books in the book corner.' On another level, less confident writers felt more able to achieve 'without being bound to writing in perfectly formed sentences'. Another teacher remarked: 'A less rigid format means they feel they are able to create pieces of writing that are as "successful" as peers they consider to be more able writers. Everyone can achieve well. Everyone is right. There are no wrong answers.'

One teacher explored the links between poetry and song. She presented one of her pupils singing her poem, inspired by 'The Lady of Shalott'. This was a particularly significant development for this child who had been very shy at the beginning of the course. The teacher felt that her growth in confidence was due to the poetry performances the class had enjoyed throughout the year.

Teachers remarked on the powerful impact of 'secret strings' in their children's enthusiasm towards new poems: 'There's a lot of fist pumping and smiling when a poem is shared to search for secret strings. The children are enthusiastic and thoroughly enjoy looking for links. Searching for secret strings has totally changed the way I approach exploring a poet's writing.'

An interesting point was made regarding the organization of in-service training: 'the fact that you get the opportunity to regularly bring poetry into your teaching ensures that the impact of this professional development is sustained'.

Conclusion

Interviewed at the end of the course, two teachers' comments reflect on the transformative power of their personal encounters with poetry over the duration of the course. For Davie, a Year 1 teacher, the experience helped to reframe his conceptualization of poetry, with a concomitant change in his practice:

> My thinking about teaching poetry has completely changed. Before I started the course poetry was something I didn't really have a lot of experience of. I hadn't really taught it to be honest. It was something I was a bit scared of. But since we've done the course, I'm much more encouraged. I'm excited about teaching it. It's shown me a lot of techniques of teaching poetry. I've been exposed to a lot more poetry, which is great, and I've actually started to enjoy it myself.

For Emma, a Year 6 teacher, the shift in her practice was from the inside out. When she started the course '[My] approach was very much involved in teaching the children metaphor and alliteration and the rhyme scheme and how many lines in each verse.' As a result of her engagement with poetry, she was able to reflect on the change, not only in her pedagogy, but also in the relationships in her classroom:

> Now we just really ride with the poems. We've been using the secret strings method a lot, looking for patterns in the poems. You don't need to necessarily give everything a label. The children, through looking at secret strings, [going from] word to word, manage to find a way into the poems themselves. And then very naturally, within conversation with the children, words such as alliteration or simile might come up. I don't tend to teach those words exclusively any more. It comes directly from the children being interested and making those links themselves.

As a result of comments such as these, I am confident that all the teachers who participated in *Poetry Right Now* over the years were able to reappraise their attitude towards teaching of poetry, despite their differing starting points. The hands-on workshop sessions and sustained enquiry into personal professional development provided a vehicle for them to explore and share ways into reading, performing and writing poetry, on their own terms. They were able to transmit the pleasure they got from noticing, experimenting and playing with language in a supportive atmosphere to their classes. They now felt freer to make professional decisions as to how they could include poetry in the curriculum, rather than fitting in with a specific scheme or framework.

I will leave the last word to Christopher, a Year 1 child:

Yoo carnt just read po ems yoo haff to heir dem and feel dem.

CHAPTER TWENTY

Engaging Invisible Pupils through Creative Writing

Emma Beynon

Introduction

The Bath Festivals' Write Team was a creative writing project designed to develop pupil confidence and engagement in their learning. The project, funded by the Paul Hamlyn Foundation, brought together an arts organization, local authority and schools to share experience and skills, in the support of those pupils who 'play truant in the mind' (Collins, 1998).

The project aimed to engage pupils 'who keep a low profile: invisible pupils who are quiet and undemanding' (DfES, 2007). The project provided a weekly programme of creative writing workshops led by the Project Coordinator and developed by writers to engage pupils and to develop their confidence and readiness to write. The Write Team lead teachers attended these weekly workshops. They recorded their response to the creative writing workshops in reflective diaries. The weekly creative writing sessions were led by the Creative Practitioner in preparation for writers' visits. Poet Mandy Coe described the impact of this dialogic process as follows: 'the pupils and teachers were ready to explore new ways of approaching writing and understand there's a different, artistic, way of thinking about the art. When we arrived they were ready to really stretch themselves and step into the imaginative and unknown'.

Eleven schools took part in the project, eager to use the intervention to address the 'guilt that the majority of teachers have about those pupils whose name they still do not know in the fourth week of term' (Write Team lead teacher). Five of these schools took part in the project for more than one year. In a Local Authority with high-achieving schools, this project focused on a key area for the School Improvement Team, namely how to support pupils who were not achieving their potential.

The programme of weekly workshops was developed as schemes of work by professional writers: poets, novelists, sports writers and dramatists. The aim of the scheme of work was to provide effective creative activities that the teachers could incorporate into their teaching practice and share with colleagues.

The writers also led INSET sessions with Write Team lead teachers, to support them in the development of their own creative writing and teaching practice: 'The schools and teachers were supportive of the project because they felt that it was trying to improve and support their practice' (Metcalfe, 2008).

Teaching poetry in the Write Team

The Write Team sessions took place in school. They contained subtle but important differences from 'normal' lessons. For example, we wrote in different colour inks: green for writing and purple for editing. Pupils were given a special Write Team folder to jot down all their ideas. They were reassured that no one would look at these folders unless it was their 'best copy' that they had chosen to edit and re-draft for publication. There is nothing magic about these interventions, but they had the effect of creating a shift in pupils' perception of their ability to engage in creative work. At first the pupils were rather nervous, focusing on presentation and trying to second guess the right answer. This was overcome through giving them small contained writing activities based on observing with the five senses. They were constantly reassured that when it comes to creative writing 'there is no one right answer'. As one of the Write Team lead teachers noted, the pupils were 'excited by the novelty and unexpected nature of what was going to happen next'.

The pupils quickly responded to the challenge of being asked to just observe and imagine, rather than focus on a fixed outcome. Pupils remarked that they found this useful: 'I liked how it didn't matter if we made a mistake and we could just use it in our way. It was nice to write and not worry about muddling things up, it just made the work more interesting. I wrote a poem where I used the word cloud with the description of a tree.'

During the early poetry writing sessions, I wanted the pupils to experience the pleasure and excitement of exploring different voices, techniques and forms. So I showed the pupils poems written by professional poets as well as poets who were the same age as them. We devoted quite some time to reading the poems aloud. Each child would read a line from the poem around the class. We would do this a number of times so that less confident readers would be able to listen to the words they would later have to read aloud. We experimented with reading the poem in a range of tones. We would whisper and then shout the lines as if in celebration. We read the poems as if we were furious or in fits of laughter. In this way the pupils experienced the extraordinary development of understanding that occurs through the repeated reading of a poem. The poems' rhyme schemes, metre and lexis were relished but never identified or analysed. I would only ask them to talk about what they liked about the poem.

I developed drama activities from the poems, inviting pupils to choose one word from a poem we had read to present to the group accompanied by an action to correspond to the word. Called 'Word in Action', this activity provided a useful starting point for drama games. It also allowed the pupils to explore the relationship between sound, meaning and tone. We found that if we asked the pupils to become a stone, a tree or even a JCB, their response was more original and exciting than ideas generated through class discussion or drawn from watching a screen. We were all surprised: 'The atmosphere was collaborative and supportive. Ideas were flying around the room. No one was quite certain what would happen next' (Write Team lead teacher).

Free writing was a technique that proved invaluable in the development of the pupils' readiness to write. Free writing consists of writing about a subject without stopping to think, edit or correct. When I first asked the pupils to do some free writing, they were understandably cautious. They were not used to being encouraged to let their imagination loose on paper or write without paying attention to the outcome. Used in a habitual but non-formulaic way, the exercise became crucial in giving pupils time to collect and develop their ideas. It provided pupils with the space to find out what they really thought as well as helped them get over the fear of the blank page. As one of the lead teachers observed: 'Children need time to think through their ideas, time to use their senses, to appreciate their environment, to observe, to notice, to think about what they are going to write. They also need time to make links and connections between everyday life, their own experience and what they are going to write.' The writer Helen Cross gave me the brilliant recommendation to use objects as a starting point for free writing. Shells, buttons, apples and even shoes: everyday objects that hold individual and archetypal meaning proved an effective way to start the pupils developing their original voice.

I also made sure that the early sessions contained lots of class discussion and modelling through writing group poems. In this way pupils became familiar with the process of writing and constantly re-drafting poems. Pupils were encouraged to trust their own judgement. In the initial stages they were not expected to read their poems aloud to the rest of the class. They were, however, invited to choose their best word, phrase or sentence to share with the rest of the class. At first the children would want an adult to confirm their choice, and were reluctant to identify their own good practice. However, they quickly developed the ability to strategically re-read their own writing and confidently identify and share the writing that really worked.

All the activities were drawn from the schemes of work which were developed by the Write Team authors. Participating teachers noticed that, far from a 'soft option', the Write Team sessions were rigorous in their promotion of critical and self-reflection:

> The children's best work in the Write Team came when they were pushed to think and consider something deeply. Often the work then became more abstract and original. The Write Team schemes of work were very good at giving little pointers, whether they were an actual poem as a model or photograph or artefact. The children were then able to scaffold their work and this gave them confidence to focus on vocabulary choices. This then led to greater satisfaction with their end product and this had a domino effect on how they approached the tasks each week. They could see that writing was a craft and they saw it as fun and enjoyable. (Write Team lead teacher)

Impact on pupil learning

After each creative writing session in the schools, I would discuss the impact of the activities upon the pupils' progress with the lead teachers. This anecdotal feedback was supported by evidence collected through pre-and post-project pupil questionnaires, as well as a letter written by the pupils to one of the authors they had worked with during the project. I have drawn directly on the pupils' feedback to illustrate the impact of the Write Team on their learning.

Pupils reported that they gained confidence from Write Team activities, in terms of both writing poetry and their willingness to participate in school life: 'The classes were great and helped my confidence levels. I liked writing poetry about the senses. I have learnt how to edit out the rubbish parts of my writing and be more selective about what I write' (Write Team pupil).

Pupils linked the increase in their levels of engagement to the way of working inculcated by the Write Team:

> I have concentrated more in lessons. Also I have started to write outside school and it has really widened my imagination. I have really liked the Write Team because I have felt more comfortable about writing generally. I feel more comfortable in lessons, and I feel I can understand more and engage more with conversations...But most of all I have loved writing poems, so much so, I have started to write my own. (Write Team pupil)

The pupils also reported an increase in their emotional stamina and readiness to engage in classroom learning as a result of taking part in the workshops: 'I've learnt to be more confident with my ideas, because sometimes you have an idea that you just sort of hide away, because you think no one will like it, but this has taught me that even if no one likes it, you won't know till you've asked' (Write Team pupil).

They became more resilient and resourceful as they gained a greater understanding of and familiarity with the creative process: 'Since I've been at the Write Team I feel more confident at thinking and writing at different times. [It] has taught me different ways of thinking up ideas when I'm stuck with my work' (Write Team pupil).

Pupils also noted that the chance to work on their writing over a sustained period of time allowed them to 'go beyond' themselves. Their feedback does not disguise their surprise at how much they achieved across the whole curriculum (e.g. drama, speaking and listening) and in learning activities outside school altogether: 'The Write Team has made me feel good when I do English at school and at home' (Write Team pupil).

Transformed practice

Throughout the project the lead teachers were invited to observe, critique and join in with all writing sessions, a process which appeared to have a marked impact on the practice of all the participating teachers and schools. As with the pupils, each teacher was given a journal in which to write their own poems, make observational notes and reflect on changes in pupils' attitudes and confidence as the project progressed. The weekly visits created the space and time for teachers to reflect on their practice over a sustained period. Through an informal action research cycle in which the teachers reviewed the writing session, tried out ideas in the classroom and discussed what worked and what did not, they were able to explore and develop new teaching techniques. This meant the workshops were valuable not only to the English departments or literacy co-ordinators but often also to the whole school.

The teachers report that as a result of their participation, they are now more willing to take risks in their practice, not for its own sake, but to promote the creative habits of mind which they have seen so powerfully modelled in front of them. They noted a transformation in their practice in three areas in particular.

Supporting the development of pupils' original voices

Firstly, they report that the Write Team sessions changed their understanding of how to respond to pupils' writing. No longer were they nervous of pupils' original ideas, even if these did not conform to the lesson plan or writing idea in question:

> I allow the children to be more original, they do not have to conform. My reaction is different. For example the children's poems do not have to have the same amount of lines. They do not have to write poems in the same style as an existing poem – allowing the children to be different, to be original and creative. Before, I would insist they all used capital letters for the beginning of each line and start each line one below the other, and now I let them shape their poems. (Write Team lead teacher)

This is expanded by the following teacher, who ends with a reflection on the construct of ownership of writing in the classroom:

> I have learnt that it is not my job to change a pupil's thoughts. It is more to ask questions about their ideas; to allow them to go on their own journey of discovery; and answer questions which can lead them to ask questions of their own and their writing. This seems to foster a willingness to redraft, to tweak and improve their writing. I always tried to steer their writing too much, before. Now they own it rather than me. (Write Team lead teacher)

Assessment

The Write Team also encouraged the teachers to review their perception of assessment of pupils' writing, prompting them to question the purposes and procedures for it:

> I think we often push the pupils to put down their ideas in writing so we can show the parents and they lose their spontaneity – it is not their best work. We need to think about videoing them or recording their ideas and stories in other ways than just writing. We should not be forcing them to lose the spontaneity of their first ideas which are often their best. (Write Team lead teacher)

Observing the creative writing classes also encouraged the teachers to change their understanding of how to democratize learning through formative assessment:

> Since the Write Team I try to be more open to choosing any pupil to work with. The children know the good writers in the class and if you use the less acknowledged writers, they enjoy that. I am now more confident to find the good in all the pupils' writing, rather than focussing on the good

or 'safe' pupils. That means the world to them. I am more open to every child in the class. (Write Team lead teacher)

Another teacher admitted to being surprised by the Write Team's lack of emphasis on outcomes and practices upon which she had previously given high status, for example handwriting, presentation and the inclusion of WALT and WILF objectives.

No longer was there nervousness, on part of the teachers, as to what constitutes 'the right answer':

> The progress we have seen in the children has been mainly due to the Write Team. It has had a big impact in terms of our teaching of poetry, and generally our approach to creativity, being more open. The pupils now have more confidence in writing poems and in their creativity. The staff has noticed the Write Team style of teaching, accepting everything, where all ideas are valid. As a result, the children put more of themselves in their writing. (Write Team lead teacher)

It is as though the presence of the creative writers in their classroom gave these teachers permission to try out new ideas, coupled to resilience to see them through in everyday practice. I argue that giving teachers the opportunity to be immersed in a process alongside other professionals reconfigured their notions of creative pedagogy itself. I call this new understanding a 'pedagogy of permission'.

A pedagogy of permission

This sense of permission can also be seen in these final reflections. In them we read of a changed attitude towards the ownership, in terms of content and style, of children's creative writing. This is evidence of a profound pedagogical shift because it is about a transformation not only of practice but also of power relationships:

> There are many ways in which I have changed my practice, from improving my questioning skills; thinking about tying in children's own experiences into non-fiction writing; the use of little bursts of writing warm-ups; using visual props for descriptive writing as well as having a different coloured pen to channel their thoughts. It has also given me great insight and experience into how to respond verbally to the children's writing – looking for something unique and inspiring from each piece of work. The main thing I have used is the use of 'Creative Thinking Time', asking the children to write in silence for a few minutes about a specific subject and then use the ideas in their written work. (Write Team lead teacher)

The project also raised teachers' expectations of their previously 'invisible' pupils:

> There is a huge difference, my confidence in my own and my pupils' writing ability has greatly improved. My expectation of what they can produce and achieve has been challenged and raised. I am much more likely to take risks or allow the pupils to take risks with their writing now, and have less fear of where it may lead. (Write Team lead teacher)

The pedagogy described by the teachers in the journals can be summarized as one of flexibility and challenge. Pupils were deliberately taken away from their comfort zones by the authors, but paradoxically this process was also made to feel very safe. Teachers consistently remarked in their journals that pupils were expected to rise to the challenges offered to them.

However, this style of teaching poetry is not without its tensions. Some teachers found that the focus on speaking and listening within the Write Team challenged their definition of a positive learning environment: 'At times it was too noisy ... I found it hard not to intervene, as I have been a teacher so long, it was hard not to want them to stop, but then they did make progress' (Write Team lead teacher).

The teachers also noticed that observing the creative writing workshops enabled them to see their pupils in a wholly new way. Writers come into school with no prior knowledge or expectations of specific pupils. This 'outsider' approach, by necessity, treats all children equally and often breaks established (and not always helpful) classroom dynamics. Write Team poets reported that teachers frequently expressed surprise at the way certain pupils engaged with the activities converse to expectations. For their own part teachers remarked how difficult it is to maintain this perspective when working with the children within the current high-stakes context. For many the Write Team was a salutary lesson in rediscovering openness and a sense of exploration in the classroom. They noticed that these were more likely to be sustained if they, as teachers, continued to write and read poetry. They noticed that the biggest transformations in pupil confidence and engagement occurred when they concentrated on pupils' poems rather than 'pupil outcomes'.

CHAPTER TWENTY-ONE

Case Study VIII: Effective Practices with English as an Additional Language (EAL) Learners

Vicky Macleroy

Introduction

Poetry can be seen as a shared way of interpreting the world with the complexity of human discourse at its heart. In discussing effective practices with EAL learners, I will be exploring why co-operation and discussion are key to developing an intercultural perspective and opening up spaces for students to write and speak about their own lives and lives of others.

I will be drawing on the work and experiences of a range of teachers and poets working in London secondary schools. The pedagogy and practices presented here include the experiences not only of newly qualified English teachers, but also of performance poets who are part of a new Spoken Word Education Training programme and who work one day a week in London schools.

Recent research on emergent bilinguals describes the interconnectivity of languages and accentuates the role of sense-making from the bilingual speaker's perspective (Garcia, 2009). This approach sees EAL learners as active agents in learning the new language and recognizes the diverse range of children's funds of knowledge: 'the object is *also* to change what counts as important knowledge so that the dominant forms of knowledge are decentred and more inclusive models of knowing – and being – are recognised and taught to all' (Thomson et al., 2008: 89).

The invisibility of EAL learners is an issue in mainstream English classrooms, as is the status and hierarchy of different languages in their language repertoire. A London secondary teacher reported on her findings from interviews with EAL learners:

> Just for these kids to actually sit down and talk to me about where they're from and which languages they speak, who they speak the languages to … some of them actually had to think about things because they were never asked about it … and I found especially with the African languages some of the kids are embarrassed to say 'I speak this or that language' because they think it's not important.

Listening to the voices of EAL learners

Diane, an NQT English teacher, reflects upon co-operative ways of working to encourage talk around texts and the importance of encouraging emergent bilingual students to have a voice in the classroom:

> Getting them to have a voice and getting them to talk is so difficult because they are in surroundings where everybody is, even if it is somebody of the same nationality, slightly more able in the classroom context than they are. It completely throws them and I think you have to build that confidence for them to be able to talk. It's one of my biggest struggles in the classroom.

Pete, a poet and spoken word educator, describes the process of working with 11–14-year-olds as helping students to 'write into the silence' and to tell their story poetically. He sees this as 'writing your insides out' and the effect on students as transformative. He reflects upon the poets' journeys into London classrooms as 'one of constant discovery and experiment'. He argues that spoken word poetry with its focus on self-expression gives students the chance to find their voice performatively and listen empathetically: 'Spoken word opens opportunities for young people to increase their cultural, social and linguistic capital, including for pupils for whom English is not a first language. It enriches the citizenship with skills of critical enquiry, communication and participation.'

In a context where the accumulation of knowledge is viewed as paramount to measure progress, these spaces for speaking and listening and experiential learning are hard to prise open in secondary schools. Teachers, above all, need time to talk and communicate with each other on a daily basis in order to implement and share transformative practices, but a language teacher new to this country expresses her frustration: 'There is no interaction. Nobody has time to talk to anybody, and that makes it all very [...] isolated. They don't really communicate with each other very well. I have never felt so foreign in my life, never!'

Who are EAL learners and what are effective practices around poetry?

Newly qualified English teachers' perceptions of EAL learners in their classes demonstrate an awareness of the complexity of developing effective practices for such a diverse group of students:

> We started off talking about the whole idea of EAL learners and tried to draw a picture of an EAL learner. We couldn't, as there are as many situations as there are pupils. They all come with different language abilities, different levels of understanding, schooling and experience in their own country. There are as many situations as there are pupils, so the issues are variable depending on who they are. (Carly)

Ela, also an NQT English teacher, is adamant that emergent bilingual learners should be exposed to a high level of language in mainstream school and should not be placed in low-ability sets on arrival: 'I think aim it high, put them in top sets, that really works. It exposes them to high levels of language which will develop their skills quickly.' Teachers also see the value of using home languages for cognitive development in the classroom to extend and develop language usage: 'getting ideas together and kind of being a bit creative. It's useful to combine that, particularly if you have got more than one student that speaks the home language'.

In discussing effective practices around studying and writing poetry with EAL learners, teachers emphasized the students' enjoyment in 'bringing out the musicality of language, the natural rhythms, stressing the tones'. Sarah, an NQT English teacher, endorsed the argument that if students engage fully with literature then they start to understand their own voice and the voices of others. This gives them 'an opening to true difference. By immersing themselves in the sole voice of another, they will start to hear their own voice, assenting, questioning, disputing, singing along, starting a new poem or song' (Senechal, 2012: 74).

Case study: EAL learners and poetry

What follows are insights taken from a case study of one London secondary school. In it the lead EAL teacher and English NQT recognize the importance of co-operation, discussion and sharing stories to support EAL learners to meet the linguistic and cognitive demands of analysing complex literary language in the study of poetry.

EAL teacher discussing EAL pedagogy

The EAL teacher, Farida, reflects upon the importance of knowing EAL learners' prior learning and understanding their cultural and family backgrounds in order to match support to their needs. Partnership teaching, one teacher working alongside another in the classroom, is viewed as the most effective practice, where teachers prepare resources together and assess students collaboratively. Farida has worked in the field of EAL for over twenty years. She draws on her experience to highlight the primacy of talk in the classroom: 'I push them to talk. Before they even write anything, there has to be discussion. Not all teachers see the value of this.' She also focuses on the importance of listening to the EAL students' stories and journeys as, if given the space to do so, these students are proud to share their language and heritage. She reports that most of the newly arrived EAL learners regret leaving their homeland, but some have found new spaces to celebrate their language and culture.

NQT English teacher discussing EAL pedagogy

Ela also highlights the importance of learning how texts work through talk: 'First they hear it, then we discuss it, just so they can verbalize their response. Then we try reading it.' In this manner she notes that students can take ownership of the text and draw on their own cultural perspectives to explore and create meaning. Sometimes these responses are communicated through drawing rather than writing, acting as a first step, or scaffold, towards full comprehension. This resulted in a much deeper analysis of the poem's constituent parts, for example its imagery, than asking for a written response in the first instance. Ela noticed these responses were often much more original.

EAL learners' writing about poetry

Immersed in a classroom culture of talking about stories and poems, three advanced EAL learners from Ela's class develop a detailed comparative analysis of Shakespeare's *Sonnet 18* and Carol Ann Duffy's 'Valentine'.

Afeefa believes that both poems 'expand the reader's imagination in different ways'. She grapples with the metaphorical language and imagery and describes Duffy's use of the extended metaphor and tone:

The onion metaphor is important, suggesting love can be wonderful, yet painful. 'It is a moon wrapped in brown paper' suggests to me that from the outside love can be seen as being dull and unexciting. The tone changes throughout the poem to show the cheerful and dreadful moments in life. I feel that tone is incredibly [important] in 'Valentine', as it changes the mood of the reader every moment, and makes them realise the true meaning of love and how it can be hazardous at times.

Humaad reflects on his own response to Shakespeare's Sonnet:

In 'Sonnet 18' love is compared to a summer's day. It gives you a calm feeling as a summer's day is warm and quiet. 'Thou art more lovely and more temperate' is talking about calmness in your mind; you think: 'calm'. Shakespeare's image is of a summer's day but that is not good enough as summer is too hot and too short.

Sannah explores the free-verse form of Duffy's poem and draws on her knowledge of idiomatic language to explain the structure:

Duffy has chosen to employ a comparatively free form. This could be because love is unpredictable. This could also be because love isn't always happy, and there will be some difficult times. This could be cross-referenced to the saying: 'love is a roller coaster ride', the ups being the good times and the downs being the unhappy times. Alternatively it could be because love has no boundaries and is free-flowing, like a conversation. This could be cross-referenced to the saying 'love has no rhyme or reason'. Additionally, maybe choosing this form allowed Duffy to mirror the sense of freedom she felt in her own life.

These EAL learners have reached a stage in their language development where they understand the nuances of the majority language and can develop personal responses to the poems. In writing about this poetry, they have developed a deep sense of the metaphorical language, the tone and mood of the language, and the structure and form.

Spoken word educators working with EAL learners

Six performance poets have implemented an approach to poetry that is creative and transformative. They spent a year working with 11–14-year-old students, including EAL learners, in a London secondary school. The poets recognized the importance of sharing experiences and stories in making poetry happen and filled their classrooms with the poetry of other poets, their own writing, and the poetry of students. Ray reflects upon his experience in the classroom:

> The first classroom I went into as a poet, I remember after my performance a student said 'that was nothing like that other poet I saw'. It turns out the other poet was a much anthologised senior British poet. The student was confused about how she and I could both be called poets, but we are both poets, despite being different in terms of our style, age, gender, race and sexuality. The students that day had now been exposed to a range of possibilities with poetry, which I hope increases engagement and deepens understanding of what contemporary poetry is and how the students themselves may fit in it. Spoken Word is not replacing the poetry of the canon, but I believe it is increasing the accessibility it currently has in the classrooms.

Spoken word poetry and EAL learners

Cat, a poet and spoken word educator, defines creativity as making, sharing and transforming worlds and finding ways to reach our good stories in the writing of poetry. This approach to poetry creates school communities where students are encouraged to bring their own identities into the classroom, where different dialects, languages and cultures are listened to, valued and explored. Cat talks about how many students feel by their voice as they have a different accent from their classmates, speak another language at home or no one seems to hear their voice:

> I believe voice-finding can be achieved through spoken word education by encouraging students to find, make, share and transform what they already know about themselves and their worlds. The pupils must be able to bridge the gap between their experience of different languages and cultures when they enter the classroom and poetry may support them to express these powerful emotions.

What different spaces can be opened up for EAL learners by this new pedagogical approach to poetry and why are these spaces important? Ray voices his concern that poetry on the syllabus is too far removed from the culture it is meant to be engaging with:

> Perhaps using the accessible tone of Spoken Word prose can deliver examples of poetry that is delivered in a voice that students are able to respond to, which can then validate the way they themselves speak in their poetry. This can increase interaction with poetry beyond the classroom. But attitudes towards poetry have to be tested. In a way poetry has to be reclaimed and I believe Spoken Word has the potential to do this.

Pete describes how the spoken word educators take part in a writing group where they share ideas on reading, writing and ways to apply their craft to the classroom. A key aspect of their transformative practice is that when they come across poems that they feel would provide a good writing prompt, they write their own version to provide a second model: 'Sharing of ourselves in this way connects with the pupils very directly and makes the experience of sharing one that is revealing, immediate and alive.'

The poets brought their own language, identity and culture to the classroom and opened up dialogue between students, including EAL learners, about their own lives and stories. There were several opportunities for students to be praised for what they know about their culture and language and for teachers to recognize how students choose to express themselves. The students shared poetry in Poetry Cafés held in the classroom. This developed over time; as Pete explains: 'the page itself should also be a safe space' where students write into the silence.

Sharing effective practice in school

Indigo, a poet and spoken word educator, believes this approach to teaching poetry in school through sharing experiences and stories leads to a co-construction of knowledge. Students' poetry is read, listened to and performed and their own writing becomes a model for others. Reflecting on her own process of writing, she says:

> I wanted to share my own experiences with my mother and the vague knowledge I have of a country I have never visited. I began to explore the facets of my story that are interesting such as the fact that I do not have a Nigerian name. The name given to a child in the Nigerian culture is very important and gives a clear indication of what family that child is from. My name however gives no such information. I am in many ways culturally homeless. I explored this in the poem 'Omo Oyinbo'.

These are the opening lines of her poem, which vividly explores colour, language and culture:

Omo oyinbo!

That's what they would call me
if I returned with my gullet emptied of Yoruba,
and my name's meaning miscarried in my mother
tongue. Since the womb I've been pushed out
of every home I've known.

Three of the spoken word educators, Cat, Ray and Dean, wrote their own versions of Benjamin Zephaniah's poem 'The British' to make explicit the process of writing and developing self-expression. They shared stories about their own identities formed across languages, cultures and continents, but also aspects of identity that link the three together: poetry, London, teaching and performing. They modelled a group poem that takes lines from their three versions and includes the following lines:

Dean: I wonder

when 'Diversity' will mean something
other than just the colour of our skin

Ray: My Britishness is keeping me quiet and I am wishing I belonged to a language more culturally assertive.

Cat: In Ireland we have a tradition,
You leave the door open.

The spoken word educators shared their poetry in the classroom and supported students as they explored their own identity, language and culture in their writing. Cat believes that spoken word education is uniquely placed to give form to feelings and meaning to often unheard voices. She argues that by bringing music, imagery, structure and story to self-expressive writing, students can start to connect and comprehend their worlds. In one of the paradoxes of both teaching and art-making, it was found that as individuals found their own voices, the stronger was their sense of being part of a community, and of finding and sharing common ground within it.

Conclusions

In the discussion of effective practices with EAL learners, I have drawn on practices in the teaching and writing of poetry that are rooted in the lives and stories of those that make up the school and its community. In this approach, creating a dynamic literate environment is seen as inclusive of local knowledge and languages (UNESCO, 2004). It also emphasizes the importance of giving students tools to write and speak about their own lives, listen empathetically and move to a deeper poetic analysis of their own poetry, the poetry of their peers and more established poets.

This approach with EAL learners is endorsed by findings from a recent project 'A Feast of Stories' presented by Dan Lea at the annual conference for National Association for Language Development in the Curriculum (NALDIC, 2012). The EAL learners' literacy levels improved dramatically in a London primary school when the focus to develop their reading was shifted to language development, oracy and storytelling. The students could record their stories in their home language and 'there's no assessment – afterwards we sit down and talk about how great we thought the story was. We just listen to it and enjoy them' (Lea, 2013: 33).

In conclusion, I argue that these practices around stories and poetry will enable EAL learners to develop a sense of intertextuality and support them in the comparison, analysis and writing of poetry.

CHAPTER TWENTY-TWO

Case Study IX: Digital Literacy

Janette Hughes

Introduction

Different technologies impact the kinds of things our students can do, including the meanings they can express, the relationships they can have, the thoughts they can think and the social identities they can assume in particular situations. Exploring poetry with and through digital media is a new literacy practice that has the potential to encourage student engagement, attention to the performative characteristics of poetry, including an increasing sense of audience. This promotes development and transformation of identity as student writers position themselves as agents of change. To explore this in more detail my colleagues and I designed a poetry unit that immersed students in digital media and poetry simultaneously.

In this chapter, we share the outcomes of the project, specifically referring to young adolescents' (ages 11–12) online and offline identities in their use of Ning, a classroom social networking site. Other digital tools used by students included poetry interactives and Apps, Glogster, Wordle, Word and iMovie. It is important to note that each of these digital tools comes with both constraints and affordances, which are two sides of the same coin. For example, one constraint of social networking tools is that we have to be particularly careful about privacy when using social networking sites (SNS) with students. Conversely, social networking tools enable students to connect with people all over the world in different ways. In this chapter, we offer an overview of the iPoetry unit and discuss the ways in which the various digital media enabled students to connect and collaborate with others, create and communicate through shifting modes of expression (which includes the use of image, sound, gesture, colour, special effects, etc.) and think critically about who they are and how they want to 'be' in the world.

Poetry snowballs

The unit consisted of five poetic forms to be covered, which were spread out over approximately 20–25 full classes of seventy-five minutes each. The five forms of poetry we chose were acrostic poetry, found poetry, postcard poetry, limericks and spoken word. The first two classes covered a general introduction to poetry and in these lessons, students learned about major poetic devices, periods of poetic history and famous/noteworthy poets. Students used iBooks (small laptop computers) and Android tablets, and particularly the Poetry 101 App for research and peer teaching during these classes. Working in small groups of three to four students, they defined the following poetic terms and devices: Group 1: Alliteration & Speaker; Group 2: Symbolism & Tone; Group 3: Simile & Rhythm; Group 4: Metaphor & Rhyme; Group 5: Theme & Sound; Group 6: Assonance & Imagery; Group 7: Haiku & Repetition; and Group 8: Limerick & Free verse. They were required to define the terms, find examples and create their own original examples if applicable, and record their work on the class Ning. They also presented their work orally to the rest of the class, who took notes during the presentations.

As a warm-up to poetry writing, students used the 'Snowball' strategy of dividing a piece of paper into quadrants and writing down a descriptive phrase in one quadrant. Students then crumpled their paper into 'snowballs', gathered into a circle and then threw their 'snowballs' into the circle and retrieved one that was not their own. They continued to do this activity writing down a metaphor or simile in the next quadrant, an alliterative phrase in the third and finally a summary sentence in the fourth. They shared the poem in whatever order they chose, reading what was written in each of the four quadrants.

In order to further apply their understanding of the poetic devices, we asked the students to create a 'Six-Room Poem' (see Figure 22.1).

Box 1: Use descriptive language to describe an image/scene

Box 2: Describe the light – bright sunlight, dim light, pitch black

Box 3: Describe the sound in this scene

Box 4: Ask a question relating to this scene

Box 5: Describe how you feel about this scene

Box 6: End by repeating some key words or sentences

Image	Light
Sound	Question
Feelings	Repeating Word(s)

FIGURE 22.1 *Six-rooms poem planning sheet.*

Here is an example of the work that was produced:

Vision
Mystical as my cousin's stories.
A dark, brown cabin.
I'd never seen it before. A figment of imagination?

The vines dripping with fresh, rain water.
Lush vines almost covering the cabin.
I walk in, curiosity taking over my mind.
Common sense left behind.

The floorboards caving in,
So timeworn,
The floor covered with fallen, dry leaves. I'm not outside?

As I pace forward,
I reach the middle,
A gleaming pool of water,
With a single beam of light shining.

As I settle down,
Around the pool of water,
I see something move.

Never before,
I get up,
Not a fish,
Stomp. Crunch. Drop. Drop

Acrostic poetry

Although acrostic poems are seemingly easy to create, we asked the students how we might make an acrostic poem 'go from okay to really interesting and informative so the reader understands a lot more about you by the end of the poem'. Rather than using single words, primarily adjectives, to describe themselves, we asked the students to use descriptive phrases to create an 'About Me' acrostic poem. Thematically, we were exploring the various ways that digital media impact students' lives, so the students used the ReadWriteThink.org's interactive acrostic-poem maker: http://www.readwritethink.org/classroom-resources/student-interactives/acrostic-poems-30045.html.

After creating their poems, they used PhotoBooth on the laptops to take pictures of themselves. After discussing the purpose of barcodes as machine-readable representations of data that relate to the object they are attached to, and how they are used in society (i.e. in retail and libraries), we talked about future uses of barcodes as they relate to human beings. We already have fingerprint, face, iris and voice recognition technologies that enable us to authenticate our identities to gain access to objects and places that require extra security. Pets and wild animals that we want to track are commonly given microchip implants. Perhaps a sort of barcode for humans is no longer just the stuff of science fiction novels. After discussing this with the students, we asked them what their barcode might look like and they created 12–16 digit barcodes using numbers they felt represented them, including their dates of birth, ages, number of people in their families, number of letters in their names, house addresses, and so on. They pieced the various components together into one file and posted them on the class Ning and the teacher also printed them out for the display board.

Found poetry

The second area focused on 'found poetry', where poems are constructed using words and phrases from an individual's environment. As a warm-up, students participated in an experiential walk around the school where they snapped pictures of found words and phrases. Here, students analysed what types of messages they were exposed to in their school and how these might affect or help shape their identity. In addition to learning the definition of found poetry and analysing some examples, students created their own using Facebook, Twitter and Ning updates. Through this, students explored and deconstructed their online identities. We asked students to consider:

- What kinds of things do you post most often?
- What are you trying to communicate about yourself based on these posts?
- Are your updates about how much fun you're having?
- Are they about how upset you are?

Based on the kinds of things they posted most often, they chose a theme and wrote a found poem using only updates and comments.

Student sample: Found poem

I really like
To be myself.
So waz up?
Try to gather awareness
Don't be scared to do it.
Say the truth with dignity.
Earn Respect
Shine brighter than the stars.
Connect to your dual-identities
Unfold your wings
And take flight.
I am me and
You were meant to be YOU.

Finally, as with all the subsequent lessons, students interacted with each other on the social networking site, Ning, to comment, discuss and critique each other's works and ideas.

Limericks

To explore limericks, we gave the students a number of examples and then asked them to answer the following questions in a think–pair–share activity:

- With your partner, discuss the lines, syllables, rhythm and rhyming pattern of Limerick poetry
- Are the lines long or short?

- How many syllables are in each line?

- What is the rhythm of the limerick poem?

- What is the rhyming pattern?

Students wrote their own limericks describing a humorous, but defining, moment in their lives. Below is one example:

> There was a good boy named Mike,
> Who kicked the ball for a strike,
> The shot was a miss,
> So he clenched up his fist,
> And rode himself home with his bike

After working through the writing process, they shared their limericks on the class Ning. We asked them to choose one of their peers' limericks to work with and copying it into a Word document, they recorded the adjectives, verbs/adverbs and nouns they found in the poem. Using these categories, they created three different word clouds in Wordle (http://www.wordle.net/) using only these words. One was an adjective Wordle, the second was a verb/adverb Wordle and the third was a noun/pronoun Wordle. They uploaded their finished Wordles on the Ning (Figures 22.2–22.4).

Molly Peacock, contemporary Canadian poet, advises teachers to begin the study of a poem by having their students 'follow the nouns down the poem' and she argues that 'if all you do then is list the nouns down the page, just in the interrelationship of those nouns, you will begin to get the essence of the poem' (Hughes, 2008: 9). Once a column of nouns is established, Peacock suggests that the students do the same thing with the

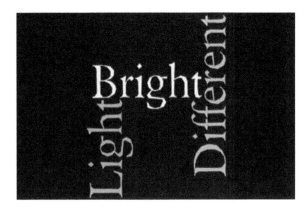

FIGURE 22.2 *Adjective Wordle.*

FIGURE 22.3 *Verb/adverb Wordle.*

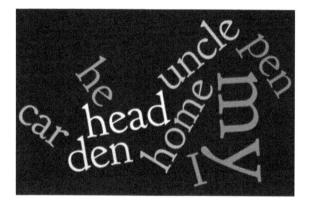

FIGURE 22.4 *Noun/pronoun Wordle.*

verbs in the poem. She acknowledges that this is usually more difficult for students but this exercise in predication helps students get beyond their fear of poetry. Peacock argues that 'in a good poem, in a great poem, the sentences are buried in the lines … But you can unbury them. The poem is a treasure trove' (Hughes, 2008: 9). According to Peacock, this type of exercise helps to take the mystery, and therefore the fear, out of poetry for those who find poetry initially daunting, in the hope that eventually it will be the 'density and intensity' that they will come to appreciate (Hughes, 2008: 9).

To reflect on the creation of the limericks, students wrote a response on the Ning in which they explained why they wrote about this particular funny moment, why it stood out in their minds and why experiences like this might help them grow as people (see Figures 22.5 and 22.6).

FIGURE 22.5 *Replies to this discussion: Markela.*

FIGURE 22.6 *Replies to this discussion: Jamil.*

Postcard poetry

After found poetry, students spent three lessons on 'postcard poetry', which is a style of poetry that relies on the interaction of images and text to reveal an intimate 'confession-style' narrative. The poem is also restricted to approximately the size of a postcard. During these lessons, students examined examples of postcard poetry, analysed a sampling of poems and discussed where in their online lives they engaged frequently in this confession-style poetry (e.g. through status updates, Twitter posts and Blog entries), and how these contributed to the development of their online identities and influenced their other identities, that is schooled or offline selves.

We asked the students to reflect on their creation of postcard poetry and to consider the following questions:

- Now that you've seen some examples of postcard poetry, how do you feel about it? Do you like the length restrictions it places on the writer – do you think it might encourage YOU to write poetry? For example, does it make writing poetry seem less scary because you're only allowed to write a certain amount? Or do you find the length restrictions difficult?

- What about responding to an image – does this make writing poetry easier for you?

- Do you think including a visual image 'completes' the poem or adds to the poem? Why or why not?

Students also worked in small groups to discuss voice and the style of art typically used in postcard poetry. We then asked students to create a collage in Glogster on the topic 'Who I Want to Be' using poetry and visual representations of who they want to be in the near-future – specifically in middle school next year. The students enjoyed postcard poetry because, as one student noted, 'you can just write any poem like, it can rhyme, it could be like a limerick … It could be basically any genre but then we just have to have a picture.'

Spoken word

Finally, students examined spoken word poetry and the poetry slam as a platform to share spoken word poetry. In the 2–3 classes here, students watched and responded to different examples of spoken word poetry performances – commenting on style, tone, voice, emphasis, structure and accessibility. To scaffold their own writing, we focused on a spoken word poem called 'We Are More' by Shane Koyczan, which we viewed on YouTube at: https://www.youtube.com/watch?v=zsq68qRexFc. We then asked the students to consider the following questions:

- What did you understand about the message of this spoken word piece?

- What are things you noticed about the spoken word style? Was it accessible or not?

- How is it similar to or different from some of the other poetry styles we have learned about so far?

- Do you like the spoken word style/format? What do you enjoy or dislike about it?

Students found their own examples of spoken word poetry and created discussion questions to share with a peer before writing a piece of spoken word poetry to perform for the class. Students created spoken word poems about their cultural identities, either as first-generation Canadians or as recent immigrants to Canada (see the following link for a student example about leaving the Philippines and arriving in Canada: www.youtube.com/watch?v=Oc3bQ2e2oeE). In this way students explored the important auditory component inherent in all poetry. Poetry is best read aloud, preferably by a strong reader, and preferably many times. As Luce-Kapler (2002) points out, 'A poem's musical character usually becomes noticed only if the poem is read aloud. Scansion exercises, which attempt to have students identify the pattern of rhythm such as iambic pentameter, seldom bring appreciation for the music of the words and lines' (p. 72). Like Luce-Kapler, Peacock (1999) refers to the music of the poem, and reminds us that 'Even though a poem is made with words, it is only one-third a verbal art. It is equally an auditory and a visual art, which we take into our bodies as well as our minds' (p. 20).

Connecting through and with a social media network

In this iPoetry and iDentity project, students explored the theme of identity through the reading, writing and discussing of a variety of poetic forms while using digital media as the vehicle or platform to do so. As there is a clear connection between literacy practices and the development of identity, Alvermann (2010) suggests that social networking platforms are the perfect arena for students to perform their emerging identities. Jones and Hafner (2012) explain that 'people's Facebook walls are like stages on which they act out conversations with their friends' and display their personal preferences, interests and activities (p. 154). This is certainly true of the Ning as well. In their exploration of the self through poetry and digital media, it became clear that students' identities are fluid, constantly shifting and multiple. Indeed, we noted that some of the students' identities were shaped even as they used social media in the classroom to examine their own identities. As these students found their poetic voices and explored their inner and outer selves, they became impassioned, and it became easier for them to participate and share. At the end of the project, we asked students to comment on how sharing and discussing their poetry online impacted them personally. Many of them found the online component very helpful in terms of their development as writers, as evidenced in these representative comments:

> Having others see and comment on posts helps so I know what I need to improve on and, sometimes, how.
> Having others see and comment on posts helps me because I can interact with others and know different opinions from different people. It also is helpful when you can't decide on something, then others will help you.
> Having others see and comment on posts helps me because then I can hear their opinion and what they've got to say. For example, when we wrote our six-rooms poem, others commented. Now we know what is really good about our poems and what we need to work on.

Other students commented on the power of the Ning to open up new social spaces for those who are typically shy: 'I got more encouraged to do stuff... Because when in real life like sometimes I'm shy, different personalities come out online. Mostly, more energetic. I talk with more people [on Ning].' Some discovered more about themselves through interacting with others on the Ning: 'I actually like found out more about myself. Like, I thought that I would be shy on Ning, like the Internet, but I'm not. So I found out a lot of things about myself.' Another student commented: 'When we first did Ning, I decided I should show my identities to everybody…I learned that, "Hey! I can be this identity in front of everybody". Like, I don't need to hide it from everybody.' Some students pointed out that discussing poetry on the Ning helped the students become more open to others: 'It made people more open. Like, in person some people don't really tell people they're creative and stuff but then on Ning, they had to respond. I don't really go up to people: "You know what? I like that, I like this", so when I had to do poems, that helped me open up.' A number of the students commented on one particularly quiet student who 'was really different' online from how she was in class. Even her teachers noticed that she became a prolific blogger on the Ning and that she initiated discussion with others by creating new groups, including one in which she encouraged all of her peers to post their favourite poems from the project. We noted that her confidence blossomed in class as a result of her activity and new-found social identity on the Ning.

The four teachers who participated in this project felt that the use of digital media helped their students connect better with the subject matter – poetry and identity. One teacher commented:

> This unit was, I think, very effective in having the students become very aware of their identities […] more so towards the end where they were becoming more comfortable, more open about where they came from, and how coming to Canada, for example, was such a juxtaposition from where they came. They really opened up. I was really impressed with the pieces that the students had written and reading their poems I learned so much about them.

Another one of the teachers noted:

> I really appreciated the way [the project] let students explore who they are and where they come from at a level that wasn't inappropriate for their age group or for their cognitive development. This is where children age 11, age 12, they're really asking themselves: 'Who am I?'; 'Where do I come from?'; 'What makes me, me?'; 'Why am I different in different situations?' So this unit was great at getting at a lot of these salient points. So I think they really enjoyed it in terms of learning about themselves and we really enjoyed being part of their journey.

One of the teachers felt that the exploration of identity through poetry and digital media was especially powerful for the students who were born outside of Canada and were trying to make sense of their cultural identities:

I think they knew who they were at the beginning but they became more comfortable talking about who they were at the end of the project. I really saw them open up about their experiences in their home countries and the juxtaposition with their identity as Canadians. I think by the end [...] they all got that they project who they are. Whether it be in-person or online, and I think that's a valuable lesson for them.

Weber and Mitchell's (2008) notion of identity as 'personal and social bricolage' views identity construction as 'an evolving active construction that constantly sheds bits and adds bits, changing through dialectical interactions with the digital and non-digital world, involving physical, psychological, social, and cultural agents' (p. 43). Through the reading, writing and discussion of identities through poetry and digital media, students were able to express themselves through multiple modes, connect with others and communicate their understandings and think critically about who they are and how they want to project themselves to others.

CHAPTER TWENTY-THREE

Commentary and Practical Implications: A Pedagogy of Permission

Anthony Wilson

Introduction

The story the chapters in this part tell is one of transformation. What makes them urgent, surprising and necessary is that they all begin in inauspicious circumstances, without great claim to outward success or to hope: a classroom of teachers self-confessedly unconfident about poetry; 'invisible children' who are present in body but playing truant in their minds; students embarrassed to hear their mother tongue mentioned, let alone spoken; students who keep their real identity hidden from the dominant culture of the classroom. These stories do not set out with much promise. Their tone is decidedly unboastful. Words like 'guilt', 'shy', 'nervous', 'invisible' and 'embarrassed' abound.

It is because they start out so shyly, yet end with such renewal having taken place, that they remind me of Brendan Kennelly's short poem about poetry 'The Gift' (Kennelly, 1990). Like the writers included here, the poem's speaker does not embark overflowing with confidence. The 'gift', such as it is, emerges 'slowly', in 'small and hesitant' steps, from places that are 'badly lit'. Likewise, these projects came into existence because their writers wanted things to be otherwise. They dared to dream of classrooms where children did not feel embarrassed to hear their first language spoken; where children did not go unnoticed; where students' classroom identities were not squashed; where the corollary of confidence in subject knowledge was not a constraining of pedagogy. They had the effrontery to take action.

From discovering a poem's 'secret strings' to the 'bricolage' of postcard poems; and from performing poems in a range of voices to adapting the models of poets facing similar issues, the reader of these stories can take away all manner of high-quality ideas for the classroom. Just as importantly, these narratives prompt the wider and political question which is concerned not only with 'how to?' but also the 'why should we?' of poetry teaching in what Emma Beynon calls our 'high-stakes context'. This is a crucial question for practitioners of all ages and range of experience, for it seems to go to the heart of what we are educating students for where the language arts are concerned.

Anecdotally, I can report that I have lost count of the times teachers, trying to maintain what Czeslaw Milosz called 'good spirits' (2005), have wearily asked me what the point of teaching poetry in school is, exactly: 'It's not as if we're training them to become poets. The economy couldn't take it.' The anxiety at the root of this problem has been neatly summarized by the American poet Stephen Dunn as the 'capitalist privileging of acquisition over contemplation' (2001: 18). Those who acquiesce in the utilitarian 'common sense' of this world-view may well feel justified in adding Seamus Heaney's words to their argument: 'Faced with the brutality of the historical onslaught, [poems] are practically useless... no lyric has ever stopped a tank' (Heaney, 1988: 107). Heaney does not leave the argument there, however. Poems 'verify our singularity' (Heaney, 1998). They may be unable to prevent tanks from advancing, but their power remains 'unlimited' (Heaney, 1998). Like the Roman god Janus, Heaney shows the capacity to look two ways at once. Even without a high-stakes context requiring measurement of outcomes against instrumental criteria, it is no surprise that the mysterious paradox at the core of his premise is enough to deter some teachers from engaging with poetry.

The power and scope of poetry

It is dangerous, therefore, to talk in terms of 'proof' being needed or sought as to poetry's 'efficacy' (Heaney, 1998). But were it to be so, the stories presented here go some way towards demonstrating the 'power and scope of poetry' (Heaney, 1980: 221) that can be found in the classroom, given the right conditions. But what are these conditions, and how can we create them? Emma Beynon and Vicky Macleroy, in their analysis of creative writers working alongside 'invisible' pupils and their teachers, remind us of the counterintuitive truth that waiting for the perfect conditions to teach poetry is, perhaps, to miss the point. The possibility for discovery and renewal of pupils' voices occurs not at the point of booking creative practitioners to make school visits, but at the moment a teacher decides there are voices to be unearthed in the first place. Collins (1998) characterizes these pupils as present in body but playing 'truant in the mind'. This chimes unerringly with another of Heaney's descriptions of the force and the joy that is to be found in making poems: 'There is a certain jubilation and *truancy* at the heart of an inspiration [...a] liberation and abundance which is the antithesis of every hampered and deprived condition' (Heaney, 1998: xviii, my italics). Truancy, both in its literal sense and when it is of the mind, is the exercising of free will to absent oneself from a classroom or other space where presence is required. The paradox at the heart of Heaney's depiction of individual creativity is that the exercising of free will creates not absence but fully realized presence and connection, with the self and with others, one which does not meet the normal requirements of time and space. In the best sense, the truancy at the heart of the stories collected here energizes the same process of inner renovation in the lives of pupils and their teachers.

This is powerfully illustrated in Janette Hughes's chapter describing how pupils merge their intuitive use of social media with poetry. The 'blossoming confidence' reported in these classrooms brings to mind the experience of glimpsing oneself in a cabinet made of mirrors. The image of the viewer is altered, front and rear as it were. In part, this shift occurs from the new perspectives afforded by the in-built capacity of the technology for transformation. In part, this occurs through the interactive element of the same technology. The viewer, seeing herself transformed, is transformed again in the eyes of the observing other. In this sense she is changed twice. The story is not just 'This is my poem' but 'There is a different me in this poem.' No wonder teachers described the impact of the project as one of discovery.

Working with poetry facilitates transformation in the lives of teachers as well as pupils. Emma Beynon has called this a 'pedagogy of permission'. This is where practitioners, having been inspired and given confidence by knowledgeable and enthusiastic others, bring poems into their classrooms and co-construct meaning with their classes instead of following preordained outcomes. Jenny Vernon describes the shift in practice that this engenders, both in terms of teacher confidence ('It was something I was a bit scared of. But since we've done the course [...] I'm excited about teaching it'), and pupil empowerment: 'The children [...] find a way into the poems themselves'. To borrow from Stephen Krashen's theory of second language acquisition (1982), it is as though the 'affective filter' of nervousness and lack of confidence and knowledge are lowered sufficiently for 'noticing, experimenting and playing with language' to flourish.

This is no less powerful for the teachers, pupils and poets portrayed by Vicky Macleroy in her chapter on EAL learners. Here, the metaphors of poetry as a new language (Koch, 1998) and a discovery of personal voice (Heaney, 1980) become blurred with the actual struggle of learning, finding and owning words for the first time. This is an effort of concentration that is demanding, both in terms of subject content knowledge and the emotions.

Cat, a spoken word poet and educator, notes that when pupils enter the classroom, many of them are not only learning in and about a new language, but they are also learning to 'bridge the gap between their experience of different languages and cultures'. Implicit in this kind of dual nationality is a daily negotiation, often unseen, of what can and cannot be admitted to. The struggle for what we so often call voice is, therefore, not just a search for accuracy and fluency; it is a quest for legitimacy, of subject matter and, in the widest sense, of identity and culture. The pedagogy of permission developed by poets and learners in classroom Poetry Cafés demonstrates that it is possible to transform cultures of schooling, replacing silence with 'safe spaces'.

As noted by all of these writers, to engage in this kind of pedagogy is to embrace risk. Too often we declare that we believe in this, without ever really defining what we mean by it. For some teachers, the move away from pupil outcomes towards honestly appraising and refining pupils' poems is too much. For others, the atmosphere generated by choosing to focus on speaking and listening, and performance in the classroom, is a threat to the established order of things. Suddenly seeing previously quiet and well-behaved pupils in a whole new light, and listening to what they have to say, can be unsettling. As Emma Beynon notes, the biggest risk of all in these teachers' stories is their commitment to transforming their poetry pedagogy whilst undergoing a shift in power relationships brought about by that change. The model to affect this change offered by these writers is based on a question implicit in creative endeavour across all disciplines: 'What if'? It is reality twisted into a new shape, not by power but imagination. They say to us: What if… we renamed this classroom a 'Poetry Café'? What if… we see where the secret strings take us? What if… this poem were a postcard? What if… I gave completely honest feedback to this poem?

The poetry wall

I conclude this commentary with a story of my own. At a school I once worked in there was a language support teacher who happened to be passionate about poetry. The teachers she worked with did not share her enthusiasm, so were happy for her to take pupils deemed in need of extra support out of the classroom to conduct these lessons. She was good at finding spaces in the school where there was not too much disruption, where pupils' voices could be heard: a medical room that never seemed to get used; a vacant office; a music library.

She found that pupils began to look forward to these lessons; they, and their friends who had heard about them, would come up to her to ask to be taken out. Her teaching style was simple. She had heard about a book on a course whose main idea she tried out. She would pass round copies of a poem, read the poem out loud, then sit back: 'Tell me what you think about it…', she would say.

News of these lessons soon began to spread to her colleagues. They asked her for her lesson plans, which she gladly copied and handed round. Then they asked her for evidence of her pupils' learning. This puzzled her. She knew that the pupils were learning; she could see it in their eyes when they talked. That some of them had even started to talk seemed not to be what her colleagues were looking for, however.

With her pupils' permission, she decided to make tape recordings of the lessons. She explained she was going to use their voices, their actual speaking voices, for a display of poetry in the school. This made the children very excited. She taped an entire lesson of the children talking about one poem. The poem, about a spider, was by a Caribbean writer. The poem was short, but their talk was long. She could not believe how long it took to transcribe onto her computer.

One week later, she put up her display. This was also simple in format. She placed an enlarged copy of the poem in the middle of the display board. Around it, using brightly coloured threads, a different one for each child in the group, she attached the typed up comments made by the children. The effect reminded her of a star. She had not corrected the vocabulary the children had used; she wanted to be as faithful as possible to the direction the lesson had taken.

The effect was electrifying. Children crowded round the display board, jostling to see their names in print next to the poem. Calling their friends to come and see their work, they swapped high-fives, laughing to recall what they had said in the lesson, thrilled to see their own names. Watching them, the teacher thought she discerned a new language being spoken, one she had not heard in the school before. It sounded similar to how the children usually spoke in the school, but was different. It was not foreign. It was English, but not as she knew it. Playtime came and went. The corridor was still jammed with children. Each day for a week that corridor was never empty.

Months later she would hear children referring back to the time she put up 'the poetry wall', as they named it. She heard children saying back to each other the words they had seen on the display board, in the order she had typed them. They were word-perfect. (She checked.) Later still, in stairwells and on playground duty children still approached her and said: 'Remember that time with the poem, Miss? That was a *good* time.'

Conclusion

Lest we forget it, the point of this story, already made eloquently by my colleagues earlier, is that engagement with poetry still retains the power to bring about change in schools and in the lives of pupils. Like that teacher displaying pupils' spoken language in front of them, poetry has the capacity to hold up a mirror to ourselves, and creates a space in which reflection, analysis and celebration may take place. I am not talking about change in the managerial sense of the word (though this may be a by-product of such work). I am talking about the vital, incremental, often unseen changes in the life of a class: children performing their work for the first time; one child translating the work of another so the rest of the class can hear it; children seeing their names on a display board which captures their first utterance in English. To bring this about does not require great resource, though this can help. A voice recorder is sometimes more than enough. All that is required is preparedness to let poems speak for themselves, and for the teacher to have confidence to say 'Tell me…'. The strangest and most mysterious paradox, demonstrated in all of the stories collected here, is that poetry is at its most powerful, and displays most potential for transformation, when the outward conditions for success are at their least promising.

CHAPTER TWENTY-FOUR

Conclusion

Anthony Wilson, Myra Barrs, Sue Dymoke and Andrew Lambirth

Making Poetry Happen can be read as a statement of intent to describe things as they could be otherwise. In a context of high-stakes accountability within education that shows no sign of abating (Sainsbury, 2009), it has never been more vital to maintain a broader cultural vision, a more creative, artistic and engaged approach to literature learning. Some readers, coming across the ideas collected here for the first time, will notice the consistency of the references in this book to ideals of education which poetry so readily promotes (and at such little cost): community, confidence, creativity, identity, empathy, permission and sharing. Poetry resists teaching to prescribed objectives, as it resists atomistic approaches to assessment. Yet, as writer after writer in this book patiently sets out, far from being an 'escape from reality', poetry can provide us with some of our realest, most deeply felt and unexpected experiences. In the words of Jennie Clark, reading and writing poetry can and does 'help make a healthy, responsive, aware human being'.

In the world outside school it is clear that poetry is undergoing an immense renaissance. After a long period when poetry seemed to have become the insular preserve of academics and intellectuals, there is now a healthy, active and popular poetry scene. The extraordinary growth of the T.S. Eliot poetry award is one proof of this renaissance. Beginning twenty years ago as a small annual event, it has grown into the biggest poetry event of the calendar, with an audience of thousands and a national tour. From another perspective, the explosion of performance poetry has shown how poetry can reach mass audiences of a different kind. The proliferation of poetry readings and poetry prizes, the immediate access to poetry provided by the Internet and the expansion of creative writing courses – all testify to a growing and a different 'readership' for poetry, one for which poetry is no longer something to look at silently on the page by yourself, but an experience lending itself perfectly to sharing and performance and fulfilling an extraordinary need.

So the importance of poetry in people's lives in the public world is growing. But in the world of school, poetry can still present a challenge to pupils and teachers alike. It has been clear throughout these two books that one of the main obstacles in the path of poetry teaching in today's schools is the lack of confidence that *teachers* experience in negotiating the medium. Their own schooling has taught them that poetry is difficult; a poem is something to be analysed to death, tortured into submission and 'pinned up in order to be pinned down'. As much as their students they often need to find their way towards a way of teaching poetry which makes it leave its lonely tower and descend into the street, where it can be sung, danced, performed, conversed with and explored. Teachers seeking to model these attitudes to their students will find encouragement in this book to lower the self-conscious filter of nervousness and anxiety in their classrooms, so clearly explicated by writers as different as Joelle Taylor and Cliff Yates.

Secondly, when we teach poetry we need to focus on its potential for play. There is no better medium for experimenting, manipulating, juggling with and revelling in language. Through the language games that we play in poetry we come to recognize our capacity for and enjoyment in making language memorable. As Sue Ellis and Amy Clifford testify, the shaping of lips, mouth and tongue around a nursery rhyme quickly creates and then strengthens the neural pathways which are necessary for developing phonological awareness, the skill of prediction and recognition of patterns of language. In practice this happens by reading and hearing the poem out loud. This mirrors Vygotsky's notion of learners internalizing their own private monologues, which develop into inner speech and – becoming increasingly abbreviated, condensed and allusive – into thought itself (Vygotsky, 1986). Thus, the outer world becomes part of the inner world. In practice this happens by reading and hearing the poem out loud. As Jennie Clark exemplifies, it is not possible to teach call-and-response refrain, alliteration and onomatopoeia in the abstract. Poetry calls out to be shared. Susanna Steele reminds us of the powerful effect of witnessing this 'sensuous apprehension' modelled to her as a child by an otherwise strict and frightening teacher. Whatever the limits of our context, she teaches us, poetry 'can find a place in the marginal spaces'. In this sense, each poem we read is a tiny revolution: the playfulness we find exhibited at its heart can literally take us out of ourselves.

In a similar vein, several of the writers in this book remind us of the co-constructed processes by which poetry can be made to happen in our lives.

Rosenblatt emphasizes (1978) that during an aesthetic reading of a poem the reader is primarily concerned with 'what happens during the actual reading event' (p. 24). A teacher who introduces her class to the art of paying attention, not only to a poem's content but also to the means by which that content is revealed in the reader's mind, implicitly acknowledges the danger of implying that there is only one meaning in the room. Rosenblatt's ideas about reader-response theory were themselves influenced by Samuel Taylor Coleridge, whom she quotes thus: 'The reader should be carried forward, not merely or chiefly by the mechanical impulse of curiosity, or by a restless desire to arrive at the final solution; but *by the pleasurable activity of mind excited by the attractions of the journey itself*' (1978: 28; Rosenblatt's italics). As this book testifies, our experience of sharing poems should be above all pleasurable.

Another habit of mind emphasized by these writers is that it is normal not to know 'all the answers' when approaching a poem. This brings to mind Keats's revelation that when he was working on a poem, he was happy to be in 'uncertainties'. This is not to say that no right answers exist, or that all poems are equally successful; it is to encourage what Cropley (2001) calls a flexible, 'over-inclusive' practice of thinking. We suggest that within the current context these untestable but vital skills appear as countercultural. In truth, they have never been more important. If we say we want a culture where empathy and divergent views can flourish, we will need young people trained in the art of listening to each other to sustain it.

The power and scope of poetry are apprehended therefore not as hegemonic forces, but as ones which hold 'attention for a space, function[ing] not as distraction but as pure concentration, a focus where our power to concentrate is concentrated back on ourselves' (Heaney, 1988: 108). This, surely, is one of the great aims of all education, not just of the verbal and literary arts. As the writers gathered here give witness, it is demanding, but never less than liberating. Poetry's capacity to thrive depends on a wide community. Its 'power and scope for transformation' (Heaney) depends on poets, and how they make it happen in their lives. But it also depends on teachers, pupils, schools and their communities, the connections they make with it and the determination and joy with which they share it.

GLOSSARY

Aesthetic and efferent readings of texts: The notion of aesthetic and efferent readings of texts was introduced by the teacher and academic Louise Rosenblatt. Her most influential writings were *Literature as Exploration* (1938) *and The Reader, The Text, The Poem: The Transactional Theory of the Literary Work* (1978). In these texts she argues that the act of reading literature involves a transaction between the reader and the text. This transaction is unique to each individual reader and in which the reader and the text continuously act upon each other. A text does not have the same meaning for each reader. The reader brings to the meaning of the text his/her knowledge and experience of the world. Rosenblatt argued that the meaning of any text can only be found in the interaction between text and individual reader. Rosenblatt described how all reading transactions sit on a continuum from what she called **aesthetic reading** – reading for the pleasure of experiencing a text – and **efferent reading** – reading to gain a meaning for a purpose other than the reading of the text itself.

Bars: A musical line of poetry. Emcee bars typically come in sets of eight, sixteen and thirty-two and feature multiple end rhymes.

Beat box: A percussive created through the manipulation of the mouth to emulate a drum and bass line track.

Composite rhyme: Rhymes constructed from more than one word. For example 'popular' with 'stopping her', 'Germany' with 'heard from me', and 'down to us' with 'astounded us' (from 'Grandad' by Andy Craven-Griffiths).

Diegesis: A fictional story-world.

Emcee: A person who writes bars to perform over a backing track or to live beat box.

Flash fiction: Very short poetic stories between 200 and 800 words in length.

Freestyle: Making something up as you go along, without reference to anything pre-written.

Free verse poetry: A poem with no set metre or rhyme scheme. A musical poem.

Full rhyme (sometimes called perfect rhyme): Rhyme in which the stressed vowels and all following consonants and vowels are identical, but the consonants preceding the rhyming vowels are different. For example 'tree' with 'free', and 'flattery' with 'battery'.

Half rhyme (sometimes called imperfect/near rhyme): A partial or imperfect rhyme which often uses assonance or consonance only. For instance, the stressed vowels and all following vowels may be identical or similar with consonants varying more. For example, 'cake' with 'face', or 'possible' with 'obstacle'.

Initiation response feedback: A type of talk initiated by the teacher during which the student tries to provide an answer which they assume their teacher wants to hear. This is then followed by some form of teacher feedback signalling whether or not the student is correct.

Mind-map: A visual diagram with which students present their ideas on an idea. The central idea is normally placed in the middle of the page and then associated ideas linked in a web-like formation around it.

National Literacy Framework: A scheme introduced in 1998 for the teaching of literacy for children of ages 5–11 and, subsequently, for 12–14-year-olds in England. It recommended that teachers teach the learning objectives in the framework in carefully constructed 'Literacy Hours' which included 'word level', 'sentence level' and text level' work. The renewed framework – **The Primary Framework for Literacy and Maths** for primary schools (ages 5–11) – introduced in 2006 was a little more flexible. Both frameworks have been abandoned by UK governments.

Open mic (short for open microphone): An event at which the microphone is 'open' for members of the audience to perform.

Pupil premium is 'additional funding given to publicly funded schools in England to raise the attainment of disadvantaged pupils and close the gap between them and their peers' (www.gov.uk accessed 26/03/2014).

Rap: Rhythm and poetry

Slam history: Slam originated in the United States in 1986, at the Green Mill Tavern in Chicago. Widely credited to American poet Marc Smith (2003, 2004), it was used by adult page poets as a way of attracting and engaging audiences. Within months of its beginning, audiences were queuing around the block to get into venues.

Slam rules: The rules vary but as slam originated in the United States many UK organizations use the rules popular there: three minutes on stage, no props, no costumes, and no music. Marks are awarded for Writing Technique, Originality and Performance. Marks are deducted for going over time, or for inappropriate language (racist, sexist, homophobic or swearing).

Syncopated rhythms: Irregular rhythms, or parts of rhythms, that deviate from the regular underlying rhythm.

Horse Shoes
The petrol of horsepower pumping my
  veins
The adrenaline headiness of being brave
Stand up, look at Joe, stick out my chest
Yeah, I'm fine, it's wicked …
you're next.

Andy Craven-Griffiths

REFERENCES

Abbs, P. (1989) *A is for Aesthetic – Essays on Creative and Aesthetic Education*. Lewes: Falmer Press.

Adisa (2002) 'What Is Poetry?', in A. Hoyles and M. Hoyles (eds), *Moving Voices. Black Performance Poetry*. London: Hansib Publications.

Agard, J. (2009) 'Toussaint L'Ouverture Acknowledges Wordsworth's Sonnet "To Toussaint L'Ouverture"', in J. Agard (ed.), *Alternative Anthem: Selected Poems*. Tarset: Bloodaxe Books.

Agard, J. and Nichols, G. (1995) *No Hickory, No Dickory, No Dock: Caribbean Nursery Rhymes*. Cambridge, MA: Candlewick Press.

Ahlberg, J. and Ahlberg, A. (1978) *Each Peach Pear Plum*. London: Picture Puffins.

Alexander, J. (2008) 'Listening – the Cinderella Profile Component of English', *English in Education*, 42(3), 219–233.

———. (2013) 'Hearing the Voice of Poetry', in S. Dymoke, A. Lambirth and A. Wilson (Eds), *Making Poetry Matter: International Research on Poetry Pedagogy*. London: Bloomsbury.

Alvermann, D. E. (2010) *Adolescents' Online Literacies: Connecting Classrooms, Digital Media, & Popular Culture*. New York: Peter Lang.

Amigoni, D. and Sanders, J. (2003) *Get Set for English Literature*. Edinburgh: Edinburgh University Press.

Andrews, R. (2008) *Getting Going: Generating, Shaping and Developing Ideas in Writing*. Nottingham: DCSF.

Angus, R. and De Oliveira, L. (2012) 'Diversity in Secondary English Classrooms: Conceptions and Enactments', *English Teaching: Practice and Critique*, 11(4), 7–18.

Armitage, S. (1989) *Zoom*. Newcastle upon Tyne: Bloodaxe Books.

———. (2006) 'Clown Punk', in *Tyrannosaurus Rex versus The Corduroy Kid*. London: Faber and Faber, 24.

Astley, N. (2002) *Staying Alive*. Northumberland: Bloodaxe.

———. (2004) *Being Alive*. Northumberland: Bloodaxe.

———. (2011) *Being Human*. Northumberland: Bloodaxe.

Auden, W.H. (2007) *Collected Poems*, ed. E. Mendelson. New York: Random House, Inc.

Auden, W.H. and Garrett, J. (1935) *The Poet's Tongue*. London: G. Bell and Sons.

Bailey, M. (2002) 'What Does Research Tell Us About How We Should Be Developing Written Composition?', in T. Grainger (ed.), *The Routledge Falmer Reader in Language and Literacy*. London: Routledge.

Barnes, D. (1976) *From Communication to Curriculum*. Harmondsworth: Penguin.

Barrs, M. and Cork, V. (2001) *The Reader in the Writer*. London: Centre for Language in Primary Education.

Barrs, M. and Rosen, M. (eds) (1997) *A Year with Poetry: Teachers Write About Teaching Poetry*. London: Centre For Language in Primary Education.

Barrs, M. with Styles, M. (2013b) 'Afterword', in S. Dymoke, A Lambirth and A. Wilson (eds), *Making Poetry Matter: International Research on Poetry Pedagogy*. London: Bloomsbury, 184–196.

Basho, M. (2013) 'Learn from the Pine', in R. Hass (ed.), *The Essential Haiku*. Newcastle upon Tyne: Bloodaxe Books.

Bauman, Z. (2003) *Wasted Lives: Modernity and Its Outcasts*. Cambridge: Polity Press.

Beach, R., Appleman, D., Hynds, S. and Wilhelm, J. (2006) *Teaching Literature to Adolescents*. Mahwah, NJ: Lawrence Erlbaum.

Beard, R. (1990) *Developing Reading 3 – 13*. London: Hodder & Stoughton.

Belloc, H. (1986) 'Tarantella', in A. N. Wilson (ed.), *Hilaire Belloc*. Harmondsworth: Penguin, www.poetryarchive.org.

Bensey, M.W. (1991) 'Growth through Group Work: Students' Self-reports', *Assessment Update*, 3(6), 7–10.

Benson, C. (2004) The importance of mother tongue-based schooling for educational quality: Background paper prepared for the Education for All Global Monitoring Report 2005. UNESCO: The Quality Imperative. http://unesdoc.unesco.org/images/0014/001466/146632e.pdf (accessed 26/06/14).

Berkavitch, J. (2007) 'A Short List of the People I Hate', https://myspace.com/berkavitchtalk/music/song/short-list-of-people-i-hate-7995486-7796670 (accessed 30/12/2013).

Berry, J. (2002) 'Seashell', in J. Berry and R. Merriman (eds), *A Nest Full of Stars*. London: Macmillan Children's.

———. (2011) 'Thinking about Poetry', in *A Story I Am In*. Newcastle upon Tyne: Bloodaxe Books.

Bishop, E. (2011) 'Crusoe in England', in E. Bishop, (ed.) *Poems*. London: Chatto & Windus, www.poetryarchive.org

Bisplinghoff, B. (2002) 'Under the Wings of Writers: A Teacher Who Reads to Find Her Way', *The Reading Teacher*, 56(3), 242–252.

Blocksidge, M. (2000) 'Tennyson: Teaching a Dead Poet at A-Level', in M. Blocksidge (ed.), *Teaching Literature 11–18*. London: Continuum, 105–117.

Bluett, J. (2012) *The Distracted Globe: A Project in the Practice of Writing Poetry*, unpublished Ph.D Thesis. Nottingham Trent University.

Board of Education (BoE). (1921) *The Teaching of English in England*, The Newbolt Report. London: HMSO.

Bolton, G. (1984) *Drama as Education: An Argument for Placing Drama at the Centre of the Curriculum*. Harlow Essex: Longman.

Booktrust. (2010) *The Motion Report: Poetry and Young People*. London: Booktrust.

Brainard, J. (2001) *I Remember*. New York, NY: Granary Books.

Brooks, C. (1971) *The Well Wrought Urn*. London: Methuen.

Brown, K. and Schechter, H. (eds) (2007) *Conversation Pieces: Poems that Talk to Other Poems*. Everyman Library: London.

Browne, A. (2010) *Through the Magic Mirror*. London: Walker Books.

Bruner, J. (1986) *Actual Minds, Possible Worlds*. Cambridge, MA: Harvard University Press.

Bruns, A. (2006) 'Towards Produsage: Futures for User-Led Content Production', in F. Sudweeks, H. Hrachovec and C. Ess (eds), *Proceedings: Cultural Attitudes towards Communication and Technology*. Perth, Australia: Murdoch University, 275–284.

Budd, M. (1995) *Values of Art: Pictures, Poetry and Music*. London: Allen Lane.

Carle, E. (1996) *The Very Busy Spider*. New York, NY: Philomel Books.

Certo, J.L. (2013) 'Preadolescents Writing and Performing Poetry', in S. Dymoke, A. Lambirth and A. Wilson (eds), *Making Poetry Matter: International Research on Poetry Pedagogy*. London: Bloomsbury, 105–115.

Chambers, A. (1993) *Tell Me: Children, Reading and Talk*. Stroud: Thimble Press.

———. (2011) *Tell Me (Children, Reading and Talk) with The Reading Environment*. Stroud: Thimble Press.

Chambers, E. and Gregory, M. (2006) *Teaching and Learning English Literature*. London: SAGE Publications.

Children's Poetry Archive, http://www.poetryarchive.org/childrensarchive/home.do

Chingonyi, K. (2012) *Some Bright Elegance*. London: Salt.

Clark, C. and Douglas, J. (2011) *Young People's Reading and Writing: An In-depth Study Focusing on Enjoyment, Behaviour, Attitudes and Attainment*. London: National Literacy Trust.

Clarke, G. (1997) 'Miracle on St David's Day', in G. Clarke (ed.), *Collected Poems*. Manchester: Carcanet.

Coe, M. (2011) *If You Could See Laughter*. London: Salt Publishing.

Coleridge, S.T. (1925(1933)) 'The Rime of the Ancient Mariner', in W. Wordsworth and G. Boas (eds), *Wordsworth and Coleridge*. [S.l.] London: Thomas Nelson.

Collins, J. (1998) 'Playing Truant in the Mind: the social exclusion of quiet pupils'. Research paper given at the British Education Research Association Annual Conference, Queen's University Belfast.

Commeyras, M., Blisplinghoff, B.S. and Olson, J. (eds) (2003) 'Teachers as Readers: Perspectives on the Importance of Reading', in *Teachers' Classrooms and Lives*. Newark, DE: International Reading Association.

Connolly, B. and Smith, M.W. (2003) 'Dropping in a Mouse: Reading Poetry with Our Students', *The Clearing House: A Journal of Educational Strategies, Issues and Ideas*, 76(5), 235–239.

Copus, J. (1995) *The Shuttered Eye*. Newcastle upon Tyne: Bloodaxe.

Corden, R. (2004) 'Learning Through Talk', in T. Grainger (ed.), *The Routledge Falmer Reader in Language and Literacy*. London: Routledge.

Cowley, S. (2010) *Getting the Buggers to Behave*. London: Continuum.

Craven-Griffiths, A. (2007) 'Grandad', http://www.youtube.com/watch?v=lh2cqpRoaTE (accessed 30/12/2013).

———. (2013) 'Horse Shoes', http://www.youtube.com/watch?v=110ViGkOWrA (accessed 30/12/2013).

Cremin, T. (2006) 'Creativity, Uncertainty and Discomfort: Teachers as Writers', *Cambridge Journal of Education*, 36(3), 415–433.

Cremin, T., Mottram, M., Collins, F., Powell, S. and Safford, K. (2009) 'Teachers as Readers: Building Communities of Readers', *Literacy*, 43(1), 11–19.

Cropley, A. J. (2001) *Creativity in Education and Learning: A Guide for Teachers and Educators*. London: Kogan Page.

D'Arcy, P. (1978) 'Sharing Responses to Literature', in E. Grugeon and P. Walden (eds), *Literature and Learning*. London: Ward Lock Educational, 137–149.

Department of Education and Science (DES). (1975) *A Language for Life*. London: HMSO.

———. (1987) *Teaching Poetry in the Secondary School: An HMI View*. London: HMSO.

Department for Education and Employment (DfEE). (1998) *The National Literacy Strategy: Framework for Teaching*. Sudbury: DfEE Publications.

Department for Education and Skills (2006) *Primary National Strategy: Primary Framework For Literacy and Mathematics*, Nottingham: DfES.

Department for Education and Skills (DfES) (2007) 'Keeping Up: Pupils who fall behind in Key Stage 2' (Ref: 00442-2007BKT-EN). London: DfES.

Department for Education and Skills (DfES). (2001) *Writing Poetry*. London: DfES.

———. (2005) *Primary National Strategy: Primary Framework for Literacy and Mathematics*. Nottingham: DfES Publications.

———. (2006) *Progression in Poetry*. Nottingham: DfES Publications.

Dewey, J. (1935/1980ed) *Art as Experience*. New York: Berkley Publishing.

Dias, P. and Hayhoe, M. (1988) *Developing Response to Poetry*. Milton Keynes: Open University Press.

Donne, J. (2006) 'The Flea', in J. Donne and I. Bell (eds), *Selected Poems*. London: Penguin.

Dreher, M. (2003) 'Motivating Teachers to Read', *The Reading Teacher*, 56(4), 338–340.

Duffy, C.A. (1993) 'Havisham', in C. A. Duffy (ed.), *Mean Time*. London: Anvil.

———. (ed.) (2007) *Answering Back*. London: Picador.

———. (2008) *Answering Back*. London: Picador.

———. (2009) *New and Collected Poems for Children*. London: Faber and Faber.

Dugdale, S. (2013) 'Editorial', *Modern Poetry in Translation*, 3(1), 1–2.

Duncan-Andrade, J. and Morrell, E. (2008) *The Art of Critical Pedagogy: Possibilities for Moving from Theory to Practice in Urban Schools*. New York, NY: Peter Lang.

Dunn, S. (2001) *Walking Light: Memoirs and Essays on Poetry (New Expanded Version)*. Rochester, NY: BOA Editions.

Dymoke, S. (2003) *Drafting and Assessing Poetry*. London: Paul Chapman Publishing.

Dymoke, S. Lambirth, A. and Wilson, A. (eds) (2013) *Making Poetry Matter: International Research on Poetry Pedagogy*. London: Bloomsbury.

Ehlert, L. (2005) *Leaf Man*. Boston: Harcourt Children's Books.

Eisner, E. (2002) *The Arts and the Creation of Mind*. New Haven: Yale University Press.

Eliot, V. (1971) *T.S. Eliot the Waste Land: A Facsimile and Transcripts of the Original Drafts*. London: Faber and Faber.

Fairclough, N. (1989) *Language and Power*. Essex: Pearson.

Fall, R., Webb, N.M. and Chudowsky, N. (2000) 'Group Discussion and Large-scale Language Arts Assessment: Effects on Students' Comprehension', *American Educational Research Journal*, 37(4), 911–941.

Fenton, J. (2003) *An Introduction to English Poetry*. London: Penguin.

Finnegan, R. (2005) 'The How of Literature', *Oral Tradition*, 20(2), 164–187.

Foster, J. (ed.) (2000) *Twinkle, Twinkle Chocolate Bar*. Oxford: Oxford University Press.

Freire, P. (1974) *Education for Critical Consciousness*. London: Continuum.

———. (1985) *The Politics of Education*. London: Macmillan.

Frost, R. (1960) 'The Art of Poetry No. 2', http://www.theparisreview.org/interviews/4678/the-art-of-poetry-no-2-robert-frost

Gabbert, B., Johnson, D.W. and Johnson, R.T. (1986) 'Cooperative Learning, Group-to-individual Transfer, Process Gain, and the Acquisition of Cognitive Reasoning Strategies', *The Journal of Psychology*, 120(3), 265–278.

Garcia, O. (2009) *Bilingual Education in the 21st Century: A Global Perspective.* Chichester: Wiley-Blackwell.

Gibson, R. (1998) *Teaching Shakespeare.* Cambridge: University Press.

Goldberg, N. (1986) *Writing Down the Bones: Freeing the Writer Within.* Boston: Shambhala Publications.

Goldsworthy, A. (2014) http://www.goldsworthy.cc.gla.ac.uk/

Goodman, K.S. (2014) 'Whose Knowledge Counts? The Pedagogy of the Absurd', in K. S. Goodman, R. C. Calfee and Y. M. Goodman (eds), *Whose Knowledge Counts in Government Literacy Policies: Why Expertise Matters.* Abingdon: Routledge.

Gordon, J. (2010) 'Talking about Poems, Elaborating Barnes', *English Teaching: Practice and Critique*, 9(2), 47–60.

Greene, M. (2000) *Releasing the Imagination – Essays on Education, the Arts and Social Change.* San Francisco: Jossey-Bass.

Grimm, J.L.C. and Grimm, W.C. (2004) *Grimm's Fairy Tales.* London: The Collector's Library.

Grogan, P. (1999) *The TES Book of Young Poets.* London: Times Supplements Limited.

Hardman, F. and Beverton, S. (1993) 'Co-operative Group Work and the Development of Metadiscoursal Skills', *Support for Learning*, 8(4), 146–150.

Hardman, F. and Beverton, S. (1995) 'Developing Collaborative Group Work in the Primary School: The Importance of Metacognition', *Reading*, 29(2), 11–15.

Hayes, N. (2011) 'The Rime of the Modern Mariner', *The Rime of the Modern Mariner*. London: Jonathan Cape.

Heaney, S. (1980a) *Preoccupations: Selected Prose 1968–1978.* London: Faber and Faber.

———. (1988) *The Government of the Tongue: The 1986 T.S. Eliot Memorial Lectures and Other Critical Writings.* London: Faber and Faber.

———. (2004) *Room to Rhyme.* Dundee: University of Dundee.

Hegley, J. (2000) *Dog.* London: Methuen.

Herbert, W.N. and Hollis, M. (2000) *Strong Words – Modern Poets on Modern Poetry.* Tarset, Northumberland: Bloodaxe Books.

Hope, A. D. 'Man Friday' accessed via the Australian Poetry Library at http://www.poetrylibrary.edu.au/poets/hope-a-d/man-friday-0418039 (accessed 22/02/2014).

Hoyles, A. and Hoyles, M. (2002) *Moving Voices: Black Performance Poetry.* London: Hansib Publications.

Hughes, T. (1967) *Poetry in the Making.* London: Faber and Faber.

———. (1978) *Moon Bells and Other Poems.* London: Chatto & Windus.

———. (1995) *Selected Poems: 1957–1994.* London: Faber and Faber.

Hughes, J. (2008) 'Poetry and New Media: In Conversation with Four Poets', *Language and Literacy*, 10(2), 1–28.

———. (2009) *Poets, Poetry and New Media: Attending to the Teaching and Learning of Poetry.* Saarbrücken: VDM Verlag.

Ings, R. (2009) *Writing Is Primary: Action Research on the Teaching of Writing in Primary Schools.* London: The Esmée Fairbairn Foundation.

Irish, T. (2011) 'Would You Risk It for Shakespeare? A Case Study of Using Active Approaches in the English Classroom', *English in Education*, 45(1), 6–19.

Ironside, V. (2011) *The Huge Bag of Worries*. London: Hodder Children's Books.

Jay-Z. (2011) *Decoded*. London: Virgin Books.

Jones, R.H. and Hafner, C.A. (2012) *Understanding Digital Literacies: A Practical Introduction*. New York: Routledge.

Kay, J. (2007) *Red, Cherry Red*. London: Bloomsbury.

Kempe, A. (1997) 'Reading Plays for Performance', in D. Hornbrook (ed.), *On the Subject of Drama*. London: Routledge.

Kennelly, B. (1990) *A Time for Voices: Selected Poems 1960–1990*. Newcastle Upon Tyne: Bloodaxe Books.

Knight, L.C. (1964) 'In Search of Fundamental Values', *in* R. de Harak (ed.), *The Critical Moment: Literary Criticism in the 1960s: Essays from the London Times Literary Supplement*. New York: McGraw-Hill.

Koch, K. (1998) *Making Your Own Days: The Pleasures Reading and Writing Poetry*. New York: Touchstone.

Krashen, S. (1982) *Second Language Acquisition and Second Language Learning*. Oxford: Pergamon.

Kress, G. (1999) 'Genre and the Changing Contexts for English Language Arts', *Language Arts*, 76(6), 461–469.

———. (2003) *Literacy in the New Media Age*. London: Routledge.

Kress, G. and Bezemer, J. (2009) 'Writing in a Multimodal World of Representation', in R. Beard, D. Myhill, J. Riley and M. Nystrand (eds), *The SAGE Handbook of Writing Development*. London: SAGE Publications, 166 – 181.

Langer, S.K. (1979) *Feeling and Form – A Theory of Art*. London, UK: Routledge, Keegan and Paul Ltd.

Lambirth, A. (2007) *Poetry Matters*, Rev. ed. Leicester: UKLA.

———. (2011) *Inaugural Lecture, Reading Voices; Appreciating Poetry Written by Children*. London: University of Greenwich.

———. (2014) 'Master or Servant? The Error of Personalising Radical Unpopular Change in Schooling', England *Considered*: Canterbury Christ Church University, http://www.consider-ed.org.uk/master-or-servant-the-error-of-personalising-radical-unpopular-change-in-schooling-in-england/

Langer, S.K. (1953) *Feeling and Form – a Theory of Art*. London: Routledge, Keegan and Paul Ltd.

Lea, D. (2013) 'A Feast of Stories', *NALDIC Quarterly*, 13, 1.

Lestrade, A. (2010) *Phileas's Fortune*. Washington D.C: Magination Press.

Levine, E. (2007) *Henry's Freedom Box*. New York, NY: Scholastic Press.

Light, J. (2006) *The Flower*. Swindon: Child's Play (International) Ltd.

Lopez, A. (2011) 'Culturally Relevant Pedagogy and Critical Literacy in Diverse English Classrooms: A Case Study of a Secondary English Teacher's Activism and Agency', *English Teaching: Practice and Critique*, 10(4), 75–93.

Luce-Kapler, R. and Sandu, G. (2002) 'The Poetics of Digital Space', in H. Roberta and Barrie B. (eds.), *Digital Expressions: Media Literacy and English Language Arts*. AB: Detselig Enterprises Ltd. pp. 67–85.

Mackey, M. (2004) 'Playing the Text', in T. Grainger (ed.), *The Routledge Falmer Reader in Language and Literacy*. London: Routledge.

Majors, Y., Mercer, N. and Simpson, A. (2010) 'Douglas Barnes Revisited: If Learning Floats on a Sea of Talk, What Kind of Talk? and What kind of Learning?', *English Teaching: Practice and Critique*, 9(2), 1–6.

Marvell, A. (1957), 'To his Coy Mistress', in H. Gardner (ed.), *The Metaphysical Poets*. London: Penguin.

MATSEC. (2013) AM syllabus (2014): *English. Malta: MATSEC Examinations Board*, http://www.um.edu.mt/__data/assets/pdf_file/0006/162834/AM10.pdf

McGough, R. (ed.) (2005) *Sensational: Poems Inspired by the Five Senses*. London: Macmillan.

McMillan, I. (2007), 'The Green Wheelbarrow', in C. A. Duffy (ed.), *Answering Back*. London: Picador.

————. (2012) 'The Perfect Poetry Lesson: how my teacher brought poems to life', http://www.theguardian.com/teacher-network

McRae, J. (1991) *Literature with a Small 'l'*. Basingstoke: Macmillan.

Mercer, N. (2000) *Words and Minds: How We Use Language to Think Together*. London: Routledge.

Merrick, B. (1987) *Exploring Poetry 5 – 8*. Sheffield: National Association for the Teaching of English.

Metcalfe, E. and Oliver, M. (2008) 'Engaging Teachers – How to Get Them to Join In', *Writing in Education*, 46, http://www.nawe.co.uk/DB/wie-editions/articles/engaging-teachers-how-to-get-them-to-join-in.html (accessed 25/02/14).

Milosz, C. (2005) *New and Collected Poems 1931–2001*. London: Penguin Modern Classics.

Ministry of Education (MoE). (1954) *Pamphlet No. 26: Language*. London: HMSO.

Montagu, M.W. (1989), 'The Lover: A Ballad', in R. Lonsdale (ed.), *Eighteenth Century Women Poets*. Oxford: Oxford University Press.

Myhill, D. (2013) 'Students' Metalinguistic Understanding of Poetry Writing', in S. Dymoke, A. Lambirth and A. Wilson (eds), *Making Poetry Matter*. London: Bloomsbury.

Myhill, D. and Wilson, A. (2013) 'Playing It Safe: Teachers' Views of Creativity in Poetry Writing', *Thinking Skills and Creativity*, 10, 101–111, Available at: http://www.elsevier.com/locate/tsc (accessed 12/9/13).

Neelands, J. (1992) *Learning Through Imagined Experience*. London: Hodder and Stoughton.

Neill, A. (2003) 'Poetry', in J. Levinson (ed.), *The Oxford Handbook of Aesthetics*. Oxford: Oxford University Press.

Neisser, U. (1967) *Cognitive Psychology*. New York: Appleton-Century-Crofts.

Nicholls, G. (2002) *Developing Teaching and Learning in Higher Education*. London: Routledge Falmer.

Nicholson, H. (2004) 'Drama, Literacies and Difference', in T. Grainger (ed.), *The Routledge Falmer Reader in Language and Literacy*. London: Routledge.

Office for Standards in Education (Ofsted). (2007) *Poetry in Schools: A Survey of Practice 2006/07*. London, UK: Ofsted.

Office for Standards in Education (Ofsted). (2009) *English at the Crossroads: An Evaluation of English in Primary and Secondary School 2005/08*. London: Ofsted.

Ogden, C.K. and Richards, I.A. (1926) *The Meaning of Meaning*. London: Routledge and Kegan Paul.

Owen, W. (2009), 'Dulce et Decorum Est', in H. Cross (ed.), *Wilfred Owen: Selected Poems and Letters*. Oxford: Oxford University Press.

Paterson, D. (ed.) (1999) 'Introduction', in *101 Sonnets: From Shakespeare to Heaney*. London: Faber and Faber.

Peacock, M. (1999) *How to Read a Poem … and Start a Poetry Circle*. Toronto: McClelland and Stewart Inc.

Pennac, D. (2006) *The Rights of the Reader*. London UK: Walker Books.

Plimpton, G. (ed.) (1986) *Writers at Work: The Paris Review Interviews, Seventh Series*. New York: Penguin.

Probst, R.E. (2004) *Response and Analysis: Teaching Literature in Secondary School*, 2nd ed. Portsmouth, NH: Heinemann.

Pullman, P. (2003) 'Teaching and Testing', in C. Powling, B. Ashley, P. Pullman, A. Fine and J. Gavin (eds), *Meetings with the Minister*. Reading: National Centre for Language and Literacy, 9–10.

Reid, C. (ed.) (1998) *Sounds Good – 101 Poems to be Heard*. London: Faber and Faber.

Richards, I.A. (1929/1973) *Practical Criticism: A Study of Literary Judgement*. London: Routledge and Kegan Paul.

Robinson, K. (2010) *The Element: How Finding Your Passion Changes Everything*. Harmondsworth: Penguin.

Rosen, M. (1997) 'Making Poetry Matter', in M. Barrs and M. Rosen (eds), *A Year with Poetry*. London: Centre for Literacy in Primary Education.

———. (1998) *Did I Hear You Write?* Nottingham: Five Leaves Publications.

Rosenblatt, L. (1965/1995) *Literature as Exploration*. New York: The Modern Language Association of America.

———. (1978) *The Reader, the Text, the Poem*. Carbondale, Ill: Southern Illinois University Press.

Rosowsky, A. (2011) *Heavenly Singing: Multilingual Verse and Song* presentation archived at: http://makingpoetrymatter.wordpress.com/seminar-3-leicester-sept-2011/seminar-3-papers/ (accessed 05/03/14).

Rummel, M. K. and Quintero, E. P. (1997) *Teachers' Reading/Teachers' Lives*. New York: State University of New York Press.

Sainsbury, M. (2009) 'Developing Writing in a High-Stakes Environment', in R. Beard, D. Author, J. Riley and M. Nystrand (eds), *The Sage Handbook of Writing Development*. London: Sage, 545–560.

Sansom, P. (1994) *Writing Poems*. Newcastle: Bloodaxe Books.

Senechal, D. (2012) *Republic of Noise: The Loss of Solitude in Schools and Culture*. Lanham & Plymouth: Rowman & Littlefield Education.

Shapcott, J. (2000) *Her Book: Poems 1988–1998*. London: Faber and Faber.

Silverstein, S. (1981) *A Light in the Attic*. New York: Harper Row.

Smith, J. (1963) *The Faber Book of Children's Verse*. London: Faber and Faber.

Smith, M. (2003) *The Spoken Word Revolution*. Chicago: Sourcebooks Publishing.

———. (2004) *The Complete Idiot's Guide to Slam*. USA: Penguin/Alpha Press.

Snapper, G. (2013) 'Exploring Resistance to Poetry in Advanced English Studies', in S. Dymoke, A. Lambirth and A. Wilson (eds), *Making Poetry Matter: International Research on Poetry Pedagogy*. London: Bloomsbury.

Spiro, J. (2013) 'Commentary: Writing Poetry, Teaching Poetry', in S. Dymoke, A. Lambirth and A. Wilson (eds), *Making Poetry Matter*. London: Bloomsbury.

Stafford, W. (1978) *Writing the Australian Crawl*. Ann Arbour: University of Michigan Press.

Steiner, G. (1978) *On Difficulty and Other Essays*. Oxford: Oxford University Press.

Street, B. (ed.) (2003) *Cross-Cultural Approaches to Literacy*. Cambridge: Cambridge University Press.

Styles, M. (1998) *From the Garden to the Street*. London UK: Cassell.

Sweeney, M. and Williams, J.H. (1997) *Writing Poetry and Getting Published*. London: Hodder and Stoughton.

Szirtes G. (2013) Review of Cosmic Disco by Grace Nichols. London: The Guardian.

Thieme, J. (2001) *Post-Colonial Con-Texts: Writing Back to the Canon*. London: Continuum.

Thompson, N.A. (2013) 'Poetry slams do nothing to help the art form survive'. *The Independent*, 1 February, http://www.independent.co.uk/arts-entertainment/art/features/poetry-slams-do-nothing-to-help-the-art-form-survive-8475599.html (accessed 01/05/2014).

Thomson, P. and Hall, C. (2008) 'Opportunities Missed and/or Thwarted? 'Funds of knowledge' Meet the English National Curriculum', *Curriculum Journal*, 19(2), 87–103.

Turner, V.W. (1974) *Drama, Fields and Symbolic Action*. New York, USA: Cornell University.

Tweddle, S., Adams, A., Clarke, S., Scrimshaw, P. and Walton, S. (1997) *English for Tomorrow*. Buckingham: Open University Press.

Van Allsburg, C. (1984) *Chronicles of Harris Burdick*. Boston: Houghton Mifflin Harcourt.

Vygotsky, L.S. (1930/2004) 'Imagination and Creativity in Childhood', *Journal of Russian and East European Psychology*, 42(1), 7–97.

———. (1978) *Mind in Society*. Cambridge MA: Harvard University Press.

———. (ed. A. Kozulin). (1986) *Thought and Language*. Cambridge, MA: The MIT Press.

Walcott, D. (2014) 'Crusoe's Journal', in D. Walcott and G. Maxwell (eds), *The Poetry of Derek Walcott 1948–2013*. Faber and Faber: London.

Walpole, H. (1764) *The Castle of Otranto (2004 edition)*. Mineola, NY: Dover Thrift Editions.

Waters, M. (2013) 'The Future of Schooling: We need a radical new education manifesto', in Teacher Network. London: The Guardian.

Weber, S. and Mitchell, C. (2008) 'Imagining, Keyboarding, and Posting Identities: Young People and New Media Technologies', in D. Buckingham (ed.), *Youth, Identity, and Digital Media*. Cambridge: The MIT Press, 25–48.

Weinstein, S. (2013) Introduction to 'Poetry in performance' session, NATE Conference, Stratford-upon-Avon, UK. June 2013.

Wells, H.G. (1894) *The Red Room*. http://www.gutenberg.org/files/23218/23218-h/23218-h.htm Release Date: 27October 2007 [EBook #23218] Last Updated: 23 August 2013. (Accessed 13/11/13).

Welsh Joint Education Committee (WJEC/CBAC). (2009) *GCSE Examiners' Reports: English and English Literature Summer 2009*. Cardiff: WJEC.

Wheeler, K.M. (1981) *The Creative Mind in Coleridge's Poetry*. Boston: Harvard University Press.

Wild, Margaret. (2006) *Fox*. La Jolla, CA: Kane/Miller Publications.

Williams, C.W. (2007) 'The Red Wheelbarrow', in C. A. Duffy (ed.), *Answering Back*. London: Picador.

Wilson, A. (2005) ' "signs of Progress": Reconceptualising Response to Children's Poetry', *Changing English*, 12(2), 227–242.

———. (2009) 'Creativity and Constraint: Developing as a Writer of Poetry', in R. Beard, D. Myhill, J. Riley and M. Nystrand (eds), *The SAGE Handbook of Writing Development*. London: SAGE Publications, 387–401.

———. (2013) 'Teachers' Metaphors of Teaching Poetry Writing', in S. Dymoke, A. Lambirth and A. Wilson (eds), *Making Poetry Matter*. London: Bloomsbury.

Wing-yi Cheng, R., Lam, S. and Chung-yan Chan, J. (2008) 'When High Achievers and Low Achievers Work in the Same Group: The Roles of Group Heterogeneity and Processes in Project-based Learning', *British Journal of Educational Psychology*, 78(2), 205–221.

Wittgenstein, L. (1967) *Zettel*, (ed.) G. E. M. Anscombe and G. H. von Wright and trans. G. E. M. Anscombe. Oxford: Basil Blackwell.

Wolff, M. (2007) *Proust and the Squid*. London, UK: Icon Books Ltd.

Woodson, J. (2003) *Locomotion*. New York, NY: SPEAK.

Wordsworth, W. (1925 (1933)) 'To Toussaint L'Ouverture', in W. Wordsworth and G. Boas (eds), *Wordsworth and Coleridge*. [S.l.]. London: Thomas Nelson.

———. (1925) 'Daffodils', in W. Wordsworth and G. Boas (eds), (1933) *Wordsworth and Coleridge*. [S.l.]. London: Thomas Nelson.

www.shakethedust.co.uk

Xerri, D. (2013) 'Colluding in the 'Torture' of Poetry: Shared Beliefs and Assessment', *English in Education*, 47(2), 134–146.

Yates, C. (1999) *Jumpstart Poetry in the Secondary School*, 2nd edition 2004. London: Poetry Society.

———. (2001) *Oranges: Poems from Maharishi School*. Ormskirk: Maharishi School Press.

———. (2006) *The Poem as Process: Theory and Practice*, Unpublished PhD thesis. Edge Hill University (University of Lancaster).

———. (2007) 'Writing Like Writers in the Classroom: Free Writing and Formal Constraint', *English in Education*, 41(3), 6–19.

———. (2009) 'Flying: A Poetics', in R. Loydell (ed.), *Troubles Swapped for Something Fresh: Manifestos and Unmanifestos*. London: Salt Publishing.

Yazedjian, A. and Kolkhorst, B.B. (2007) 'Implementing Small-group Activities in Large Lecture Classes', *College Teaching*, 55(4), 164–169.

Yeats, W.B. (1952) 'The Lake Isle of Innisfree', in W. B. Yeats (ed.), *The Collected Poems of W. B. Yeats*. London: Macmillan & Co, and www.poetryarchive.org.

Yolen, J. (2000) *How Do Dinosaurs Say Goodnight?*. New York: Scholastic.

INDEX